MANAGING CAREERS
Strategies for Organizations

MANAGING CAREERS
Strategies for Organizations

Andrew Mayo

Institute of Personnel Management

First published in 1991

Phototypeset by Intype, London

and printed in Great Britain
by Biddles Ltd. Guildford, Surrey

British Library Cataloguing in Publication Data
Mayo, Andrew
Managing careers.
I. Title
331.702

ISBN 0–85292–467–4

Casebound 0–85292–467–4
Paperback 0–85292–481–X

CONTENTS

PREFACE

'I didn't get where I am today by relying on someone else to manage my career . . . hard work and seizing opportunities are what it is about.'

Most people have heard something along those lines from a successful executive. Yet is it really as simple as that? Is corporate success about ensuring the right personal visibility and availability with the right people at the right time? Or is it about fostering key relationships? Or just luck?

One view, then, is that people make and manage their own careers; the organization's role is just to provide a supportive environment. Why should an employing organization worry about succession planning and career management? Those who have ability will naturally rise, those who do not will not; those with drive and ambition will push forwards and upwards – and, as long as an organization has a culture that supports meritocracy and rewards performance – then careers will look after themselves . . .

Some studies have been made of people at the top, and how they got there. Professor Alan Mumford in his book on *Developing Top Managers* observes that, whereas learning from experience was the universal description of how top managers described their development, this learning was 'an unplanned, relatively disorganized and unreflective process'. Few outside some areas of the public sector would say 'the system, which exists to recognize performance and potential, got me where I am today'. They made it through achievement of results, opportunism, gaining visibility and being in the right place at the right time.

So should we assume that the intervention of the organization in sharing the management of careers with individuals is redundant and bureaucratic? Should managers of human resource development abandon their dreams of integrated systematic approaches to the inevitability of natural and market forces, and focus instead on facilitating self-development?

Here are five reasons why I believe the answer is no, and why this book has been written:

1. The prime assets of every organization are the capabilities of its people – *all of them*. So developing employees to the maximum of their potential in harmony with the needs of the organization should be a significant concern. Most organizations probably use less than a third of their available potential. Understanding what capabilities the organization needs to meet its objectives, and how to match its people resources with that requirement, should be an essential part of the planning process. There is no logic in providing a greater degree of planning for products or services than for people development.
2. People develop through a combination of training and experience. While investment in training is considered normal, by far the majority of personal growth and development comes from experience. Look back on your own personal development and ask what have been the really significant training courses, and what have been the milestones of experience – a particular job, a special project, an unexpected promotion, a particular boss, a reorganization – that caused your knowledge and skills to take a leap forward? Experience usually provides the lion's share of development, so the management of experience is a prime issue for organizations, and cannot be left to chance.
3. Nearly every human resources manager who is familiar with opinion surveys and exit interviews is aware of unfulfilled expectations in career growth and prospects. Most jobs lose their capacity to motivate and generate new initiative after four or five years; and for some people it is less. Even if those at the top need no help, most of us are never going to be in that group. Most of us are not high flyers with dedicated ambition to rise at all costs above our fellows. That

does not mean we do not care about having a career or about self fulfilment, or that we are not going to try and influence our careers and take initiatives. But a message that our career growth is important, and that practical help in planning it is available, is motivational and influences our loyalty and sense of self esteem.

4. The cost of losing, hiring and retraining people is the great unsung cost of organizations. It should be a separate item in the profit and loss account for all to see. More people probably leave (voluntarily) through frustration on career development than for any other reason. An effective framework of career management does not solve all problems but it helps.
5. The 1990s will be years of interesting demographic change and mobility within Europe. Organizations will have to spend more time and effort in planning manpower and skills than they have done in the past, and know how to react to changes on more parameters than previously. Maintaining the career growth of women and older employees will be key issues.

So this book is about how organizations and individuals can work together to maximize personal growth for mutual benefit. Although it is primarily based on my own experience, I have taken a continuing interest in what others have written. Research in this area can be categorized as (1) looking at career planning from the individual's point of view (2) studies of particular groups such as chief executives (3) general books on management development which cover aspects of career management (4) writings specifically from the organization's point of view. In the UK the first three are plentiful but the fourth category is quite sparse. Most books in this area have been written in America, particularly since 1980, almost entirely by academics, and most not easily transferable to European cultures.

Struggling through some of the more turgid American writings can be exasperating – many words are spent stating the obvious or restating other people's findings. Notwithstanding that one must pay tribute to the pioneering thinking of people like Ed Schein at MIT, and to the extensive knowledge of specialists in the field of career development like Douglas T Hall.

I have never been an academic or a consultant, so this book will be short on theoretical models and, I hope, long on practical issues of implementation. It is not the fruit of rigorous and detailed research and it contains a number of personal points of view which should not necessarily be taken as those held by the organizations for which I have worked. It is written from a background of 25 years business experience and, although most of its ideas will be transferable to the majority of organizations, it does not pretend to throw special light on career management in, for instance, the professions, academia, or the arts.

The word 'organization' is used a lot as a convenience. But such an impersonal body in itself does nothing. Key people within it make things happen and can make 'it' change its value system and do things differently.

The aim is to provide a practical handbook of ideas and tools to set up and implement a framework of 'career management'. I have chosen this term to cover the subject matter – for it is more than just career planning, more than succession planning, more than having career structures. The term career management embraces the total framework within which personal growth through experience should be managed. Developing the potential of ALL the people in line with the objectives of the organization is key to success, and the book is not confined to issues for management development only.

It is hoped the book will be of value to all those concerned with helping their organizations manage the personal growth and careers of employees. The generic term 'careers manager' is used in the text, although it is understood this responsibility may be a part of a wider job scope.

ACKNOWLEDGEMENTS

This project started at the 1989 IPM Conference in Harrogate. Michael Armstrong invited those who had spoken at the seminar he led to a dinner, where I met Anne Cordwent and Matthew Reisz of IPM Publications. They have been a constant help and encouragement in both getting me started and in realizing completion. To attempt such a project in parallel with a job that itself demands 60 hours a week does not make for a balanced life, but one learns, as always, from experience . . .

I am especially grateful to my colleague Peter Kennedy, who was my best critic and made many helpful suggestions, and also to Alan Mumford who has not only been a source of much learning over the years but gave me valuable advice.

In a book of this kind shaped by so much of my own experience I owe the greatest debts to those who especially assisted with my own development, by providing me with an environment of challenge and experimentation and by the learning opportunities they gave. My initial years with Proctor and Gamble were particularly formative, helped by managers who were trained to care about development, such as John Nicholls (my then works manager) and Eric Hopkinson (my first manager). Along the road I owe much to Roger Crabtree of Philips, Dick Page of BOC, Don Beattie and Tony Hadaway of ICL, who provided specific growth opportunities, and to my many colleagues who have provided stimulation and ideas.

Last but absolutely not least, the support of my wife Elisabeth has been tremendous, gently applying the pressure to get me started while on the island of Paxos in summer 1990 and putting up with many hours of non-communication and piles of paper at home.

GLOSSARY OF TERMS

To avoid semantic confusion, I have tried to use a standard language throughout the book. It may help the reader to define these terms at this point.

Career aiming point	A type and level of job within a *career direction* to be aimed for in career planning over the next five to seven years
Career anchor	Term used by Schein for a person's natural career inclination
Career break	A period of time spent away from the organization but maintaining links with it
Career bridge	The move from one *career stream* to another
Career counselling	The process of helping a person decide on their preferred *career direction*
Career direction	The main type of occupation followed by an individual
Career guidance centre	As for *development centre* but specifically concerned with longer term potential career guidance

Career ladders	see *career structures*
Career manager	Person whose role is totally or part concerned with the implementation of the *career management framework*
Career management	The design and implementation of processes that enable the careers of individuals to be planned and managed in a way that optimizes both the needs of the organization and the preferences and capabilities of individuals
Career management framework	The integrated set of processes available for career development and personal growth
Career path	The actual sequence of jobs an individual follows
Career phase	A major period of an individual's working life, with common characteristics
Career plan	The types of job and approximate timings that will take an individual from today's situation to an *aiming point*
Career resources pack	A pack of relevant data on career structures and development processes for use by managers in *career counselling*
Career stream	A specific occupational career within a main *career direction*

Career structures A series of jobs of increasing value within the same technical or specialist area, with descriptions of the requirements for each level

Development centres Events designed to assess potential and evaluate personal development needs

Development position A position that an individual can enter without previous specialist experience and be effective within, say, three months

Personal growth profile A person's accumulation of relevant knowledge, skills, attitudes and experience to date

Person specification The knowledge, skills, attitudes and experience required of a specific job or generic group of jobs

Potential The capability to do a bigger and/or broader job at some time in the future

See the following diagram showing how these concepts are interlinked.

INTER-RELATIONSHIP OF TERMS USED

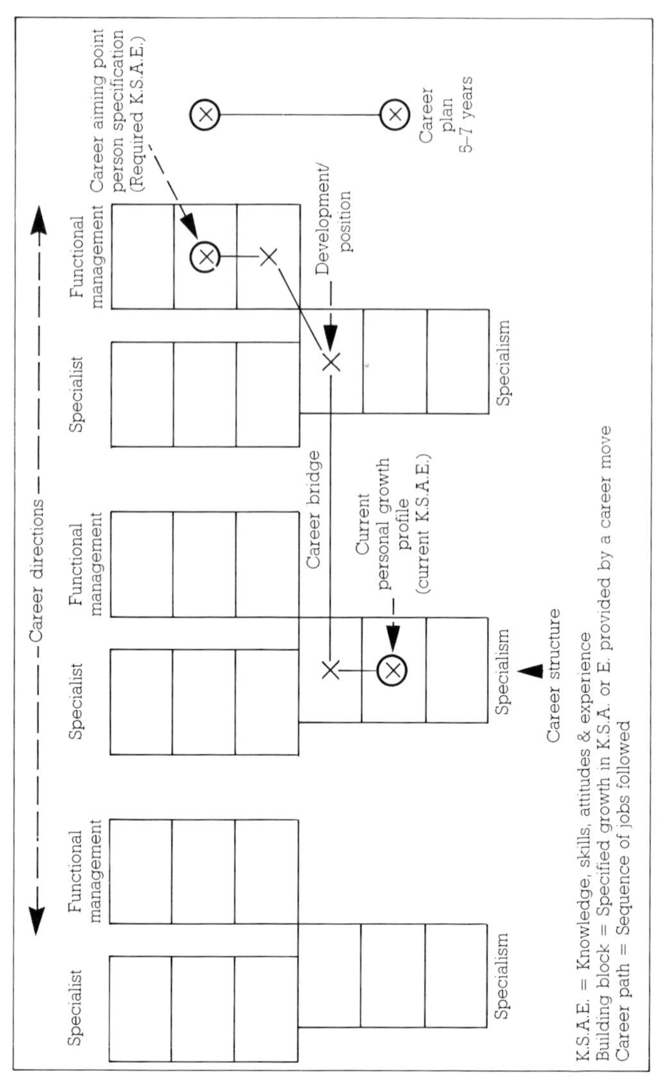

Inter-relationship of terms used

1. WHAT DOES THE ORGANIZATION NEED?

Different organizations have different needs, and no book of this kind can provide a set of answers to suit every one. My background has been all in companies with business orientated objectives – seeking to maximize benefits to shareholders, customers and employees through making profits. All organizations, however, share the need to grow their people and provide for future specialist and managerial leadership based on their objectives. This first chapter considers what the organization needs in three ways:

- The demands of the future,
- The demands and issues of today,
- The particular needs of different types of organization.

Organizations have more or less permanent policies that define the way they want to be run; these reflect their history, ethics and values, and the beliefs of senior leaders in the organization. Policies and needs should clearly be in harmony; a re-evaluation of the latter may cause the former to be changed. The next chapter examines the issues of culture change in more detail.

What do we mean by 'needs' in this context? What are the outputs that we would like to achieve that would result from the way we manage people growth and careers which in turn will enable the organization to meet its objectives? Examples of how we might define targets are shown in Table 1.1, although each organization will have its own list.

Table 1.1 Examples of targets appropriate for strategies of people growth

	MANAGEMENT	SPECIALIST
NUMBERS OF STAFF	**N**	**eg 4N**
CAPABILITIES OF STAFF		
Knowledge	Customer requirements Global competition Industry structure Financial literacy	Technical state of the art Relevant legislation International taxation
Skills	Team leadership Multitasking Delegation Public presentation	Problem solving Numeracy Systems analysis Detail accuracy Benchmarking
Attitudes	Political sensitivity Cultural sensitivity Strategic vision People are key	Cost-orientated Results driven Quality conscious
Experience	Different functions Second country P&L responsibility	Particular situations
	(eg)	(eg)
% of staff replaced by internal movement	90%	80% mid-levels 90% upper
% with experience in >1 function	60%	10%
% with experience abroad	20%	10%
International mix in homebase	10%	15%

THE DEMANDS OF THE FUTURE

An organization should only do those things that contribute to its objectives. The problem is to know what does and what does not.

This is not a book about business planning, but the subject cannot be ignored. Career management is making sure that the organization has the right people with the right skills at the right time. We need help to determine what is right, and that means that both our set of processes for career management AND the actual decisions we make in developing people must be in line with the strategic direction of the organization.

In addition to the regular operational review processes, every organization needs to take stock from time to time and check how it is doing against its goals, how it is meeting the expectations of its owners, its capability to cope with internal and external change, its competitive standing, and what it needs to adapt and reset in the light of these.

An organization must have:

- A clear idea of its purpose, which is best written down in some form of 'mission statement'.
- A clear idea of where it wants to be within that purpose at a point in time in the future, namely some long term objectives. These are usually in financial or market positioning statements.
- Strategies for reaching the objectives – these will be (for a business) in marketing, product sourcing, distribution, pricing, customer care, financing, human resources, technology, collaboration and so on.
- Some milestones to measure progress along the chosen paths.

For a business organization the objectives may be articulated as achieving a particular size, established in a particular place, having a particular market share, achieving a certain return on investment and so on. For a public sector body they might be measured in desired levels of service. There are clearly levels of objectives – for the organization as a whole and then for subdivisions. Each objective that is defined will have impli-

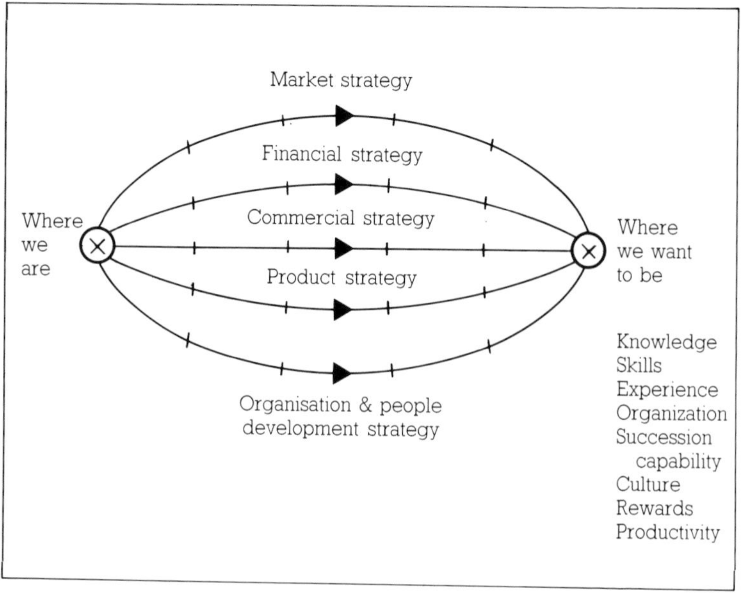

Figure 1.1 Objectives, strategies and milestones

cations for numbers of people and the knowledge, skills, attitudes and experience that will be needed by these people; for organization structure; for cultural values, and for a range of human resource management issues that arise from these. Understanding the objectives and the matching functional strategies enables human resources strategies to be set – including that for career management. Figure 1.1. illustrates this. There will always be a set of these which applies to the whole, but the level of detail depends greatly on the nature of the organization – whether it is integrated or decentralized.

All the objectives and strategies should be arrived at in the context firstly of the external environment, i.e. the political and economic outlook, competitive and technological trends; and secondly by an analysis of the organization's internal capability.

Management consultants specialize in providing models for analyzing strategic positioning. I have found the simple SWOT approach to stand the test of time: given the environmental outlook, what are the Strengths and Weaknesses the organization has in facing the future, and what Opportunities and

Threats can be foreseen. The aim is to capitalize and increase the strengths to maximize the opportunities available, and at the same time create action plans to overcome weaknesses and avert the threats as much as possible. The resetting of objectives and strategies follows such analysis.

This can be applied to issues for people and organization as effectively as to any other area, although the main business strategies should be formulated first and their implications for human resources evaluated subsequently.

There is a plethora of gurus and consultants willing to provide scenarios against which to do this planning, and plenty of books are written about the future – whether it is the 1990s, for the year 2000 or beyond. But in practice people may only pay lip service to the study of the future environment, and organizations are more comfortable in extrapolating their past experience as the main guide to what they can achieve in the future. Where short term operating or stockmarket pressures have a significant impact on decisions, managers may lack faith in long term strategic plans. But all would agree that long range planning should be done.

The main objectives and direction need clear commitment, even though implementation may be pragmatic and oscillate along the way – see Figure 1.2. The important thing is that the right people – that is, those who will have to implement the strategies – are involved in the analysis and choice of objectives and it is not left to backroom planners. Senior teams responsible for businesses or comparable organizational units in the non-commercial sector need to spend at least some time each year thinking about the future and sharing their personal perceptions. The human resources director should be there – but he or she earns the right through their personal understanding of what the organization is trying to achieve, and their consequent contribution.

FUTURE TRENDS AFFECTING ORGANIZATIONS

What trends are particularly relevant to our subject? Much has been written – the Ashridge Research Centre studied nine major European companies and published their findings in early 1988

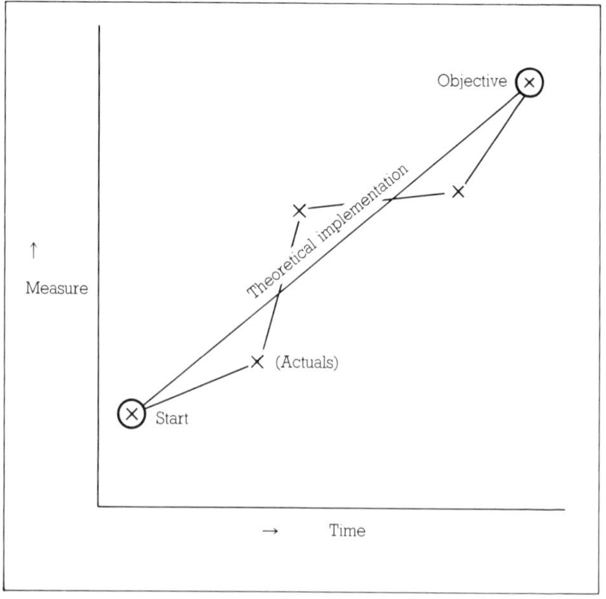

Figure 1.2 Maintaining a business direction

as *Management for the Future;*[1] ten major US and two British organizations formed a joint venture with the Sloan School, MIT, from 1985–1990 and published their work as *The Management in the 1990s Research Program.*[2] (This group included organizations such as the Inland Revenue Service and the US Army.) Their objective was defined as 'To develop a better understanding of the managerial issues of the 1990s and how to deal most effectively with them, particularly as these issues revolve around anticipated advances in Information Technology.'

The conclusion to be drawn from these and other studies is that the following will have a significant impact on organizations in the 1990s:

Increasing rapid and complex change

So what is new? Nothing, except that those organizations which have felt themselves relatively immune from external and internal change will find that they cannot continue like that. Factors fuelling this include the globalization of product sourcing, the development of the single European market, increasing cross-border mergers and acquisitions activity, deregulation in previously protected industries, and a host of others.

The *Management in the 1990s* findings laid great emphasis on the changing nature of work itself. It is not just that routine tasks become automated but that the whole structure and system of skills and inter-relationships will change more rapidly than before. The manager in the years ahead will need to be personally competent in exploiting the new technologies, and in organizing work and human interfaces in new ways. The emphasis on education, training and work design to support this will most certainly need to increase.

This change and turbulence requires not only managements capable of reacting to change, but of initiating and exploiting it. Organizations must plan for a future that they have already tried to anticipate and be ready with their strategies for winning in their field. The rate of management learning needs to keep pace with the rate of change.

Emphasis on customers, service and quality

Marketing strategies that start from the requirements of the customer are now much more of a reality than a mere statement of intent, and the old days of 'second best will do' are disappearing. The change in thinking required of most employees to adapt to this is substantial and cannot be underestimated. Personal empowerment for customer and supplier interfaces is becoming normal.

The key to success is in meeting customer needs faster than the competition, and providing world-class price/value and quality standards. Niche marketing is an essential capability – expertise to meet specialized requirements of groups of customers and aligning the organization with them. Total quality management is needed – radically different in concept from the old style quality assurance. Service management and customer care cease to be the mop-up parts of the organization and have a new strategic significance, needing new skills. Marketing no longer does its best to sell the latest ideas of technical whizz-kids, but specifies, together with technical consultants and customers themselves, what products or services are needed.

Decentralized accountability and integrated strategy

The trends of the late 1980s to decentralize responsibility and provide matching authority will increase. Along with this will come flatter, less hierarchical organizational structures – requiring innovative, entrepreneurial, team-based yet independent managerial skills. However, the risks of fragmentation must be balanced by integrated strategies which can take advantage of the maximum economies of scale where needed, and provide synergy of particular competences. Information technology will be increasingly crucial to exploit and will lead not only to the greater autonomy of sub-divisions of the organization but also of various kinds of individual knowledge workers who will be managed in quite different ways. Flexible networked organizations will need to be created, which may extend beyond traditional organizational boundaries.

Openness of communications

Information technology will bring new opportunities for speedy and universal communications to members of organizations. This will certainly include the availability of data: such things as organization structures, vacancies and so on being fully in the public domain and not locally filtered. Informality and a reduction in both functional and hierarchical barriers will increase, across cultures. Increased information leads to increased involvement in decision taking.

People the most precious resource

This has always been the case but why is it increasingly obvious? How does a firm gain competitive advantage? There are many answers to this question, but the traditional 'hard' advantages of easy access to raw materials, financial muscle, local manufacturing economies, etc, are rapidly taking second place to the acquisition, retention and development of the best people – who are needed to make decisions, to design and operate in a smarter way than the competition. The need is increasing to retrain constantly in parallel with career movements or job broadening.

The development of individual potential in creative ways will not only be essential for the maximum use of scarce talent but will be expected by individuals.

Continued globalization and opening of markets, leading to alliances of product providers and, increasingly, of service providers

Strategic alliances are driven by economic realities of low cost sourcing and efficient distribution. The opening up of markets favours the efficient producer over the less efficient and increases greater international interdependence. The global alliances that are well known in the major industries will become more and more common as wider economies of scale are sought. It will be a minority of organizations – small local entrepreneurial ones -- that have no international connections in the future. Cross-cultural understanding and management skills will have a premium. Service providers are following the same trend – consultants, accountants, insurance etc – and the single European market is specifically set up to enable simpler, more competitive cross-boundary trading and alliances.

Demographic changes

The change in the age population in the Western democracies – both in more older people and fewer younger people – is well documented. This trend will cause reviews of policies regarding older workers; more creative recruitment policies that will act across borders in Europe; a more detailed assessment of the role of women and their careers (and dual career family units); greater premiums on scarce skills and more training initiatives for young people to attract them to a particular career. There are many statistical predictions available – such as the Institute of Manpower Studies Report on the European Labour market as a helpful example.[3]

IMPLICATIONS OF ORGANIZATIONAL STRATEGIES

Figure 1.3 shows diagrammatically some of the main areas of impact that future organizational objectives may have on policies and practices of managing people growth, together with the pressures from the external environment.

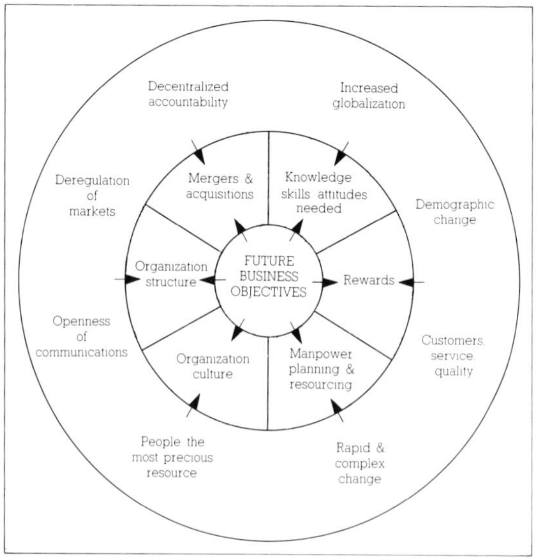

Figure 1.3 Influences of organizational strategies on human resources

Manpower planning and resourcing

At its crudest level the achievement of a certain objective can be translated into the *numbers* of resources required. In business plans these are derived from profit and loss calculations and desired productivity ratios. From them will come downsizing and restructuring requirements, or expansion needs. Models for this purpose have been developed by organizations themselves, and by the Institute of Manpower Studies, but every organization needs to customize its own. Models need to be applied to the whole organization, to its constituent parts and to different functions.

Some of the manpower planning questions (discussed in Chapter 6) to be modelled might include:

- What should the intake of young people be in the coming years?
- What pools of potential do we need to resource healthy succession?
- What ratios of managers:specialists will be needed?

- What percentage of posts would we like to be internal promotions and are we going to be able to achieve that?

The numbers of staff need then to be analysed to determine such factors as:

- Ratios of direct to indirect staff,
- Numbers and levels of managers,
- Geographical location,
- Full-time and 'buffer' resources.

As we make comparisons with where we are positioned today, we will be able to determine our strategies of resourcing, and, following on from that, our need and capability to grow people.

We may need to modify our desired strategies in the light of the external environment that we anticipate. We need to take into account the availability of resources, and in western countries we are well aware of the demographic changes that will influence this. The mobility of labour within the single European market could turn out to be a mixed blessing, as young people and those with scarce skills migrate to countries with the highest pay levels. In respect of career management this analysis has far-reaching importance. Personal development is about tomorrow's needs and being able to grow to meet them.

Figure 1.4 shows the basic steps required in manpower and skills planning.

Knowledge, skills, attitudes and experience required

Numbers in themselves are only a start. The numbers should be broken down into skill types, and all such plans need to be recast in the light of the other factors looked at below. Particularly important is the question of what type of people we should be bringing into the organization. In one company in which I worked, graduates had never been hired for the manufacturing division, and management had been traditionally promoted from the shopfloor. However, the future plan called for radical changes in the increase of automation both in production and in logistics management, and a different profile of person would be needed. The divisional director, therefore, instituted an ambitious programme for graduate recruitment, both for techni-

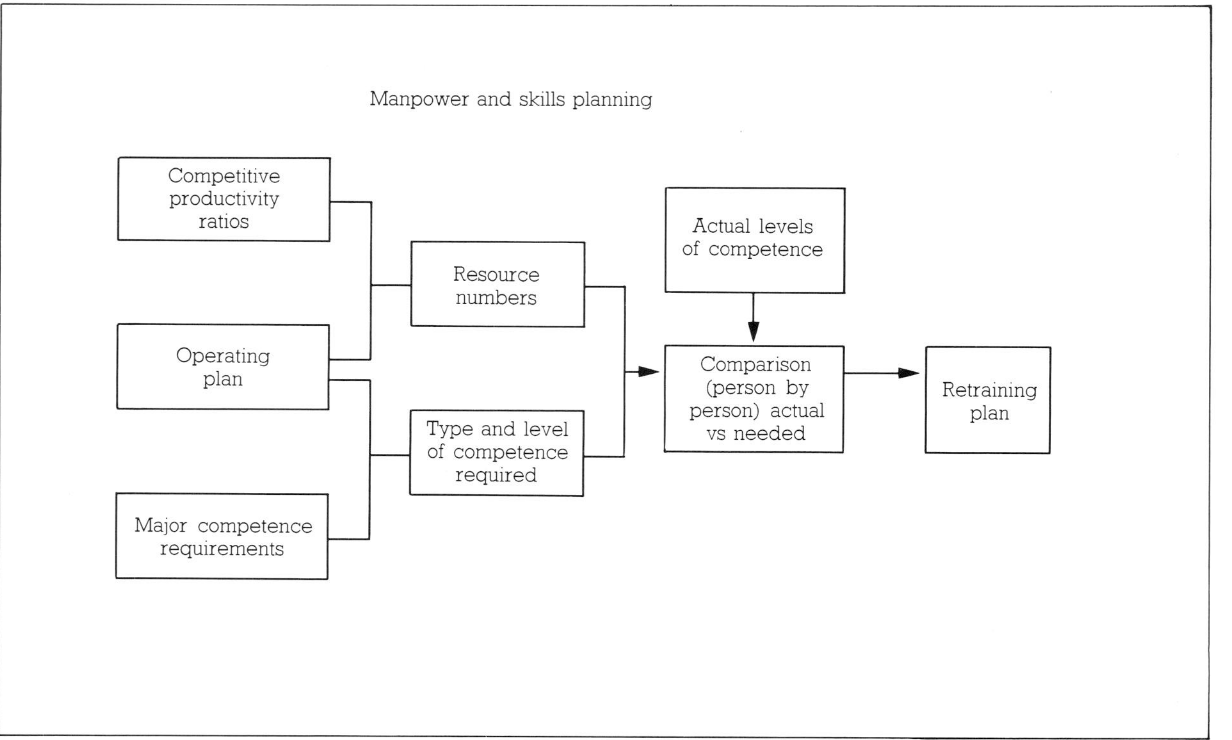

Figure 1.4 Steps in manpower and skills planning

cal support functions and for supervisory responsibility, and began a process of changing the entire skill profile of the division.

This book uses the terminology 'knowledge, skills, attitudes and experience' in preference to more general terms like 'competences'. It is essential that we ask what the organization's strategies will need in these terms for various groups of people in the years to come. It takes time to build these capabilities and so a people development strategy pursued over a long period is needed. In practice it is a difficult task, but at least we should define *generic* shifts that we know certain categories of people will need. In addition we should attempt to define the knowledge, skills, attitudes and experience required for success in *key jobs* so that this can be used as a target for the planning of individual development. Thus the task is:

> *'Describe the engineer, investment analyst, general manager, etc, of tomorrow'.*

The analysis of the answers is key to career management strategy.

Great effort is currently being expended on attempts to define managerial and other competences and the subject is addressed more comprehensively in Chapter 3. Each organization has specific needs, particularly the experience dimension which, I suggest, is far and away the most important. So, for example – how important will international experience be in the coming years, and what impact does this have on our current approach to international transfers? How important will it be to have had direct customer experience? What kind of knowledge and capability must our people have to exploit the information technology available to them in the future? Will there be a greater need for conflict management, the ability to manage trade-offs and contradictions, the ability to respond more quickly to external change? Should we be deliberately training managers, graduates and others from different countries together? Questions such as these help to define the capabilities we must develop.

We should certainly be deriving training plans from the business plans. It sounds so obvious, but too often training depart-

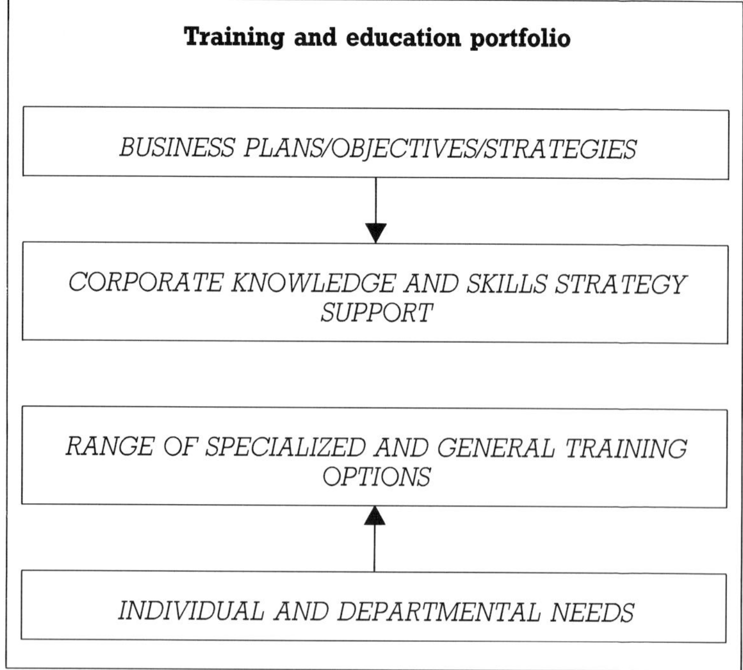

Figure 1.5 Relating training needs to the organizational objectives

ments are working in ignorance of the real business requirement. The question should always be asked at every milestone along the strategic road – 'and what are the implications for training both in order to get to this stage and when we get there?' Few organizations work so systematically – but at least they should have some kind of annual training plan. Is it 'bottom up', ie, largely composed of a synthesis of individual requirements? Or is it 'top-down', ie derived from the business priorities? Or is it (correctly) both? This is illustrated in Figure 1.5.

Organizational structure

Organization structures that match and are responsive to the business strategies are of critical importance and fundamental to our consideration of career management.

Table 1.2 looks at some positive and negative characteristics of different structural approaches for organizations, particularly with personal career growth in mind. Flatter structures are becoming more and more frequent; with the deliberate reduction of managerial levels. These yield real problems in people development, as the size of the jump in responsibility from one level to another becomes so much more significant. They reduce bureaucracy, assist better and faster communication, save layers of managers, encourage devolution of authority – but they reduce opportunities for promotions. Decentralization and the resulting increased autonomy have many benefits, but the accompanying reduction in central positions reduces the opportunity for positions which provide valuable overviews of the organization. Narrowness and parochialism are strengthened while opportunities to gain strategic breadth are fewer.

In the early 1990s some organizations are experimenting with cross-functional teams or networked organizations. The argument is that flatter structures basically perpetuate the old organizational issues of functional myopia, narrow skill building and bureaucratic, hierarchical administration. The answer lies in bringing teams together under variable leadership to meet specific challenges. From a people development point of view the possibilities to gain accelerated and varied experience are significant. This approach is being used at the higher structural levels of large complex organizations: units networking with one another rather than going through a central hub and responsibility for parts of a business being distributed rather than controlled hierarchically. Lower down in the organizations more traditional structures may be mixed with this networked approach. Companies like Rank Xerox, BP and ABB Asea Brown Boveri Group are working towards this at the time of writing. ABB describes[4] its structure as follows:

> *'Each business area has worldwide responsibility to allocate its resources. It decides where to produce what for which market. Operational execution is assigned to over 1300 operational units, which are wherever possible, separate legal entities with a clearly defined responsibility within the framework of the respective business area strategy. National policy and coherence is assured by*

Table 1.2 Characteristics of some different organization structures

	+	–
MULTILAYER PYRAMID	Clear hierarchy and clearly defined job responsibilities	Rigid communication lines Parochialism; lack of cross-functional development
MATRIX	Shared objectives Increased communication Integrated strategies Cross-functional exposure	Confused accountability 'Passing the buck' Duplicated roles
FLAT	Decentralized accountability; more opportunities for autonomous P&L experience Short communication lines – to staff and customers	Fewer staff positions and therefore fewer opportunities for an overview of the organization Large promotional jumps Less attention for each individual
'Y' STRUCTURES	Clear promotion paths Recognition of technical/specialist careers Fewer wrong management appointments	Vertical people growth Less cross-functional understanding – parochial mentality
FLEXIBLE – BUILT AROUND PEOPLE	Optimizes use of talent/skills Evolves with business needs Provides variety of learning options	Risk of unclear accountabilities May not be the most economic
CROSS-FUNCTIONAL TEAMS/ 'NETWORKED'	Shared understanding and commitment Development of broader skills/ knowledge Optimum resource use	Keeping coordinated direction in line with objectives

> *holding companies, whose employees are familiar with local cultural, social and political institutions. Functional guidance is provided by specialized corporate staffs with corresponding specialists assigned throughout the group. Project execution and key customer contacts are so important to the company that responsibilities are assigned to specific executives. Such a multi-dimensional matrix cannot be drawn up on a piece of paper. It can only function if the people at the various responsibility "nodes" understand their and others' roles, and have the matrix entrenched in their minds as they go about their tasks.'*

So the aim is to cut out bureaucratic controls and achieve innovative responses to business needs. The opportunities for personal and career growth (even if not by traditional up-the-ladder promotion) would seem to be extensive in such an organization.

The strategic plan not only raises questions about organizational philosophy, but may require organizational structures that are quite different from today, depending on how much change is anticipated in the plan. Thus we may be planning to dispose of some parts, combine others, go for substantial growth in one area, in another cease manufacturing and buy in instead. We may be creating more or less autonomous units; be planning joint ventures, collaborations, mergers or acquisitions; be opening up in new countries; restructuring a headquarters. All these have their impact on the management of careers.

Understanding what these plans mean in managerial and skill requirements is vital. We should be able to answer the following questions:

- Will our need for general managers increase or decrease?
- Will our need for international skills and experience increase or decrease?
- Shall we need to face possible losses of key skills because of closing or moving a location?
- Shall we have more or fewer positions suitable for developing high flyers?
- Shall we find it more or less difficult to manage cross-organization development?

Mergers and acquisitions

Plans can never be precise about which of these will take place; statements will be made about the intention to grow, diversify, vertically integrate or whatever through collaborations of various kinds. Although joint ventures, mergers and acquisitions tend to be put together as if they were the same, every one is quite different and a range of skills is needed.

These may include:

- **Pre-acquisition analysts**. This is a good entry point for MBAs, and an excellent growth opportunity for those with good analytical skills who need an overview of total business as part of their development.
- **Integration managers**. The greatest challenge in mergers and acquisitions is successful integration. Secondments to such posts, usually for a few months, provide tremendous learning opportunities (see Chapter 7) which should be used to develop individuals.
- **New positions in general management** – particularly of joint ventures.

Such activities bring a new population of skills and talent into the organization and enrich the potential available. Keeping that talent and bringing it speedily into the career management framework is one of the measures of success of such a venture.

Organization culture

We look at this in some detail in the next chapter as specifically related to career management. Although a cultural change programme is a long term process, from time to time it is essential to evaluate 'the way we do things around here' and decide whether it is consistent with supporting the stated objectives and strategies. When Robb Wilmot was in the process of turning round ICL in the early 1980s, he had to come to terms with this factor. After a year of stating clearly the objectives and strategies of the 'new' ICL he found he was getting nowhere fast and concluded 'the enemy is us'. As a result he defined and started a culture change programme that he knew would take many years but was essential for the achievement of the objectives. It involved changing the way managers thought and made decisions – a reorientation from, for example, internal to customer focus; to market driven products rather than technical excellence for its own sake; to becoming a global competitor rather than a UK exporter; and instituting quality fanaticism rather than 'second best will do'. Several components helped in this process, including the design and publication of a statement of values, and a major management development and education programme.[5]

Some of the questions to ask include:

- How different are the characteristics that describe the organization today from those that are needed to describe it in the future?
- Do people here understand and share a common set of values; do we know what these are, and are they the values that will help us to succeed in the future?
- Is there a consistency in decisions taken both vertically and horizontally in the organization that support a shared vision of the future needs?
- Are the processes and systems of the organization integrated with and supportive of the strategies?
- Do we operate as if people are a cost or an investment? Do we make it clear that people growth is a priority?

Rewards

An organization must ask whether its reward structures are positively supportive of the strategies. Does our vision of the culture we would like include high performance by individuals or by teams? Do we reward in line with whatever that is? Do we want people to make longer term strategic efforts? If so it is no use rewarding them only on the short term results. Do we want certain parts of the organization to be more innovative? How are we going to encourage that to happen?

We are not necessarily talking about money – it may be forms of status, opportunities to travel, receiving recognition and so on. But it is certain that if the organization does not specifically say 'we believe this is important' relatively few will achieve their levels of capability through loyalty to the organization alone.

This is an area where external pressures can be significant –

market movements in pay and benefits, international comparisons, government policies on taxation, profit sharing and other matters.

THE DEMANDS AND ISSUES OF TODAY

The demands of the future are in many ways the most difficult to understand and articulate and yet the development and career management of people is about the future, and about preparing people for those demands. However no organization can say 'well, we are meeting all our current needs perfectly and all we have to do is to see what the future requires and work out how we need to control the process of change'. So we need to examine those parts we are happy with and the factors we are unhappy with today as well. Each chapter of the book has a section at the end which gives some possible indicators of success for each of the processes – systems and procedures – described. But does every organization need them all?

Table 1.3 lists some common problems for career management in organizations. It is not an exhaustive list; if none of the problems are present in your organization then this book is going to be of academic interest only. But each problem has a cost – in terms of the bottom line, in lost productivity, morale or creative contributions. It is worth examining these costs further.

Productivity – judgements are sometimes made about the percentage of available potential in people that is in fact used by organizations. A speaker from Marks and Spencer – a model to many of a caring, productive organization – once said that its estimate was not greater than 20%.

Let us suppose that, through better investments in people development, better attention to identifying and growing potential, fewer mistakes in appointments, helping people find their right career direction and planning progress with them, we could increase productivity (output over a given input) by just 10%. That is, 10% more revenue or 10% better service for no extra cost. Compare that with the cost of the resources, training or organizational processes needed to make it happen.

Table 1.3 Common problem areas in career management

Symptoms of a problem	Possible causes	See chapter
High turnover of graduates	– Trainee programme causing frustations – Job content lacks challenge	4 (many causes listed)
Successors not available for key posts	– Lack of succession planning	6
	– Lack of planned careers	5
	– Growth outstripping ability to grow people	1
High potentials leave in 30–40 age group	– Rigid organization structure and lack of development opportunities	4,7
	– 'Plateaued' managers blocking upwards mobility	6,7
	– Mismatch of responsibility and authority	2
	– Inadequate or unchallenging rewards	2
Top specialist people leaving	– Inadequate career ladder and recognition for specialist people	4
General managers lack experience other than in their 'base' function	– Narrow development paths and lack of career *management*	4,5
	– Unwillingness of individuals to deviate from what they know and understand	5
Lack of knowledge of who has potential for what	– Inadequate assessment and control of data on individuals	5,6

Good people are unwilling to serve away from the home base	– People fear loss of visibility	2,6
Returning expatriates are difficult to place	– International experience not valued – Career planning for the individual not matched with organizational planning	2,4 5
Divisions unwilling to share their high potentials	– Integrated career management not accepted – Lack of trust in the organization	2,4
High failure rate among first line management appointments	– Inadequate potential assessment methods – Failure in development, coaching and counselling	5 7
Frustration amongst 'plateaued' managers and low performance	– Failure to attend to needs for continuous development	7
No resources allocated for career management	– Chief executive unconvinced of necessity or value – Philosophy of 'self-development'	2, 8 4,8
High losses of acquired staff in mergers and acquisitions	– Failure to understand the values and culture of acquired staff – Failure to apply individual career concerns in the new wider context of the organization	2 4,5

Losing good people and replacing externally – because the costs of replacing good people are wrapped up in different parts of the accounts of an organization the true costs never get the visibility they deserve. All human resources people who care about the business side of their organization should be familiar with the reality of these costs. Table 1.4 lists the costs that should be taken into account. Some of these also apply to internal replacements but they still need to be known. As a rough guide a year's remuneration is the cost of a replacement – more if a substantial training investment is needed before productive output. When asking the question 'What is my prime contribution to the business as a personnel manager?' the answer always came as the 'attraction and retention of the best people'.

Table 1.4 Costs of staff replacement

Direct costs	Indirect costs
–Advertizing	–Management time in selection
–Agency or search fees	–Time given in induction and training of new person
–Applicant expenses	– Learning curve productivity loss
–Personnel department time in managing recruitment	–Opportunity loss due to vacancy
–Recruiter's expenses	–Risk factor in recruitment decision
–Testing and assessment costs	
–Training costs	
–Possible relocation costs	

Good career management must not only help to retain people but also provide ready replacements in the event of loss. Again, do the calculations for your organization. Say that the loss rate can be reduced by a third through an effective career management policy, and the need to replace externally (above a certain level) by one half – what does this mean in savings?

Each problem identified in a list like Table 1.3 should, therefore, be costed as a means of determining a priority for dealing with it. The solutions proposed may also have a cost in implementation but, the balance should be a positive saving.

A list of possible benefits to be realized from a framework of career management is shown in Table 1.5. Describing the benefits is in reality easier than achieving them. The ability to create a credible, integrated set of career management processes depends on where we are starting from, on the capability of those specialists whose job it is to make them work, and on the conviction of senior management that a part of organizational success really does depend on getting this area right.

Table 1.5 Possible benefits to be achieved through career management

Building organizational capability for the future
Fuller use of staff potential
Top management involvement in resource management
Individual career challenge, motivation and care
Greater productivity through planning and control
Broadening and deepening of experience of individuals to match career goals with organizational capability needs
Fewer wrong appointments
Higher percentage of internal resourcing of vacancies, saving wasted costs in recruitment and retraining
Greater flexibility and ability to adapt to changing demands
Improved data available for decision making

THE NEEDS OF DIFFERENT KINDS OF ORGANIZATIONS

The third part of answering the question about what the organization really needs is to note how requirements can differ, depending on the character of the organization. We cannot be exhaustive here, nor should we attempt to be so, as no solution that is right for one organization is likely to be right for another.

Lynda Gratton and Michel Syrett have made a special study

of this aspect in the context of succession planning[6], looking at the practices of some very different organizations.

Organizations may be distinguished using dimensions such as:

Size – the larger the organization, the more formal the career management framework needs to be, the greater number of separate career structures it is likely to have and the greater variety of career opportunities. Small and medium sized organizations need to be more creative in using learning opportunities which do not involve job changes.

Integration – the organization may have a number of smaller autonomous units, or it may be integrated with central dependencies such as research and production, or policy making if in a service business, with branches spread geographically.

The latter gives the greater scope for careers development; in the former some staff functions and general management may be regarded as 'of corporate interest' but otherwise careers develop within the unit.

Competition/pace of change – these two factors are inter-related: the stronger and the more complex the competition, the faster the rate of change in the organization and the greater the turnover of staff. This leads to faster promotion possibilities and the need for greater attention to effective potential assessment and career planning. Long established organizations like those in the public sector, the armed forces, the larger banks and major companies are likely to have the most systematically established career management frameworks.

Public sector organizations that have been privatized are finding their traditional approaches to career management and required skills need rapid reassessment.

Growth – an organization that is static or declining has special problems but still needs good people. The management of its best talent is critical to its continuing future.

When IBM fell on difficult times in the late 1980s it launched a policy of retraining as many 'overhead' personnel as possible to become revenue earning. This made a radical change to the established career patterns and gave new and broadening opportunities to thousands of people.

Technology – organizations that are highly specialized or technical have their own needs in career management to ensure that they retain and grow the best in their area. They have to distinguish the need for effective management and the requirement for technical excellence in different career structures.

Internationalism – not all organizations operate beyond the boundaries of their domestic base. For those which do, there is a special set of needs that have to be considered in developing careers and future management. There are a variety of different ways of operating internationally and each places different demands on career management:

- **Foreign subsidiaries** – in this case local organizations are legally constituted in the country and there may be a local board of directors.

  Many organizations today have a policy of management of subsidiaries by local people, in which case the need is for a substantial emphasis on local development processes. Expatriate managers need a great deal of encouragement to develop indigenous capability, particularly in countries that are themselves developing.
- **Local sales offices** – effectively export office branches, employing a relatively small number of people.
- **Via local agents, dealers and third parties**. The difference here is that this is a trading relationship and the people employed belong to other organizations.
- **Via joint ventures and collaborations**, where the staff employed may belong to a different company although one may still have management control and responsibility.
- **Local purchasing offices**, where a small number of staff may be based for the purpose of ongoing purchasing for import to other parts of the organization.

In these latter cases it is in the management of the situations either locally or from a central point that provides the challenge.

A number of measures may be used to assess the success of an organization becoming international. One is the mix of nationalities to be found in the top 2% of the organization, the decision makers. What percentage come from the homebase country? And what has happened to the careers of the few who may have been imported from foreign subsidiaries? One of the measurable objectives that can be set to improve internationalization is the percentage of decision makers not from the home country. Table 1.6 shows examples of these differing needs. An organization should benchmark itself against competitive organizations, to ensure that its own understanding is not out of date, inappropriate or putting it at a competitive disadvantage.

INTEGRATING THE NEEDS ANALYSIS

There is no common answer to how an organization should approach career management, as there is no common set of needs. Effective managements think through their policy and their strategies in areas that affect them, and have processes and systems to support such a policy. The career and personal growth of employees as an area of interest is common to all, and so the questions to be answered are:

- What are our current policies?
- What are our particular needs, taking into account future requirements, current issues and the particular nature of our organization? (reference Table 1.1)
- Should we change any of our underlying policies?
- What strategies should we pursue to meet the organization's objectives?
- What new processes and procedures do we need to support those strategies? (The processes of career management are outlined in Chapter 3, Table 3.1.)
- What existing processes and procedures need changing to support the strategies?
- What processes need changes in the measures or criteria used – for example the way potential is described, or the assumptions in manpower planning?

Table 1.6 Requirements of different types of organizations

Characteristic	Important career management issues (and chapter covered)
Conglomerate – HQ level	Senior succession planning (6) Functional development (4)
Large, integrated with similar subsidiaries	Cross-functional development (4, 5) Potential identification and career planning (5) Structured career paths (4)
Small, high added value	Flexible organization structure Development through changing team membership (7) Mentoring (7)
Fast organic growth	Managed on-the-job learning (7) Management selection (6) High flyer management (4) Manpower planning (6)
Acquisitive; JVs	Management selection (6) Managed on-the-job learning (7) General manager development (7) Potential assessment for general management (6)
Strongly international	Expatriate policies and management Career planning (5)
Static, declining	Outplacement (5) High flyer management (4)
Public service	Clear career framework/structures (4) Manpower planning (6) Potential assessment (5)

Answering these questions – using the conclusions drawn from looking at the future, the present and the nature of the organization – will enable us to answer the question posed in the chapter heading.

SUMMARY

Linking strategies for human resources to the objectives of an organization has rightly gained more attention in recent years. Before we embark on changes to our strategy for career management, we should examine closely what the organization needs on three dimensions – what the future demands; what problems of today we need to solve; and the special requirements of our particular type of organization.

In all processes of change we start from one point and want to get to a different point: there is a gap to be closed. We need to define systematically those two points on various dimensions, analyse the gaps that exist and decide which strategies to follow and which processes to put in place. This book covers a range of options that might be chosen in career management.

Time and resources are required to achieve real results. It takes years to see the success of effective potential identification, effective career planning or carefully planned individual development. It requires continuity of policy and effort, and consistent commitment from top management until it forms part of the culture.

PLANNING FOR ACTION

Problems of reality

1. Human resources strategies are often not given the same attention and level of importance as other organizational strategies, and when strategies in other functions can be shown to be impossible to achieve for human resource reasons the issue is ignored.

It is not always natural for all senior managers to act as if they believe that such issues are critical to success – even if intellectually they do agree. The first essential, however, is for the HR person to show that the organizational priorities are truly understood – the nature of the business or other purpose is comprehended in such a way that discussion can be held on the same terms. It is more than asking a few apparently intelligent questions: it is **demonstrating** an understanding. That may require some investment in personal learning, and argues the case for HR people to have had practical line experience in their own career.

The resulting credibility, plus an ability to present options and arguments well, helps with this problem. It differentiates the mature contributor from the ones with limited capability.

2. Managements are not very interested in the intangibles of future scenarios.

Managements are interested in what is practical. Strategic planners are interested in futures. As Mumford says[7] in his book about top managers regarding two quite different organizations he studied, 'Both organizations had a strong requirement for formal corporate plans, which like many others were long on analysis and hope and short on competitor understanding and implementation. In both cases they showed how the company was going to move into an era of great success'.

The issues of the future are important, however, and they have to be analysed intelligently and then presented in terms of 'what needs to be done', with the risks to the organization's achievement if the appropriate changes are not made. That practical presentation will be in terms of the needs of different kinds of organizations.

The evaluation of the issues of the present – which can be illustrated with real problems – can be combined with those of the future to produce one practical change programme.

3. Strategic plans often lead to organizational restructuring and, in the process, ownership for the career growth of individuals is disrupted. The same thing happens with mergers and acquisitions. The result is that the individual is thrown back on his or her own resources.

This is real enough and one frequently hears individuals complain that they have had several bosses over a small timescale and lacked consistent direction in their work, let alone their careers. It argues strongly for making the basic framework of career development as wide as possible across an organization so that it overrides structural change.

Individuals carry with them to a new boss a career plan that is tuned in to the values and processes that lie behind it. Likewise it argues for a coordinating resource at the highest level that guards the framework.

Starting again from scratch is a painful and lengthy process. In mergers and acquisitions one should respect the 'acquired' systems for a period and plan carefully to integrate over time – faster if the employees have much to gain from the integration and the necessary manager training can be done.

Indicators of success relating to issues in this chapter are listed in Table 1.7 on page 32.

Action for those responsible for career management

1. Ensure that you, and all the specialists involved, know and understand the mission, objectives and strategies of the organization.
2. Check against the 'indicators of success' list, and describe the areas which need to be more effective; make a realistic plan of each that might be achieved.
3. List all the constituent parts of the organization's career management framework, and check for appropriateness under:
    - The needs of the future,
    - The demands and issues of today,
    - The needs of the type of organization itself.

   Make plans for those that need improving and, from the analysis of the needs, list those that are not being met well enough and the corresponding processes that should be introduced.
4. Make estimates of staff-replacement costs using a table such as 1.4; then make up a table such as 1.3 and estimate the unnecessary costs resulting from each item; work out possible solutions, and the cost/benefit of each solution proposed.

Table 1.7 Indicators of success checklist

Assessment of future needs	1. The human resource implications of organizational objectives and strategies needed for future success are assessed on a regular basis. 2. Current HR strategies, policies and processes are examined and modified as needed to ensure the desired success. 3. Changes proposed are supported and reinforced by senior management.
Review of current issues	4. The effectiveness of current policies and processes is measured against current needs at least annually and adjusted as needed. 5. The criteria used in the various processes are revalidated at regular intervals.
Understanding of the particular needs of the specific type of organization	6. The characteristic needs for the type of organization are articulated and benchmarked against the best practice externally.
Organizational change	7. The effect on human resources availability, on development opportunities and on the needed skills is taken into full account in proposals of organizational change.
Human resources costing	8. The cost factors of improved productivity through more effective people and of replacing a lost employee externally are fully understood by management.

REFERENCES

1 *Management for the Future,* Ashridge Management Research Group 1989

2 *Management in the Nineties Research Program Report,* Massachusetts Institute of Technology, Sloan School, 1990

3 Pearson R, Andreutti F and Holly S., *The European Labour Market Review: The Key Indicators.,* Institute of Manpower Studies Report 193, 1991

4 Gasser, T. P., *Managing Without Boundaries – The Challenges to Business,* Paper given to Annual conference of European Forum of Management Development, June 1991

5 Mayo A. J., *Business Strategies and Management Development,* Industrial and Commercial Training, March 1989

6 Gratton L. and Syrett, M., *Heirs apparent: succession strategies for the future,* Personnel Management, January 1990

7 Mumford, A., *Developing Top Managers,* Gower, 1988

2. THE IMPORTANCE OF ORGANIZATIONAL CULTURE

Although we may have assessed the needs for our organization comprehensively, no programme of change succeeds if it does not take careful account of the way things happen, ie, the 'culture'. Taking somebody else's good ideas and imposing them on an organization that is not in a fit state to take them does not work. It is like trying to change the behaviour of an individual – it is a process requiring care and there are limits to what can be done. The culture of an organization is like its personality – just as distinct and difficult to change. So before examining all the practical aspects of career management we need to understand those aspects of culture that will affect our endeavours.

The defensive reaction 'It won't work here' is inadequate if the business strategy requires new policies, processes, commitments and value sets to meet its objectives. We may have to embark on a cultural change process to adapt the environment and it may take some time to achieve.

The simplest definition of culture that I know is 'the way we do things around here'. The real way things are done may be quite a long way from what is written down as the official way. It is a combination of:

- Values and beliefs,
- Norms of behaviour that are acceptable or otherwise,
- Written policies,
- Pressures and expectations coming down from the top,
- Formal and informal systems, processes and procedures,
- Networks.

It is a product of a number of influences – the history of the organization, including mergers and major influential senior figures in the past; the leadership style of the chief executive; the systems of reward and punishment – and is seen first in the values, messages and behaviour of the top management.

Many organizations write down a statement of values or beliefs and provide it to all current and prospective employees. Chief executives wishing to establish a new culture find it useful to crystallize the characteristics of the company they would like to have in such a way. These formal statements are to be recommended as they provide an anchor-point for new initiatives in the organization, a reference point or sounding board to give some consistency. Nevertheless, the reality of the way people behave may be a long way from the desired expression, because a statement in itself changes nothing. Some examples of cultural value statements are shown in Table 2.1. Note how many similarities there are, but it is the total blend that counts. Incidentally, only one of the five shown in the table features people development.

ORGANIZATION CULTURE CHANGE

Any reassessment of objectives and strategies demands a reassessment of the organizational culture, and we may as a result deliberately embark on a culture change programme. That is, we want people to share a new vision, to adopt a set of new values, to change the way they behave to each other and to customers. We may want to create a new environment of performance rewards, or of accelerated personal growth. As we will see later there are factors which encourage and factors which constrain the development of people. To meet the needs identified in Chapter 1, we must be an organization that:

- has these beliefs (e.g. 'Everyone has the potential to grow and it is in our mutual interest to maximize this potential')
- has these supporting policies (e.g. policies for appraisals, expatriates)
- communicates these messages to all (e.g. 'Self-development goes hand-in-hand with career planning')

Table 2.1 Examples of cultural value statements

ORGANIZATION	HEADINGS OF VALUE STATEMENTS
CADBURY SCHWEPPES 'The character of the company'	Competitive ability Clear objectives Taking advantage of change Simple organization Committed people Openness Responsibility Quality
CMB PACKAGING 'CMB Packaging values'	Obsession with **each** customer's needs Confidence in **each** person in CMB Demand for best results in **each** CMB business Partnerships – keeping promises Accountability to shareholders Loyalty – solidarity – quality
ICL 'The ICL Way'	**Seven commitments of all employees**: Excellence Change Customers Teamwork Achievement Productivity showcase People development **Plus 'Ten obligations of every manager'**
HONEYWELL 'Honeywell principles'	Profits Quality Integrity Decision-making Customers Integrity Citizenship
DIXONS	Pride Competition Excitement Evolution Profit

- has these expectations of managers (e.g. 'All managers are expected to be trained in coaching and counselling skills, and to use them')
- invests in these activities (e.g. development centres, specialist resources in career management)

- encourages these experiences (e.g. acting roles, multinational task forces)
- operates these processes of people development (e.g. succession planning, potential assessment)
- is known for these areas of expertise (e.g. international management, specialist research, merger management)
- measures these indicators of success (e.g. internal replacement rate, reputation for quality and excellence).

A comparison with where the organization is today on these factors leads to the prescription for a change programme.

Figure 2.1 shows a simple model of cultural change, based on the concept of three interlocking circles. Each circle must be in place or change will not be effective. You cannot, as so many visionary specialists have found, introduce new processes into an organization if there is no commitment to make them work from the top. Equally, without a programme of communication **and** education, they will not be able to work as intended.

Top management vision and determination is absolutely essential. However full of insight and vision the human resources function may be, if there are no end goals that are both shared between the top management and owned by them, so that they visibly drive and articulate the changes needed, then little will happen. In Peters and Waterman's *In Search of Excellence* [1] the theme comes through constantly of a top executive or management team spending every opportunity to communicate, even preach, constant messages. People take their cues from above, and the chief executive is likely to have the biggest impact on cultural change in an organization.

An example can be quoted from Dixons PLC [2] – whose chairman Stanley Kalms constantly restates key messages. In one annual employees report he laid out the meaning of his philosophy in practical terms, concluding 'Above all, my most abiding hate is bureaucracy; it stifles initiative and people. We must keep it out of Dixons Group.' With such conviction from the top, I imagine staff people think twice before they introduce a new form . . .

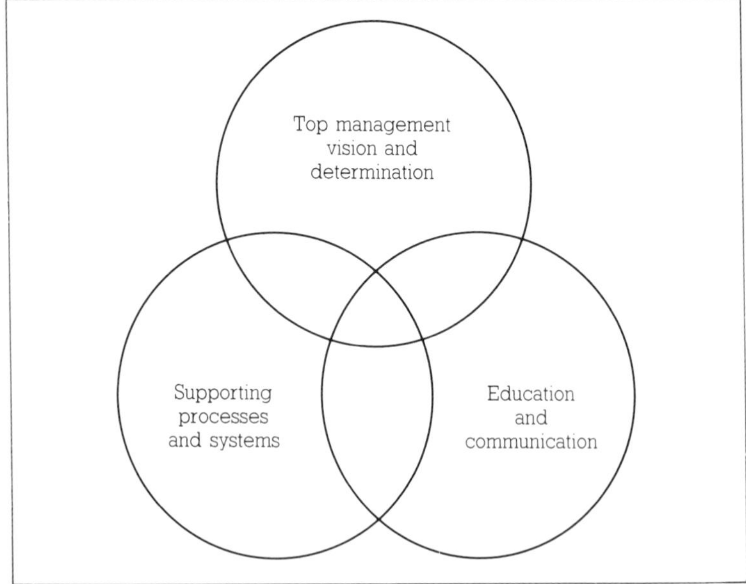

Figure 2.1 A model of cultural change

Similarly Jack Welsh of General Electric describes in the 1989 annual report his 'dream of a boundary-less company, where we knock down the walls that separate us from each other on the inside and from our key constituencies on the outside'.

Education and communication is the second circle. It is not enough to communicate in fancy brochures or videos what kind of an organization you want to be. That is important, but you also want to change the way people think in the organization and this requires educational programmes; first for management and then for all staff. They have to think through the implications of the desired culture for themselves and work out what they must do personally in progressing along that long road.

British Airways is an example of an organization which invested an immense amount in cultural change through education in the 1980s, first through its 'Putting people first' programme for all staff and later in the 'Managing people first' series. The chief executive, Colin Marshall, realized that nice statements about customer service changed little – it was necessary to reach the attitude base, the mindset, of all employees. He personally attended nearly every course to reinforce his beliefs in the cultural messages. The management courses were used to define a vision of the future, and apply the mission statements in practice.

ICL provides another example of a chief executive recognizing the key part education had to play in cultural change.[3]

Systems and processes are the lifeblood of the organization that affect every individual: the laid down methods of doing things – information systems, procedures, authority levels and so on. Processes concerned with the management of people are a significant percentage of the total, and they show to people what kind of organization we really are – how much individuals are trusted, the openness of communication, the match between authority and responsibility. (For instance, in one company a regulation on claiming expenses in the UK was 18 closely typed pages long and used the word 'authorized' 43 times. . .). Making changes in this area is essential to support the other two circles and conversely is a problem if it is done in isolation from them.

SOURCES OF INFLUENCE ON ORGANIZATIONAL CULTURE

Any culture has layers of influence that have helped to form it. The four main layers are as follows:

- National influences,
- Influences specific to the type of organization or industry,
- Influences from a parent organization,
- Influences arising from the history and characteristics of the local organization.

What works in one country may not work so well in another; different industry sectors have their own characteristics. Culture grows and changes like a person with the passage of time and the relative strengths of the influences.

National influences

One expert in this area is Gert Hofstede, of the Institute for Research in International Cooperation, in Arnhem, Netherlands. He has developed dimensions[4] for measuring national cultural characteristics as follows:

Individualism versus collectivism This is about individual self-sufficiency versus social and group dependency. Highly individualistic countries include the USA, Australia, UK, Netherlands; Japan is midway on the index and places like Greece and Portugal are more socially integrated.

Power distance This refers to the degree of equality or inequality in society. Highly collectivist countries show a high differential of power, whereas the reverse is not necessarily so. The USA, Australia and the Netherlands are low on this factor; France, Germany and Scandinavia are higher but all below the average of the measure.

Uncertainty avoidance Some societies are relaxed and feel relatively secure; others are always trying to 'beat the future'. Laws, regulations and strong religious forces characterize some countries, whereas others are tolerant and easygoing. Japan and Germany are low risk-taking countries; the USA and other Anglo-origin societies are more comfortable with risk and experiment.

Masculinity/femininity Are traditionally masculine roles more or less dominant than traditionally feminine roles? Japan comes out strongly masculine; the Scandinavian countries and France are more feminine in characteristic.

In organizations Hofstede suggests that the key dimensions are uncertainty avoidance and power distance. He describes the different approaches to a problem when given to French, German and British students at Insead – the French solution tended to rely on authority levels; the German on the definition of clear rules; and the British on discussion and negotiation. Hofstede concludes, and explains why, that the most successful international corporations have been Dutch, Swiss and American. Readers concerned with a multinational dimension to people growth and career development are recommended to study his work in terms of the countries in which they are interested.

Another professor who has studied this subject is Andre Laurent, of Insead. In his lectures he consistently used a blue pen and a green pen to depict two types of societies – the blue is time-conscious, systematic, task-orientated whereas the green is more relaxed and things get done more through relationships and by evolution.

Some of the dimensions of particular relevance to our subject are these:

- The degree of emphasis on the individual,
- Systematization vs relationships,
- Openness and personal behaviour,
- Hierarchical and power structures, alliances,
- Respect for age,
- Organizational loyalty,
- Traditions in recruitment and development,
- The educational system,
- Interaction with other nationalities.

The individual and the organization

In the USA and similar societies that place a premium on self-actualization, the individual is dominant – his or her freedom, rights and equal opportunity come above most other considerations. Providing the individual with a multitude of facilities for career counselling in a totally open way is common; flexibility and mobility the norm, and key values are self-care and personal achievement. Any kind of unfairness or discrimination on grounds other than merit is not tolerated. Open discussion on issues is expected and encouraged. Americans particularly are also obsessed with analyzing relationships, and whole books are written on exploring relationships at work in the finest detail. For this reason relatively few books in human resources translate easily to cultures that have less overt emphasis on individual rights, although many books on management itself have worldwide currency.

Organizational loyalty is relatively low and career changes, internally or externally, are expected fairly frequently. Americans are more willing to start a completely new career later in life than almost any other nationality.

The opposite culture, although this is changing, can be found in Japan where loyalty to the organization is far more important than any individual. Foreigners are rarely trusted to take any position of responsibility in a Japanese organization due to a distrust of conflicting value systems and not being 'one of us'. Age is respected – and is still the normal base for remuneration scales – and criteria for promotion are certainly not based on success in the most recent assignment. Openness is constrained by the importance of maintaining and saving face, and of seeing the status and success of the organization as more important than anything personal.

In Europe we find differences and diversity – particularly between north and south. The extremes of American culture are despised as childish and patronising (particularly in the UK; less so in, for example, Holland). There is a more overt internal self-sufficiency – and a great variety of historical traditions. The UK is characterized by a level of cynicism which appears to live comfortably with a loyalty to an organization; such a combination can be totally paradoxical to foreigners. In the UK the network of interpersonal relationships between individuals (often quite independent of status or hierarchy) through whom one can get things to happen is dominant, whereas in Germany the network is much more based on understood levels of professionalism and competence. In France authority, power and hierarchy are the stronger dimensions.

During my time as a personnel director for Europe, I worked first under a Yugoslav (naturalized as a Swede), then under a Frenchman and latterly an Englishman. The first, who had worked in Swedish and American organizations, had a variety of styles, most typically American, but the Frenchman was unswervingly French. Some of his expectations were revealing and culturally educational – for example it was quite natural to him that there would be no question of us finding a job for the son or daughter of an important contact or customer in France, regardless of the ability of the young person concerned. His respect for the views and statements of his superiors was noticeable, as was his assumption that the laws of France were the best guide to justice in situations.

In developing countries personal relationships (particularly family) can dominate any more formal systems, and multinational companies which like to believe that what is good at home is good everywhere can meet real problems here. Frequently qualifications bestow a status quite out of balance with experience. Whereas the multinational seeks to retain its normal standards of meritocracy it can find its people poached by local organizations and given positions of immense responsibility, based on the credit attached to being trained by 'a big name'.

Approaches to people development

One of the most helpful recent studies on comparative development practices (for managers) is *The making of managers* by Charles Handy and others.[5] This study was of management education, training and development in France, Germany, USA, Japan and the UK. It concluded that, despite its international record, the UK had the least well educated management population and the least systematic approach to development. It was this report that caused subsequent activities that led to the Management Charter Initiative. A wealth of information is clearly summarized in this informative study. (I particularly liked the table showing the number of qualified accountants in the UK as against Germany and Japan – 120,000 plays 3,800 and 6,000 respectively.)

All countries value experience as the real basis of development, although it is the most formalized in Japan and least systematically planned in Europe. Self development (self enlightenment in Japan) is strongly encouraged everywhere. In France organizations are required by law to spend a certain amount on training – many spend much more than the minimum. Much of it is funnelled through chambers of commerce, which are in touch with local needs. In Japan the organization itself is seen to be the prime provider of education through on-the-job training, which is systematically managed and continues throughout a career. The Germans have a long preparatory period for work, often not starting an organizational career until they are 27 years old.

In a book edited by three Insead authors (Doz, Laurent and Evans, 1989) entitled *Human Resource Management in International Firms*,[6] four different types of management development models are described, characteristic of four different national cultures. They provide useful illustrations of the different approaches to recruitment and progression. (These cameos apply more to large, established organizations than to smaller, entrepreneurial ones.)

1) The Japanese model is based on the recruitment of an elite from the best universities. For the first five to eight years no further distinctions are made; thereafter fierce competition takes place and the graduate's ultimate fate will be written through performance in a number of horizontal job rotation assignments over the next few years. Total dedication from the individual to the firm as his (or, less likely, her) life's calling is expected. The average time in a post is typically twice as long as in western cultures and it may be 15 years before junior middle management is reached. Overseas assignments are normally given as a sign of trust and recognition of future potential. Career management is planned and directed from the organization, with a low degree of individual choice. The equivalent of mentoring – which is heavily orientated to coaching – is normal, with one coach for someone's career and another for current performance.

2) In France the high value placed on intellect means that the school attended probably matters more than anywhere else in the world. Entry is based on prowess in quantitative techniques, problem solving and mathematics and is fiercely competitive. The large organizations compete for the best graduates from the Grandes Écôles (either engineering or administrative), and starting salaries are related to the prestige of the school in the annual league tables. The smaller organizations place far less value on the intellectual elite. The Ecôles de Commerce have moved steadily towards an American model of management training over the last 20 years.

Career success for those picked is almost guaranteed. Maintaining links with peers is an important element in continued success, along with astute political self-promotion. Systematic post-entry development is by no means the norm, although there are exceptions.

3) The typical Germanic model is less attached to the early identification of a management career, and the early years are characterized by technical or professional career paths including a job-rotation type apprenticeship for the first two years or so. Functional careers, relationships and power structures are the norm, so that it is quite common in Germany and related coun-

tries to have two leaders – one, for example, for commerce and technical and one for finance and administration. Problems experienced outside an executive's area of expertise may proceed up a professional hierarchy and reach quite a high level before cross-functional discussion takes place.

4) The fourth model described is Anglo Dutch. Here recruitment is typically decentralized for functional or specialist posts, although the importance of degree discipline is relatively low. People progress in their own part of the organization for five to ten years and then may be subject to some form of potential assessment for management. Thereafter they are likely to be monitored by some central corporate body. Relatively few organizations – an exception is the retail industry – have direct entry to generalist management training schemes.

In the UK the nature of the degree studied at university has less significance than the quality/reputation of the institution or course. Thus degrees in arts subjects have been quite acceptable as entrance to management training schemes, or professions like marketing and personnel.

In America it is more common to recruit people specifically for management careers at the outset, particularly from those with MBA qualifications.

The Insead authors observe that the generalist approach leads to the development of people with good strategic overview and understanding, and good networks of contacts, but with shallowness of understanding of any subject in depth and of the processes of people management. The German/Japanese models produce solid expertise and achievement through dedicated implementation, but lack breadth of thinking; they foster organizational rigidity.

Implications for multinationals

The multinational has a number of issues to come to terms with, as it considers the spectrum of:

Total cultural conformity throughout the world	Local cultures dominate – minimum results reporting required only

McDonalds, for example, has a business totally built on a standardized quality image that the customer can understand anywhere in the world. Thus, against advice from many cultural gurus, they introduced the same model into France – the home of serious eating – and into Japan and Russia. They were very successful.

However, a more complex business with a variety of local interfaces has to find a balance on the spectrum – between overwhelming the local processes and norms with those of America, France, UK or wherever and having no consistency in the way things are done. Thus the nature of the 'corporate umbrella' needs to be determined. Which values and processes do we believe are important enough to our success to be applied throughout the world?

That importance has to be sold locally so that it is owned by local management. Many years ago I was taught Proctor and Gamble's way of dealing with quality and productivity, and people did not question the American origin of what seemed to be excellent ways of doing things. On the other hand the local Manchester culture lived side by side with some worldwide principles in people management processes. I later found that the organization had a good system of collecting ideas from all over the world and modifying its processes accordingly, so that the perception was of 'the company way' rather than 'the American way'.

When ICL was faced with trying to consolidate some common principles out of a plethora of different appraisal schemes, it decided to launch a set of manuals on people and performance management processes to apply to all employees at all levels, and throughout the world. The series was entitled *Investing in People* and achieved high acceptability with managers and employees alike. The company felt that the processes of individual performance and development management were so much the key to business success that it should be part of an otherwise fairly thin 'corporate umbrella'.

However, André Laurent asserts from his research[7] that the assumption that national differences can be subjugated under the unifying culture of large multinational corporations is false. Deep-seated values regarding power, hierarchy, control and coordination remain. Laurent believes the successful culture of the future will be the one that has a minimum level of consistency but is able to capitalize on the strengths of the diversity of its national cultures.

Another issue for multinationals is the transfer of staff, particularly managers, in terms of acceptability. This is particularly an issue in Europe where on the one hand there is the movement towards a United States of Europe, and on the other are the strongest historical and cultural differences. One could draw up a matrix of each nation by each nation and mark with a tick which nationality is acceptable to manage an operation in which country!

Career management processes are made to operate by many multinationals across all boundaries but the effective careers manager will be sensitive to the influences of each national system on the formation and aspirations of the individuals in the local organization.

Influences due to industry sector or type of organization

Working in, for instance, a start up electronics company is immensely different in culture from working in the government Department of Social Security. Each sector of industry and commerce, each group of organizations with broadly the same interest, has different histories, different pressures and, therefore, cultures of their own. There is a natural tendency for job movements between organizations to be predominantly within a sector, especially if the sector has a unique technological base. So one finds 'computer people', 'motormen', 'management consultants' and 'retailers'. There are interesting natural bridges existing between sectors, a study of which is outside the scope of this book.

The particular aspects of culture that are affected by this group of influences include:

- The pace of change,
- The dominant players,
- Average size of organization,
- Extent of internationalism,
- The nature of competition,
- Barriers to entry,
- Age profiles,

- Norms and policies regarding promotion,
- Equal opportunities.

If the reader thinks of the sector in which he or she works against these parameters, and then asks 'is this combination of answers unique to my sector?' the answer will probably be yes. Most sectors have leading players who set the pace for the others, even though this may not be overt.

For example, the Information Technology sector is almost universally characterized by a relatively high labour turnover. This has the effect of frequent creation of opportunities and encourages career movement of all kinds. The average time in position is often not long enough to consolidate very much personal achievement, so the importance of seizing opportunities for promotion when available is seen as high. Reorganizations to meet the constantly changing technical and competitive environment are frequent and create their own opportunities. The smaller companies tend to have great informality, with very little hierarchical distinction and a young age profile. Most of the larger ones have developed distinctive cultures that pervade across national boundaries. Where supply and sales are on a global scale, internationalism is a major issue.

Competition is fierce and, therefore, reward systems are incentive-orientated and remuneration levels are high. Most of the typical jobs suit men and women equally, and so entry into the sector of women is relatively high. There is a large number of firms of all sizes in which to gain different kinds of experience, and many opportunities to start up a business arise.

By contrast an industry like industrial gases is characterized by a very small number of large, dominant firms, each of substance and solidity in the process chemical industry. Turnover is low, the pace of technical change is well controlled, organizational loyalty is high – and as a result the time spent in a position is longer and careers move at a slower pace. Although technology is global, markets tend to be locally defined by the economics of the industry, and the transfer of staff around the world is limited to less developed countries and technical exchange. The need for broad general managers is low, competition is limited and well understood, and it is primarily a man's world.

Both these examples from industry are likely to share values of meritocracy in promotion policies and reward structures. Organizations more in the public sector may be more formal and less flexible in terms of stepping outside accepted career patterns and reward structures. Careers may be more general and may cross boundaries more easily where administrative capability is a common denominator. Much is changing in parts of this sector but the differences in culture compared to the private sector are quite visible.

Another influence in this group is the structuring of firms or similar organizations into common interest groupings – both for employers and employees. Such bodies may set standards, provide some common processes and approaches, common training programmes for young people, etc – and may even constrain individual firms in some ways.

Because many career moves take place within the sector, norms and values develop which can make it difficult for outsiders to adapt. 'The problem is that he or she wasn't brought up in this business' has been heard many times. In people career management practices, competitors often share and collaborate in the common interest of the sector as a whole.

Influences from the parent organization

If there is an owning organization it may be quite separated from the local one where things actually happen. The distinctions between the two will depend on the level of centralization/decentralization allowed in the organization in cultural terms. Even though authority and responsibility may be decentralized, cultural issues in 'the way things are done' may still be strongly controlled. In some American multinationals very similar cultural values will be found everywhere in the world, dominating local national norms with the views of acceptable behaviour and effective systems promulgated by the great corporate headquarters of New Jersey or Massachusetts.

A parent organization may have a strong influence on:

The level of directiveness in career moves – particularly at senior levels, centralized planning may predominate and subdivisions be told whom they should receive and whom give up.

Internationalization policies – are commonly defined and often managed centrally, so that people from various parts of the organization are treated in the same way.

Processes of appraisal and potential identification – often not centrally prescribed, but similar principles and paperwork may be applied throughout an organization for consistency.

Manpower planning – organizations may wish to prescribe classifications of people and skills for the purpose of statistics and planning.

Job evaluation and grading – a common language of grading may be imposed, especially in organizations that are basically integrated. This is much less common in conglomerates.

Brand image – the positioning of the organization for the purpose of marketing to graduates is of great importance, and if a common 'brand' name is used then this is likely to be controlled centrally for each country.

Senior management development events – the provision of training and education may serve a number of subdivisions of the organization, but certainly for the senior management group a corporate approach is likely so that they share in the values and objectives of the parent.

Issues of corporate identification and loyalty – Goldsmith and Clutterbuck quote[8] the case of the proud and prestigious Jaguar Cars Company being instructed by their owners that the switchboard should announce to callers that they were 'Leyland Cars – large assembly plant number one'. Jaguar flags were replaced with Leyland; the company was split between two new Leyland divisions. Sir William Lyons, the founder, removed his portrait from the boardroom in protest. Fortunately, the more enlightened Sir Michael Edwardes reversed this attempted subjugation of a local culture.

In summary there is immense variation; organizations with subsidiaries in the same business will be more prescriptive than those holding companies whose only interest is in the bottom line. However, as the pool of management talent in an organization is one of its primary assets, it would seem unwise not to have some focus on the development and use of that pool. How far one goes in prescribing common processes depends very much on the organization's philosophy of management.

History is critical – parents and local organizations that are the product of mergers and acquisitions, demergers and disposals, can have a weaker coherence in their culture than organizations which have a long, uninterrupted history. This can be both a strength and a handicap.

Influences from the local organization

This should be the strongest set of influences of all and normally is. The local management, their example and value set, the observation of what counts, the practical systems and processes defining the way things are done – these are what the employee will observe and be part of. Particularly important and overriding from the local scene will be:

The behaviour and expectations of the chief executive and his or her team – these are the interpreters of the desired culture. Most of all, the chief executive (or the most senior local person that a group identify as representing the organization) plays the key role. What is it that gains his or her praise? His or her displeasure? What pressures does he or she put down the management chain? What are the things he or she gives active support to, ie frequently asks questions about and checks progress, as opposed to those things he or she just goes along with and thinks are fine things to do? Alan Mumford quotes in his study of reality at the top of organizations, *Developing Top Managers*[9], the case of the CEO who marked the draft corporate plan 'filed unread'. This became known, and the credibility of the corporate planning process thereafter followed a predictable path! Examples abound of positive signalling – Lord Sieff of Marks and Spencer once said that his first impression of a store was always gained by visiting the toilet facilities – if they were well looked after, it boded well for customers . . .

The real level of openness and sharing This may well be a corporate value, but how does it work in practice? What local styles of management and interaction with individuals are encouraged?

The level of parochialism Every sub-division has the opportunity to filter, reinterpret and modify the directives and procedures that may be given to it. What is submitted upwards (succession plans to HQ, lists of people with high potential) can just be an exercise to satisfy 'them' and may bear little reality to the truth. My experience is that if 'they' show no further interest or ask no questions, then trusting written data by itself is naive. If, however, they show a genuine supportive interest, looking to add value, then it is likely to be different.

Parochialism, or looking after our own interests, is the most natural occurrence in the world and to criticize it is like blowing in the wind. Nobody wants to expose their best talent for poaching elsewhere; no one wants to be told how to manage; nobody wants to be given the impression that others think they know more about their patch than they do. When people understand that benefits are two way, then some progress may be made. However, sometimes it cannot be two way – the centres of excellence in the organization have to support the less developed areas and have to accept their role as nurseries for the corporate good.

Promotional processes at the lower levels – everyone starts their career in some local unit, distant from the decision and policy makers in any organization of size. The way local management looks after individuals' early career and personal development can shape their whole future. Local cultural norms affect these significantly.

Recruitment and training policies – recruits are the potential future of the organization. The standards of selection and the professionalism of their training are thus critically important. The amount of effort and investment made may vary considerably. Some local units provide exemplary induction programmes; others give the person a desk and some manuals and tell them to get on with it. Some local top managers regard training as the first candidate for cost reduction when the squeeze comes; others see it as sacrosanct. A common conflict scenario in organizations is the difference between the wonderful story told by central graduate recruiters regarding the trainee programme and the neglect that actually happens when the new entrant arrives.

In summary, the interpretation of corporate policies and directives reflects both the commitment of the top team and the historical traditions and values of the local management.

If the local organization is part of an integrated structure such as a national sales organization with a lot of mobility between sites, there will be probably little difference between the local and parent culture. However, if it is in a different country, or it is a distinct self-standing unit like an R&D establishment, or a specialized factory, or most of all a subsidiary company whose relation to the mother organization is only one of ownership – then quite distinct differences may be present.

Summary of influences

Table 2.2 shows the relative strength of these influences on aspects of career management. The weaker the sum of the influences, the less resistance to change may be expected.

Table 2.2 Aspects of career management related to cultural influences

	national	industry	parent org.	local org.
Chief executive values, messages etc	L	L	M	H
Formality of process	M	M	M	H
Level of direction given on career moves	L	M	H	H
Organizational decentralization	L	M	H	H
Line/personnel role	L	M	H	H
Openness of individual discussion	M	L	M	H
Visibility of career paths	L	M	M	H
Speed of movement of people	L	H	M	M
Age profiles	M	M	H	M
Mobility	M	H	M	H
Equal opportunities	M	H	H	H
Internationalization	L	H	H	M
Organizational loyalty	M	M	H	H
Potential identification	M	M	H	H
Importance of qualifications	H	M	L	L

(L = low, M = medium, H = high)

CULTURAL DIMENSIONS AFFECTING CAREER MANAGEMENT

Having looked at a variety of influences on the organization, we need now to focus on the major cultural dimensions that will affect our ability to meet the needs we have derived from Chapter 1. On each we will look at the opposing ends of a spectrum and discuss ways of managing change from a current position. The dimensions are:

- Chief executive commitment
- Formality of process
- Promotion and movement
- Decentralization
- Resources

Chief executive commitment

The section on local influences demonstrates the importance of the values and messages coming from the chief executive. Some clarity may be needed on the use of this term – for there may be a hierarchy of chief executives in some organizational structures.It depends from where we are trying to influence. Thus, if I am in a region of a bank, say, the key person for me may be the regional executive director. If I am in the HQ of a large, dispersed organization it will be the company chairman or managing director. In all organizations the chief executive at the top is key; however, the relative power and influence of local

Passive commitment only	Full, active commitment
– May or may not agree to processes but takes no active interest in their effectiveness (signs the introduction to the booklets only) – Espouses beliefs such as 'good people will rise to the top anyway' – Invests little or no personal time in people development matters – Unwilling to invest resources – Regards succession plans, etc, as bureaucracy	– Makes clear his/her support for each process to everybody – Has a regular review of plans/status/progress/issues – Personally involved in potential assessment, mentoring, development centres – Proactive in needs analysis and policy development – Sets objectives or standards for his/her managers in people growth – Budgets deliberately for resources and activities

Figure 2.2 The commitment spectrum

executives on people development issues will vary from case to case. It is important to recognize that, even with processes that are designed to be organization-wide by the HQ, their practical application and real usefulness is in the hands of the local management. The two extremes of commitment are shown in Figure 2.2.

How does one influence a shift from left to right? Sadly, there is no recipe. Erudite books have been written, such as *The Change Masters* by Kanter[7] to which readers are referred. But there follows a simple checklist for attempting to influence changes in 'mindset':

- Determine what is important to the executive and show that the change will give benefits in the relevant areas.
- Achieve a level of credibility through personal commitment to the executive's own, and the organizational, objectives so that one will be listened to.
- Work through others who have stronger influence, either internally or externally.
- Make it easy for the executive to show more active commitment through solid supportive work.

This last point is particularly important – through preparing material in a concise way, having clear statements of where decisions are needed, being an efficient secretary at review meetings, and so on.

Finally, perhaps it is easy to prejudge and label an apparent lack of interest when what the influencer really needs is more confidence to get the dialogue going in the first place.

Formality of processes

Every self-respecting dynamic individual, whether in management or in a specialist role, will say that he or she does not support bureaucracy. However, effectiveness depends on some form of order and discipline in the way things are carried out.

Some organizations thrive on having little written down in the way of formal processes and procedures. To invent a new form is anathema. Others have a process or procedure for everything. Most managers find bureaucracy suffocating and do their best to get around it. They soon learn the processes that have sanctions attached and those that do not. One of the most difficult things for an organization to determine is the balance between the disciplines necessary for organizational effectiveness and the avoidance of those that have 'built in non-conformance', ie,they are designed in such a way that people will bypass some elements to get the job done. In the processes of people management the balance is critical, because short cuts are highly undesirable and yet, if too much is requested, this is what happens.

Processes are visible and this is important for openness and trust in the organization. So the aim should be to make them simple, easy to manage, monitor and implement. Like everything else initial managerial commitment is crucial for them to work in reality – it is surprising that a number of specialists introduce new processes and systems without asking any 'customers' to try them out first.

This does not imply a need for complex bureaucratic form-filling: the level of formality must be consistent with the culture of the organization. The emphasis is on a systematic framework, as opposed to a laissez-faire abdication. The extremes of formality are shown in Figure 2.3.

Informal laissez-faire	**Systematic framework**
– No clear policies for personal growth and career management. – No understood processes or procedures for assessment, development or planning. – No regular reviews of succession or future needs. – Career moves are opportunist. – Appraisals focus on the current job only. – Appointments based on networks.	– Clear policy made public to all. – A framework of processes and procedures has been designed for the particular needs of the organization. – Personal development and career moves are a planned and managed process. – The potential in the organization is regularly checked and compared with needs.

Figure 2.3 The formality spectrum

Shifting to the right of this spectrum will fail if it is too far from the norms and expectations that are acceptable. The style of the HR specialist is critical – if that style is to sit in an office and seek to create more formality through paper it may well prove a failure. Most managers respond better to a face to face discussion – including the persuasion of the benefits of change, however erudite the paper that outlines the case. Likewise they will participate better in systematic processes with good supporting assistance – it's no use crying that 'they **ought to want** to do this'.

Some long established organizations may find they are so far to the right of this spectrum that the need is to create greater flexibility and give greater responsibility to the individual. This can be more difficult to achieve than the moves towards greater systematization.

Promotion and job movement

The way promotion and job movements happen in the organization may be more or less **directive** – meaning the extent to which the organization determines in its own wisdom who should be moved where and when, as opposed to the freedom of individual choice. The latter freedom is both for individuals taking an offered move, and for managers in their choice of candidates. Typically cradle-to-grave organizations have historically been more directive – banks, oil companies, some large multinationals and some public sector organizations like the armed forces. The extremes of the directiveness spectrum are shown in Figure 2.4.

Directive	Non-directive
– Publication of opportunities limited to those expected to go to outside press. – Selection chosen by committee and based on records. – Very special reason needed to reject proposed move by individual. – Data on potential, etc. used for centralized planning and strongly controlled. – Personnel role is strongly managing.	– All vacancies openly made available to all. – Selection interactive, discursive; final choice by recruiting manager. – Individual free to turn down an offer; not held against him/her for future reference. – Data confidential, owned mutually, used as an input to options. – Personnel role is advisory and supportive.

Figure 2.4 The directiveness spectrum

However, it is probably true that career management is much more difficult in the non-directive style. For example, managers like to work with known quantities rather than the unknown, so to put the case for the bright engineer needing sales experience to the sales manager – who can choose some already proven salespeople – is quite a challenge! The non-directive style can result in a low value given to international experience – of what use is it to the majority of the home-based managers? If the culture is non-directive, there is a need at least to define a 'corporate umbrella' which says 'there are some subsets of our organization that are of corporate interest, and we, the top management, want to know and approve what is happening to people in those subsets'. This is discussed further in Chapter 6.

Making a shift in either direction is very much associated with corporate philosophies of individual accountability and personal freedom. The tendency of organizations (in the UK) is to go from left to right – the careers manager must work within the culture that exists or initiate a process of change in a difficult area.

Centralization versus decentralization

Organizations have generally moved over recent years towards greater decentralization, putting authority and responsibility further downwards. This is accompanied by less resource at the central points. The characteristics of the two extremes are illustrated in Figure 2.5.

Centralized	Decentralized
– Common policies and procedures can be operated. – Information in consistent formats. – All resources corporately owned. – May demand layers of specialist resources and unproductive liaison. – Cross-divisional moves easier to implement.	– Control of development activities limited to the 'populations of corporate interest'. – Cross-divisional movements difficult. – Ownership of talent parochial. – Freedom to innovate new people development processes. – Short term demands may overshadow longer term considerations.

Figure 2.5 The centralization spectrum

Career management can be made effective at any point on this spectrum, with adaptation as needed. A balance is ideal – of local autonomy and ownership, and yet with just enough interaction with the centre to ensure that the needs of the main organization are met and that the individual has the maximum opportunity of career development options.

Resources

A larger organization is more likely to have the resources to invest in the design, publication and implementation of a more comprehensive system than a small one. However, we do not need to confuse comprehensiveness with complexity, and all organizations ought to determine what is right for them and then use whatever is necessary to implement the need.

There is a debate to be had, nevertheless, about the value of specialist resources. Cultural attitudes may be polarized as shown in Figure 2.6.

People management is the task of line managers, and a minimum of specialist advisers is needed, if any.	**People management should mostly be handled by personnel specialists so line managers can get on with running things**
– Line managers take full responsibility for people development – appraisals, training, career planning. – Personnel people provide administrative support.	– Personnel look after career counselling, job selection, training needs. – Personnel specialists design and manage the processes of people development, and control all movements.

Figure 2.6 The spectrum of cultural attitudes

Each organization needs to determine where it wants to be on the spectrum. For most it will be in an in-between position. A good principle to start from is that managers are responsible for the development of their people. The soundest way of building this into the culture is in the design and implementation of the appraisal system – which is perhaps the most powerful tool available.

The role of personnel should be that of professional expertise, ensuring that things happen, providing additional guidance and counselling where needed, analyzing the data available, recommending courses of action – but with the line manager making and communicating the decisions.

The reality is that even with the best training, managers are going to be variable in their ability both to analyse the development needs of their people and to spend the necessary time on doing something about it. The understanding of each manager of the processes he or she is supposed to follow, the knowledge of the wider organization and its opportunities, the skill in analyzing needs and synthesizing development plans – these are bound to be dependent on the style and interest of the manager.

Professional expertise is needed then in a) the design and coordination of the parts of the system (if it is not coordinated and maintained it will have a good chance of dying out) and b) providing individual added value in working with managers on the development of their staff. Statements about 'overhead resources', 'decentralization of management decisions', 'avoiding unnecessary duplication' and so on are frequently heard. The application of these in practice must be put in context with the needs related to the objectives of the organization and the cultural environment that supports it.

The dimensions considered above are the most significant. The following are also relevant:

Reward systems

People are usually quick to work out 'what counts around here'. Is it who you know, who you cultivate? Is it getting good numbers? Is it working hard? Is it doing a spell in a particular department? Is it expected that a period of operating abroad is a necessary route to promotion? Are there grade thresholds that become an obsession to be reached, regardless of broadening en route, because of the status they bring?

We may have many apparently effective systems and processes, but underlying cultural norms and reward systems such as bonus and status benefits undermine them.

The pace (and acceptance of) change

The faster an organization changes, restructures, etc, the greater the opportunities that open up for career management. Conversely it makes it more difficult to career plan systematically.

If an organization has a relatively high loss rate of staff this obviously increases opportunities, but management needs to understand the reasons for those loss rates and ensure they are not because of bad management.

An environment of fast change creates it own mindset in people so that they look for change and seek out their next opportunity. That opportunity may not be upwards promotion, but may be getting new experiences from a different job at the same level. But a culture with a high pace of change can lead people to become restless if they have been in the same post for more than a year or two, and too much change can lead to a lack of achievement and consolidation.

The more static organization finds fewer options for growing its people, although this is often given as an excuse for minimal action. Every organization that **thinks** it is static should regularly look back five years and see how much **has** changed – it is a good lesson, and one can usually assume that the coming five years will be more and not less turbulent.

International perspectives

Chapter 1 showed some of the ways in which organizations operate internationally. However, the level of international thinking in the homebase culture where major decisions are made can vary considerably. For example, how is foreign service valued in the organization? Are certain levels of position barred to those who have not served outside the homebase, and is this barrier enforced and accepted? Or is it the case, regardless of statements and policies that apparently encourage foreign service as being important to the internationalization of the organization, that the best people avoid it and are encouraged to avoid it by their advisers; that expatriates struggle to get reestablished on return; and that no preferential value is in fact attached to such services in consideration for posts or promotion subsequently?

Good procedures for transfers and assignments are essential. But having these, and good policy statements, will not achieve an internationally minded culture. Clear objectives and rules have to be set and top management has to abide by them consistently for a period of probably at least five years until people begin to believe that 'this is the way things are around here'.

Equal opportunities

Scarcely an organization can be found today in the developed countries that does not have a policy of equal opportunities. Not many extend this to positive affirmation as at the time of writing.

This becomes a practical business issue in the 1990s regardless of any other pressures, as the shortage of skilled staff will intensify. So organizations are developing policies designed to make it easier for women to leave and return to work. However, in the context of careers there are still big issues. Nearly every organization has a lower percentage of women managers than is consistent with the intake levels of women to the organization. Partly this is due to the historical process of development and the percentage of younger women who show potential for management is greater than it was. Therefore one might assume that this ratio will steadily increase.

The real cultural question is whether there are non-explicit discriminators in terms of the criteria for selection (derived mainly from studies/analysis of existing male managers), and in terms of the hidden disadvantages of the career break in putting women managers behind in the competitive race. This is sometimes termed 'the glass ceiling'. Women who have specialist careers – in, for instance, personnel, finance or various kinds of public sector work are not affected as much by these issues, because expertise always has its value.

Commitment to training and development

The real commitment to training and providing a message that people are regarded as an investment rather than a cost, is a crucial cultural element for success in career management. This is not seen in one off programmes but in an ongoing recognition that all staff need constant inputs to their development. It is an attitude of mind and, as it costs money, is seen also in more tangible commitment. So one would look for explicit norms of annual number of training days per person and budgets compatible with these norms.

A highly desirable country house available for in-house training does not equal commitment in itself – and it may not be in the organization's business interest at all.

However, there needs to be a significant level of interest from the top management team in the priorities and content of development activity, for their support and attendance at presentation/feedback sessions and for them to make it clear to their own operations that they regard the activities as important. Such a team would always do the appraisals of their own managers, and find the necessary time and money to spend on their development.

Committed individual managers can always be found. But the question is whether the example is set by all because it is part of the value system of the organization.

SUMMARY

The culture of an organization is a product of history, a variety of external and internal influences, and the priorities and values of key people in it. It must be supportive of the objectives for the future and may need to be changed to enable the strategies to be realized. There is a set of beliefs, policies, messages, expectations of managers, activities, processes for people development, areas of expertise and measures of success – that needs to be in harmony within itself, and with the future needs.

We looked at the sources of influence on an organization's culture. In seeking to make changes in it we have to start with top management's vision and commitment of where it wants it to move to, back it up with communication and education, and then change the systems and procedures of the organization to be consistent with the new state.

Those responsible for careers management have to succeed in their endeavours within the cultural environment, and adapt appropriately to it to be effective. They may well influence the process of change personally, because the areas of intervention touch so many aspects of the cultural make-up of the organization. We selected five major aspects from many that affect career management: the importance of the commitment from the most senior executive; the level of formality in process management; the level of directiveness in job movement; the amount of decentralization of authority, and the role of personnel and line management.

The use of opinion or attitude surveys to assess how people perceive things is recommended as a way of checking progress. This is mentioned further in Chapter 8.

PLANNING FOR ACTION

Problems of reality

This chapter has been all about reality anyway! But one or two problems for completeness:

1. There is often a multitude of local cultures. The careers manager may be providing a service over a fairly diverse range of local organizations all of which have different sets of influences, different priorities and different needs.

This is bound to be true; it emphasizes the need for the careers manager to focus on dialogue, discussion and on-the-ground help rather than paper processes. We still want to be systematic and retain the same principles and policies throughout, but the local organizations will move at a different pace. In my role as personnel director for ICL Europe with responsibility for a large number of countries, this was a familiar problem. I could observe countries going forward under a keen general manager aided by a professional human resources manager for a while, then losing months of impetus when a key player left. I could see the effects of the French environmental culture as against the Danish for example, working on the same issues in quite different ways. But I had my 'blueprint' of where we wanted to go – revised and reassessed with changing circumstances – and that provided the cohesion and direction.

2. People growth and career development is a long term process. You cannot change the framework and processes often – they need time to be effective. Yet an organization may be subject to frequent changes of chief executive and/or human resources director, each of whom has different ideas and emphasis.

Perhaps the most difficult problem of all is creating a framework that will last. Very strong cultures (like IBM for example) are bigger than any individual contributor, and what has been carefully decided to be the right direction cannot be overturned by a mere single player. If there is a solution, it lies in getting commitment from the whole management team to the framework and components of career management – so that if one or two members of that team leave (however important) there is the residue who still own the framework for themselves and can influence newcomers.

Indicators of success relating to this chapter are listed in Table 2.3.

Table 2.3 Indicators of success checklist

Cultural influences	1. The cultural influences from the different sources are understood and have been evaluated.
Cultural measurement	2. The organization is measured along a spectrum of key cultural dimensions – determined specifically for the organization – at least annually. 3. In addition the desired state is noted as indicated by the needs from the strategic plan.
Cultural change	4. Any gaps arising form part of a carefully planned cultural change plan
Operating a career management framework successfully	5. Successful measures can be shown on the various processes of people development in each of the cultures where they are applied.

Action for those responsible for career management

1. Compare any written down values of the organization with reality, and assess their impact on the policies, processes and actual practice of career management.
2. Measure the relevant cultural dimensions using a tool like Figure 2.7.
3. Integrate the conclusions from the above with the conclusions from the actions of Chapter 1 to formulate, if necessary, a cultural change plan that will provide the environment for the career management framework that the organization needs.
4. If you are seeking to manage a career framework over a variety of cultures (several countries for example) what considerations need to be taken into account for each?

REFERENCES

1 Peters, T. and Waterman, R., *In Search of Excellence*, Harper and Row, 1982.

2 Pye, A. and Mangham, A. L., *Review of Management Training*, Working party No 3, BIM/CBI, 1987

3 Mayo, A. J., *Business Strategies and Management Development*, Industrial and Commercial Training, March 1989

4 Hofstede, G., *The Cultural Relativity of Organizational Practices and Theories*, Journal of International Business Studies, fall 1983

5 Handy, C. and others, *The Making of Managers*, NEDO, 1987

6 Evans P., Doz, Y., and Laurent, A., *Human Resource Management in International Firms*, Macmillan, 1989.

Evans, P., *New Directions in Career Management*, Personnel Management, December 1986

Measuring the Cultural Dimensions

Place a * measuring where the organization is **today** and a + where the organization would **like to be**.

Chief executive commitment

Low | | | | | High

Formality of processes

Low | | | | | High

Directiveness

Low | | | | | High

Decentralization

Low | | | | | High

Availability of specialist resources

Low | | | | | High

Supportive reward system

Low | | | | | High

The pace of change

Low | | | | | High

International outlook

Low | | | | | High

Equal opportunities

Low | | | | | High

Commitment to training

Low | | | | | High

Figure 2.7

7 Laurent, A., *The Cultural Diversity of Western Conceptions of Management,* International Studies of Management and Organisation 1983 Vol XIII Nos 1/2

3. LAYING THE FOUNDATIONS

This chapter lays some foundations in career management, demonstrating how to establish a framework and a language within which we can build a set of processes.

THE SCOPE OF CAREER MANAGEMENT

My own definition of career management is as follows:

The design and implementation of organizational processes which enable the careers of individuals to be planned and managed in a way that optimizes both the needs of the organization and the preferences and capabilities of individuals.

Two dimensions emerge from this – those relating to the organization and those relating to the individual. A spectrum of activities can be drawn up from one extreme to the other: corporate succession planning can be seen as a process primarily for the benefit of the organization, and third party career counselling as specifically for the benefit of the individual. Then there are processes like appraisal which bring the two together. At this interface the role of an employee's manager is fundamental. The aspirations of the individual may neither match the organization's view of his or her capability nor meet its real needs – hence the importance of not letting the two parties operate apart from one another and making sure mutual objectives are agreed and aimed for.

Figure 3.1 shows a list of the processes that might be found; the majority of organizations have some of these in name but with varying degrees of effectiveness. There is a significant

Career management processes (Numbers in brackets indicate chapters in the book where the process is covered in detail)		
Individual career planning processes	**Joint career planning processes**	**Organizational processes**
– Occupational choice assessment/counselling (5) – Career planning workshops (5) – Self-development plans/activities (7) – Pre-retirement courses – Use of career resource centres (5) – Careers seminars – Use of computerized career planning (5) – Writing CVs and personal growth profiles (3)	– Appraisal and development reviews (5) – Potential assessment centres (5) – Career guidance/ development centres (5) – Mentoring (5) – Career counselling/career planning (5) – Outplacement (5) – Career breaks and alternative methods of employment (5)	– Appointment processes (4) – Career structures (4) – High flyer schemes (4) – Organization/grade structures (4) – Succession planning (6) – Creating opportunities for experience (7) – Manpower planning (6) – Expatriate policies (7) – Defining person specifications for jobs (3) (adapted from T Hall [1])

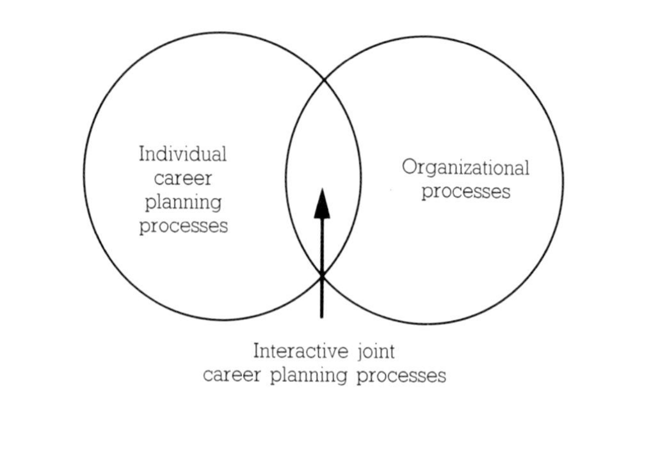

Figure 3.1 Career management processes

difference between having an appraisal system nominally in place and one that really achieves all its objectives. But effectiveness comes from integration and cohesion. The outputs of one process flow as inputs to another and there is added value both from individual processes and from the overall integration.

This book is written with the role of organizations primarily in mind, and its objective is to look at ways in which organizations can manage careers for the benefit of their objectives. This is not to denigrate self-development, which is a key factor in the total success of career management. What is important is to have integration of the processes in use. So manpower planners do not work in isolation from those concerned with career planning; employees participating in career counselling exercises are not totally distanced from the organization, and so on.

The term career management implies that somebody is doing the managing. Who should that some one be? Line managers are usually expected to assess, advise and counsel their people in their development and careers and rightly so. However, we should expect human resources specialists, including those working in a generalist role, to see this as a part of their special contribution. It is asking a lot of most line managers to have the level of professional and organizational knowledge to cope effectively other than in the function or unit they know best. Also a measure of the importance of an issue is whether an organization believes it worthy of some dedicated responsibility (for the small and medium sized firm it is probably not realistic to have a full time person). A balance is needed however; there is a risk that line managers devolve their entire responsibility to the specialist whereas the responsibility **must** remain with them.

A dedicated resource, in terms of a 'careers manager', provides continuity and consistency, drives and educates the various parts of the organization to fulfil their roles in managing careers, and develops the constituent components of career management, keeping them in line with the needs of the organization. The careers manager initiates, influences, coordinates and manages. (If specialists in this area lose touch with reality and get tied up with their own ideas of interest then they can expect the organization to lose sympathy.) Such a role is frequently found in institutional organizations and usually in major corporations, although not always dedicated to career management alone.

Unfortunately, too often this is the type of role seen by many chief executives as an unnecessary overhead, either because 'people should look after their own careers like I did' or perhaps 'we don't want a lot of overheads at the centre'. Not enough human resource directors have a background in people development and so this is not top of their agenda. However, the benefits of managing 'people growth' effectively are an essential logic of business prosperity.

The term career management is distinguished in the total context of people development from those training and development activities that are more concerned with performance enhancement. Whereas developing managers is probably more complex and demanding, growing the potential of all employees in whatever direction is also appropriate.

THE INTERACTION BETWEEN CAREERS AND OTHER LIFE AREAS

A lot has been written, particularly in America, about life balancing – between work, family, and leisure or other interests. In a landmark book published in 1978,[2] Ed Schein – a much respected writer at the Sloan School, MIT – discussed what he called the biosocial life cycle and particularly the interaction of work and family, and work and self-development issues. He argues that career management must take account of the whole person and his or her environment. The three components of the interactions have their own cycles – moving through long stretches of smooth waters but from time to time encountering turbulence. Life moves inexorably forwards, with points of choice along the way, aiming points and milestones. The evidence that many people find untapped potential and abilities later in life is quite strong, and encouraging in the context of career management. It seems that individuals strive in the earlier years to come to an equilibrium with their environment – to understand what they are good at and what they are not so good at – and to realize they have a place and can be accepted as they are. Once people have passed this point it becomes a tough job to change behaviour related to personality – even though new knowledge and active skills may be absorbed. Some people give up learning about themselves and adapting behaviour in their early 20s; some never do.

Many employees, particularly in Europe, would regard their personal lives as an area to be kept to themselves and separate from work. However, family life becomes of significant interest to the organization in some circumstances – such as relocation, expatriation and maternity leave. People also change in their values and priorities with age; the importance of career ambition changes also and anyone concerned with career management must recognize that people have different needs at different times.

Career phases

The demands on a career management policy differ as a career progresses through different phases, as does the practical way that we apply processes and systems and provide counselling to individuals. Shakespeare identified seven ages of man; Schein made it nine; I am going to focus on three. The so-called mid-career crisis has occupied many writers in the last ten years, but I would argue that it is the earlier years that are too often neglected and that are so critical.

A career may last approximately 40 years, spent earning a living and building up some way of living comfortably in retirement. Concerns about a career are concentrated in the earlier half of this period and the divergence between the needs of individuals becomes increasingly marked in the latter half. It is often assumed that the term career implies 'ever onwards and upwards', and once a ceiling is reached in this climb someone's career has reached a halt. Worse still is to have the label 'has reached his or her level of incompetence'. Certainly, ambitious individuals can reach a point of frustration as they see the way ahead blocked, but a career must be seen as the continuation of personal growth rather than progressive hierarchial steps upwards. This is absolutely fundamental in an approach to career management – the alternative limits our understanding of potential and restricts the population in which we will take interest.

The great majority of young people when they join an organization look forward to some kind of advancement. (And an organization should not employ them if they don't – to run out of personal growth ambition before one has started is bad news indeed!) Some want to be managing directors, some good, respected professionals, some to make a lot of money – and many actually have not thought about it very specifically but have a generalized ambition to make progress. Much more important at this stage is the quality of training provided and the feeling of 'fit' with members of the organization whom they have met. Nevertheless, within a year their vision of a future has begun to take a different shape. It will be heavily influenced, for good or ill, by the positive and negative perceptions of their older colleagues who have had their own different histories of career advancement and personal experience.

The three main phases are set out in Figure 3.2.

Phase one – the discovery phase

Lasting approximately the first ten years, this is a period of adapting to work, discovering capabilities, absorbing knowledge, seeking experience – and beginning to understand firstly the general direction one's career should take and secondly how far along that chosen direction one might reasonably set as a goal. In the UK relatively few people follow the career they thought they had embarked on when they joined their first organization, as one often points out to the graduate being interviewed who says his or her first priority is 'to use my degree'. In countries where the educational system prepares people more thoroughly for a specific career, the opposite is the case – it is not so easy to make a change in the early years.

The organization needs to concentrate attention on people in this phase. Working with individuals to help them in their choices – however varied or limited – is a most worthwhile activity, particularly in the critical choice of specialist/professional or managerial career. Both parties should find out the core areas of capability of the individual, be able to identify the most appropriate career path, and form a view of the realistic speed of career progress and growth potential. If there is a policy of providing opportunities for individual career choice assessment, those in the discovery phase should have total access to them. Too often people change jobs and move up the

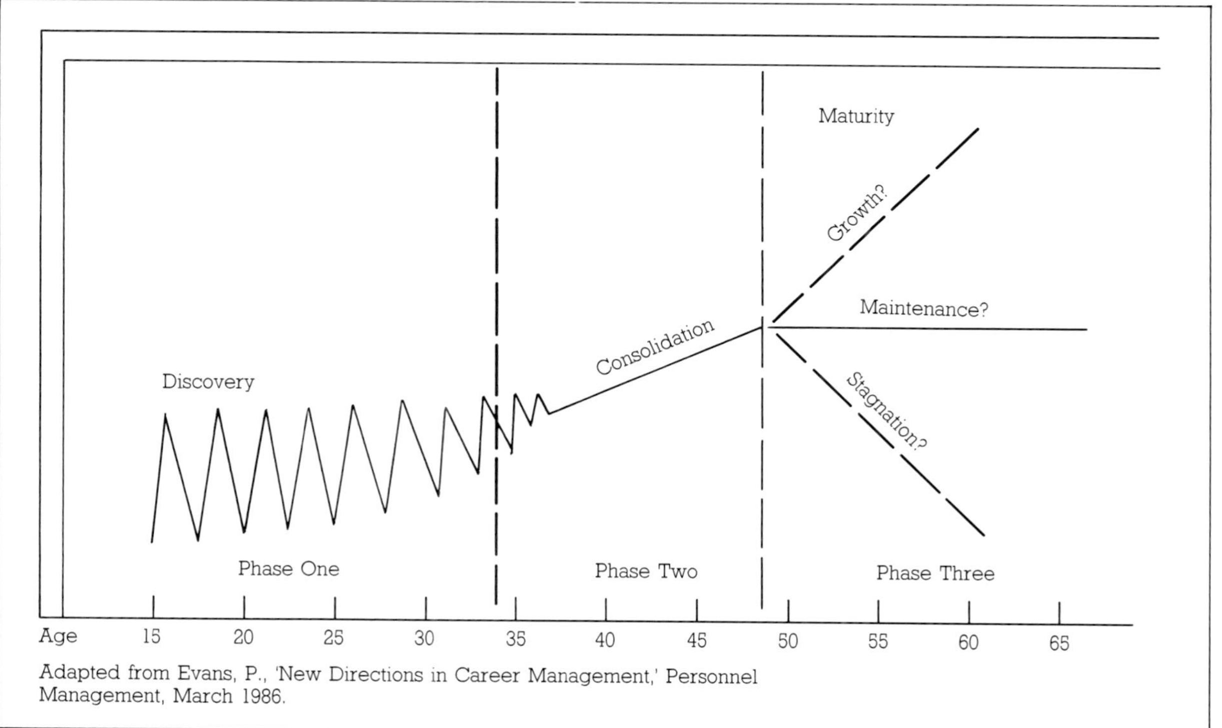

Adapted from Evans, P., 'New Directions in Career Management,' Personnel Management, March 1986.

Figure 3.2 Stages in career development

ladder without really assessing if it is right for them and, by their mid–30s, they have achieved a level from which lateral development becomes difficult to achieve.

It is a time when individuals are most likely to leave the organization they first joined. The phenomenon of the two or three year itch prevails in most organizations. People leave because of frustrated expectations, being left to stagnate in some forgotten part of the organization, being advised by some very junior personnel person who knows almost as little about the organization as the disenchanted individual, having a manager who has no time to spend with them . . . these are familiar and not forgiveable experiences. Losses for these reasons in the early years is an unsung and hidden cost. However, other reasons may be discomfort with the type of career or organization that has been chosen – a reassessment of their true career anchor, or because the relative comfort of being a trainee has ceased and now they must stand on their own feet. Many such partings are quite the best thing – the individual and the organization do not match and it is best to cut any losses before this phase is completed. Too few organizations face up to such issues honestly and forget that the earlier some partings are made the better it is for both parties.

The chapter on cultures showed how different nationalities typically view the time spent in a job. In the more turbulent and fast moving organizations a real risk is that young people change responsibilities before they have had the chance to learn, consolidate and apply their learning to some real achievement. Most jobs require at least 18 months for this process, often two years or more. It is important for development of the individual that the cycle of learning through experience is completed wherever possible.

It is a time of life when people are most mobile. They are likely to be the most keen to gain international experience – and this is often a personal goal in itself. How many MBAs have enjoyed themselves and matured enormously in remote parts of the world in the oil or construction industries – but suddenly find they have no career path, so choose an MBA as a new starting point? But this mobility is a great asset – it provides opportunities for giving lateral and unusual experience which cannot be given so easily in later life – when status and ties restrict.

The professional careers manager will concentrate on this group just as much as the more senior people, for herein lies the future leadership of the organization. He or she may not know every individual personally, but should be satisfied that good processes are being applied effectively.

It is the time of life when most will marry, begin to own property, and develop lifestyles. Women in this phase follow the same pattern as men but for many another choice is going to be made – to have children or not, when, and how to reconcile this with other life objectives? An organization must have policies which take account of this, not because it is fashionable to do so but because the needs for skilled resources demand it.

Phase two – the consolidation phase

This is a period approximately from 30 to 50 years old, sometimes starting or finishing later. It is about realizing (or not realizing) ambition and finding the level of one's contribution. Many people go on to higher things after the age of 50 – Churchill did not become Prime Minister until he was 66. But most people have either reached their level, or know what it is going to be by this age.

Whereas in phase one the major concerns are choosing a career direction, the majority of people towards the end of phase two experience a constriction of opportunity. If in management, the narrowing of the pyramid is an obvious cause; if in a specialist role of some kind, the level of recognition of expertise has probably peaked. So most people experience a plateau of one kind or another – American writers describe this as a crisis as if it is inevitable, but it need not necessarily be so. Professor John Hunt of the London Business School referred to it as the 'managerial menopause'[3] and it is a subject that has fascinated many (mainly academic) writers.

It is quite a natural phenomenon. The reality is that people follow personal growth paths as in Figure 3.3.

The number of people in the various bands is governed by a normal distribution. Thus about 5% follow the fast growth curves; about 5% make very little progress and the majority of the people level out somewhere in the middle of the organiz-

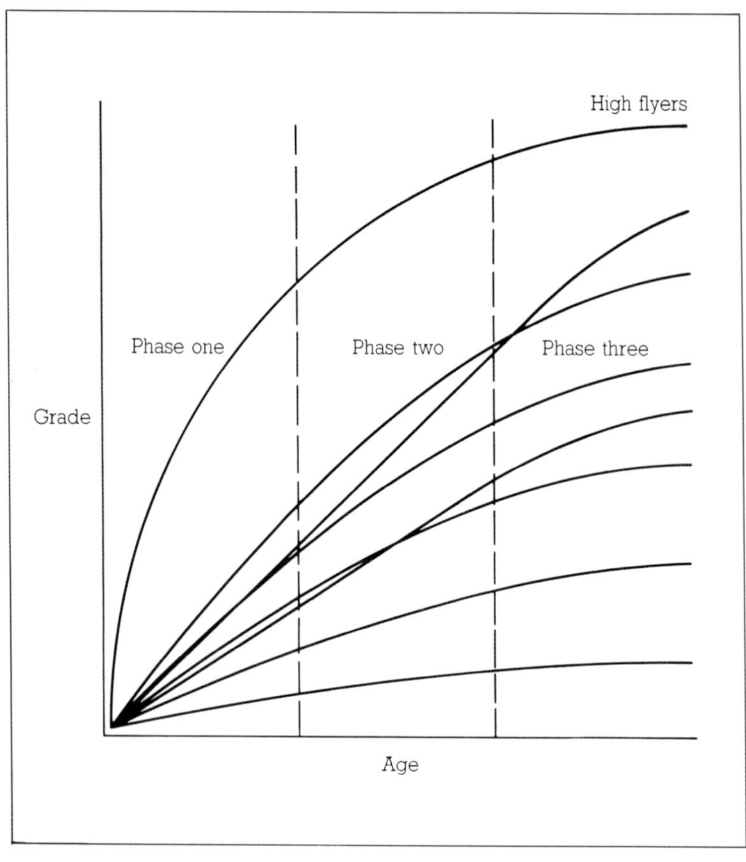

Figure 3.3 Typical career paths

ation around the age of 40 to 45. However, this natural characteristic is exacerbated in many organizations by the tendency to reduce levels of management, particularly in the middle. The move is from a hierarchical organization to a more horizontal one, where problems are solved by ad hoc project teams; business units are smaller and more autonomous. Personal development needs, therefore, to be more horizontal also – accumulating new knowledge and skills from new situations rather than from having bigger numbers to manage. In time, this should reduce the feeling of being on a plateau.

Douglas T Hall in the chapter on career development processes in his textbook on human resource management [4] describes a number of varieties of career path models and these are reproduced in Figure 3.4. They are more or less self-explanatory.

Does the general phenomenon of plateauing lead to a large number of frustrated individuals? Not necessarily so – most of the people on this plateau know they have reached their limit of competence (in terms of level of responsibility), or they are secure and comfortable and do not wish additional stress or workload, or they have imposed other constraints on themselves. It is a time when the balance of family/leisure/career is more than likely changing – children growing older and perhaps leaving home; spouse's career reaching maturity also perhaps; assuming positions of responsibility outside work or work related but in an external environment.

There may be some frustration nevertheless. There are those who have been led to believe, falsely, that the top is still reachable, yet they watch others taking precedence. There are some with the real ability to take top responsibilities – but opportunities are limited; they may wait patiently but if the organization cannot provide enough challenges they will seek them elsewhere.

There may be uncertainty and ambiguity about the way ahead but both the organization and the individual should see this as a time of 'investment return'. Whereas people may level out in hierarchical terms this should not mean the end of personal growth. Indeed this phase is a challenge for the organization in many ways, for example:

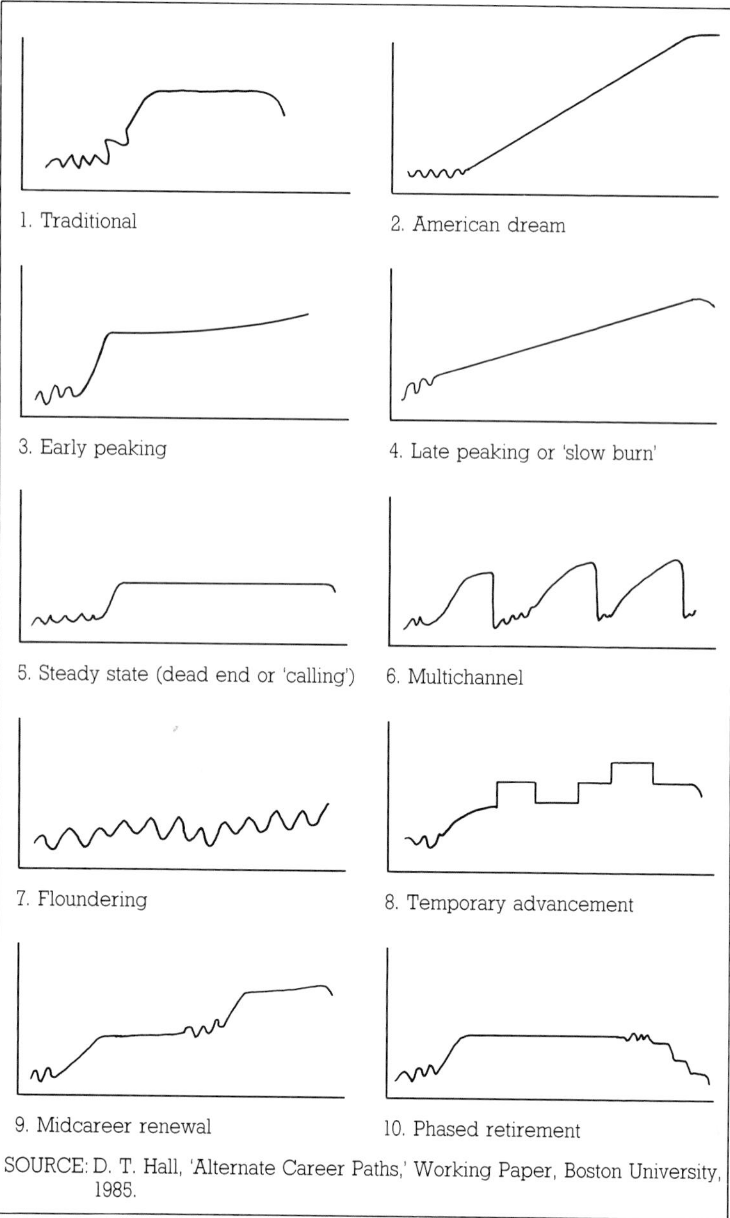

SOURCE: D. T. Hall, 'Alternate Career Paths,' Working Paper, Boston University, 1985.

Figure 3.4 Alternative career path models

- To try and ensure that we understand the capabilities of and make way for those people who do have the highest potential, and manage their experience.
- To be flexible enough in structuring opportunities and tasks in the organization to provide continual challenges for those who have reached a 'glass ceiling'.
- To use flexible and broad based people to cope with the varying demands that the organization faces, for example in mergers and acquisitions.
- To provide in reward structures the opportunity to return to a specialist or professional role for some managers who have reached hierarchical limits, without loss.
- To use the experience of these people in mentoring and helping younger people.
- To maintain the self-esteem and personal growth of those who have reached their hierarchical level of competence.
- To provide the means of integrating career break facilities for women, or for any staff.

This is a period of life when values become firmly established. Mobility is often reduced for various reasons, most commonly children's education. Ambitions become muted and balanced against other satisfactions in life. A level of financial stability is normally reached and the rationale of making decisions on the basis of how much money a change will provide decreases as this phase progresses. Status is, nevertheless, important to people, and this often governs a decision to make a change – as does anything that gives the visibility of status, like a bigger company car.

Phase three – the maturity phase

It is a tragic mistake to write off people over 50. Some do lose flexibility, fail to understand changing values, changing environments, lose steampower, and become old-fashioned. But people in this phase do have a substantial accumulation of knowledge and experience. The challenge for the organization is to capitalize on that experience. It may not always be within the organization – it may be some external body where representation is of some benefit to the organization, eg an official on an industry or academic committee with related interests.

In the US it is illegal to discriminate in the area of job opportunities on the basis of age. In the UK, the Institute of Personnel Management has made a statement on both the unfairness and illogicality of discrimination, especially in the light of current demographic changes. The statement[5] asserts that correlations between age and performance or mental ability have no substance, and that discrimination is wasteful of particularly valuable resources. Tony Buzan, the 'brain training' expert, quotes research that the brain increases its effectiveness with use, and that, even with the loss of 10,000 brain cells a day from birth, only 3% are lost by the age of 80. Like most aspects of the human condition, however, 'conditioning' has an effect – older employees who are led to believe through subtle or unsubtle messages that their time is past may eventually start to play that part. So the organization needs to show that all its employees are expected to learn, innovate, perform at a high level and grow. In the US the Hudson Institute followed up its landmark report *Workforce 2000* two years later (1989), drawing attention to the folly of policies of early retirement for good workers in the light of the shortages that will arise in the 1990s. A large proportion of retired people return to the workforce – often their previous organizations – on a part time basis.

A survey by KPMG Peat Marwick Management Consultants, jointly with the Institute of Personnel Management, was entitled *Age . . . has its Compensations*.[6] Out of nearly 3000 respondents (20% public sector) aged over 40, most wanted a flexible retirement date between 51 and 60 followed by the opportunity for part time or temporary assignments. 45% could not recall any personal development opportunity over the last five years, yet 85% still had some form of aspirations for personal growth or career progress.

In Japan age is highly respected within and without organizations. The whole national system of values looks on age as an accumulation of wisdom and experience. Phase three, therefore, should be an age of achievement in personal terms rather than rejection.

Phase three typically lasts 10 to 15 years depending on the nature of the organization and retirement policies. Many organizations have made attractive provisions for people in their 50s to leave early, and provide space for others to progress. (Some are recalled as consultants, because the organization has realized it needs their experience and knowledge.) For the individual it may herald a new mobility, a desire to experience things not achieved earlier in life such as working abroad, or to try something new knowing that a career or the mortgage is not under threat. It is a time when planning for retirement is important also. It requires a different approach from the organization from the other two phases: not an approach that ignores this group as beyond the need for help, but a recognition of the options available and assistance with them.

These phases are important when we consider the methods available to manage personal growth. Our priorities, choices and methods will be different if we want to manage effectively, and not many organizations are structured to recognize these realities fully.

A COMMON LANGUAGE FOR PEOPLE DEVELOPMENT PROCESSES

Integrating processes in human resource development needs a common language to describe capabilities of individuals and those required of jobs or groups of jobs. The study of what people actually do, particularly managers, has been extensive in recent years. Henry Mintzberg[7] and Rosemary Stewart[8] have probably been the most helpful analysts of what managers actually do, and the mythical manager engaged on systematic planning, detailed investment return calculations and strategic visioning each day has been shown not to exist (an uncomfortable reality for the business schools). Such activities are undertaken, but often in close association with supporting staff.

In the many studies made of top people, neither personality nor academic achievement equates with success – although a level of intellectual application, and of numerate and verbal fluency do in themselves. That is not to say that personality does not affect the choice of someone for a position. Indeed, personnel professionals often despair at the senior manager who chooses people on the basis of a feeling that they will fit in well, rather than on the recommended careful analysis of laid down criteria. Many a senior manager is frequently justified in the rightness of the choice – he or she is probably being more analytical than appears on the surface as a result of long experience. Activities, roles, personal qualities, intellectual attributes, personality profiles – all these things are less important than what a person can actually do.

In the UK the study of competences has been a great preoccupation in recent years. Stephen Bevan of the Institute of Manpower Studies[9] has described competence as the capability that results from the combination of knowledge, skills and attitudes. A further helpful definition of competences can be attributed to a firm called Advanced Technology Ltd and is as follows:

- Competences are descriptions of the core skills which result in effective performance at key job levels
- They provide a structured way of describing behaviour, allowing a common language for the organization
- They form the basis for consistent managerial development, providing a clear focus for assessment, appraisal and development.

The latter statement can be expanded to say 'providing a clear focus for integrated human resource processes'. For we can create a language that links recruitment criteria, appraisal of strengths and weaknesses, development planning, skills training, potential assessment, job profiles, team building and so on. Wendy Hirsh in her study of this subject[10] points out the importance of having a language that is owned by the organization, that relates where appropriate to its history – rather than taking something off the shelf. The offerings available from the shelf are many and varied – variations of labels on the same essential concepts – from individual organizations, from consultants, and from the national study work in the UK known as the Management Charter Initiative. An illustration of the linkages that a common language makes is shown in Table 3.1.

A language may just consist of a list of skill names with suitable definitions or these can be grouped in various clusters. Table 3.2 shows the clusters that Advanced Personnel Technology has

Table 3.1 Integrating a common language into human resource processes

Major process	Application of a common language
Skills planning	Skills and manpower classification
Person specification	Description of knowledge, skills, attitudes and experience required by the job
Selection	Criteria-based interviewing techniques Assessment and test specification and analysis
Performance appraisal	Description of strengths and weaknesses Training objectives for enhanced job performance
Personal development	Personal development objectives Learning objectives
Potential assessment	Criteria for development centres or career guidance centres Career planning

derived, which is one of many available. These are illustrated not for the reader to take them away and use them, but as an example; a set should be derived for each organization that builds on the historical language used in human resource processes.

Competences

The Management Charter Initiative was formed in July 1988 in the aftermath of two major reports[11] on the state of management development in Britain. Within two years it had some 7000 employers as members wishing to participate in its work. It has attempted to describe, measure and provide a basis for training

Table 3.2 Generic skill groupings

LEADERSHIP	
Delegation	Delegation for development and efficiency; allocating tasks and responsibility
Management control	Developing systems and procedures for monitoring, controlling and organizing
Motiving others	Setting the goal; providing a vision and sense of direction for others; acting as a role model
Developing others	Giving feedback and appraisal; knowing staff as individuals; identifying development needs and addressing them
Management accountability	Management identification; responsibility and accountability
TEAM WORK	
Communication	What to communicate, when and how; clarity, questioning and listening
Credibility	Professionalism; impact; earning respect; assertiveness
Cooperation	Being supportive of peers, pulling towards a team goal; adapting and cooperating
Rapport	Showing empathy, understanding, warmth and humour; establishing good working relationships
Influencing	Persuading, selling, lobbying and negotiating
ACHIEVEMENTS	
Planning	Prioritizing; planning and organizing; turning ideas into a way forward
Thoroughness	Checking the details; quality control
Productivity	Goal orientation; working towards results; delivering quantity
Administration	Written communication; organization of paperwork; use of systems/ procedures

Resource management	Juggling resources; focusing on efficiency and value; cost effectiveness
DECISION MAKING	
Problem identification	Fact finding; spotting problems; investigating and questioning; probing
Reasoning skills	Logic and analysis
Judgement	Reaching conclusions; considering options and making decisions
Problem solving	Turning a problem into a solution; devising an effective answer or way forward
VISION	
Creativity	Innovation; novel ideas and approaches; lateral thinking
Initiative	Adding value; resourcefulness; looking for ways to improve; entrepreneurial approach
Strategic perspective	Perceiving opportunities; identifying own goals; long term perspective; strategic approach
COMPANY FIT	
Flexibility	Positive outlook; willingness to try; quick to learn; adaptable
Motivation	'Buy in' to corporate objectives; determination; commitment
Organizational outlook	Company knowledge of systems/approaches/other departments; networking
Business perspective	External knowledge; knowledge of the market place and economic position
Customer orientation	Providing a service and meeting needs internally and externally

and assessment of the skills needed by managers to do their jobs effectively. The framework is built around four key roles regarded as fundamental in causing an organization to meet its objectives:

Meeting customer needs (internal and external)
Managing people
Managing financial resources
Managing information

These roles are broken down into units (typical tasks) and elements (practical activities) developed as at the end of 1990 for the two levels of first-line management and middle management with plans to expand to supervisory and senior management. For each element a set of performance criteria is defined in terms of what managers are actually required to do. Overlaying the functional roles is a model of personal competence. A series of certificates and diplomas are being created, based on assessment against the standards. Controversy naturally exists as to the real value of these qualifications – but the work is being taken up by several large organizations (the retail company Safeway was the first to receive MCI endorsement for a management training scheme based on the approach), and many small and medium ones are joining. However, others may find the result all too descriptive; there is danger of a whole new bureaucracy emerging and the truth that real learning comes through experience being neglected.

Determining the requirements of a job

PE-Inbucon was one of the pioneers of the concept of competency modelling. This is defined as matching people and jobs, and building superior performance. It provides a method of defining and measuring those characteristics that lead to the highest levels of performance in the organization, as observed currently in those who demonstrate it.

A number of different languages have been developed for describing essentially the same thing. Thus Merck, Sharpe and Dome have described[12] an approach of 'templating' the requirements of jobs in terms of the skills required and the 'motivated abilities' – a terminology invented by Marlys Hanson, a Californian consultant. The principle is the same – a common language of describing job requirements and people.

A set of competences can be derived in various different ways to be relevant to a specific job or group of jobs in a specific organization. It is not enough to just look at the generic groupings of competences based on levels – different roles, functions and environments have different demands. For instance:

Model performance observation and analysis
This requires finding the best examples in the role and studying what characterizes them. The problem with this is the separation of the job requirements and the individual capabilities – an excellent employee can show the same set in a variety of jobs. It is, however, only part of the equation – skills in themselves do not guarantee high performance. Circumstances in the environment; the team of which the individual is part; the competence of his or her staff – all these make such analysis complex. The superior performers of one year may be the falling stars of the next.

Brainstorming
A group of individuals familiar with the job or generic job group identify, through brainstorming and subsequent sifting, the characteristics and skills needed. This can be effective – provided real experience of the target job is present.

Repertory grid
This is the name for a technique in clinical psychology for finding distinctions and similarities between activities and their importance. The method is described by Andrew and Valerie Stewart[13] who used it extensively to find the criteria for use in assessment centres. It is a sound method, but in-company practitioners tend to prefer more pragmatic approaches.

Performance questionnaires
These are lists of up to 100 items with scales of observable behaviour on each item that a selection of people familiar with the target job fill in. Thus a series of statements might be given on the characteristics of an effective performer in the job such as:

He/she asks for his/her people's ideas before making a decision	He/she takes decisions without consulting his/her people

This requires skilled analysis and careful distinction between the individual's managerial style and the specific job requirements. There is also an assumption that managers always behave in the same way – life would be much easier if they did!

Selection from a defined list
This consists of a list of skills, either as a straightforward list or grouped, which is given to a selection of people familiar with the target job. This should include people at a level above it, and may include job incumbents also. Each is asked to choose the eight to twelve most important requirements for effectiveness for the particular job. These are then consolidated to give an average set. Where an organization has created a common language this would be a frequently used approach, resulting in a set of criteria that are readily understood. The averaging suffers from the assumption that all participants have an equally valid perception of the job – this may not be so, and the boss's views should perhaps be favourably weighted.

Job analysis
This method requires detailed analysis of the tasks and accountabilities of the job and translation into the knowledge and skills needed to do it.

Constraint within the common language is helpful, provided the language is rich enough to embrace all the diversities of the organization. Terms like 'judgement' and 'leadership' mean a variety of things and are inadequate descriptors. Examples of behaviour illustrating the characteristic are to be recommended. (see Table 3.3).

It is not enough simply to define an element without some form of capability level qualifier, and here we run into difficulty. For instance, every manager needs the ability to plan ahead, but everyone *is* able to plan in some way. How do we define strength or weakness and how do we relate it to the expec-

Table 3.3 Illustration of behavioural examples

Work organization

- Specifies objectives, plans and priorities in advance of action.
- Accurately schedules own or other's work.
- Delegates action or decision making based on the readiness of subordinates.
- Organizes and runs meetings effectively.
- Known for meeting deadlines and being punctual.
- Knows where everything is; competent user of systems.

tations at different levels of responsibility? The chief executive has a much harder task of prioritizing time than the warehouse supervisor, although that specific competence might appear in the specification for both. We need some description of the environment and complexity within which the competence will be demanded for completion.

For this reason it seems that the element of **experience** is a crucial ingredient of assessing the personal value and growth of an individual – if, for example, a person has spent three years as an accountant for European Operations, and the evidence through appraisals and so on is that this was successful experience, then we can draw some good conclusions about specific knowledge, skills and (probably) attitudes developed as a result of that experience.

This book uses the elements of knowledge, skills, attitudes and experience rather than the more generic term of competency.

Knowledge refers to those parts of the organization's activities that we have particular knowledge of, plus professional or external knowledge that is relevant. We cannot list all the things a person knows; it is those relevant to their personal contribution and career progress that we are interested in.

Skills – refers to the capabilities of the individual, those things that the person is particularly good at doing; the effective application of knowledge. They may be manual, specialist, technical or managerial in nature. This is about what a person can **do**, rather than what he or she **knows**.

Attitudes reflect values and emotions. They are not a fixed part of personality but do change with time and experience. They are about the way a job or situations are approached.

Experience is a separate category, even though the other elements have mostly been acquired through practical experience. The environment, the context, the scope of experience in which knowledge and skills were gained is important and relevant.

General management capabilities

Mainguy[14] surveyed in 1987 the key characteristics of 1016 managers across Europe, asking them what they saw as the key characteristics their CEOs should display, as against those they actually showed. The five most desirable attributes were seen as:

- Effective team-builder.
- Listener.
- Self-sufficient decision maker.
- Retainer of good people.
- One who surrounds him or herself with good people.

The five attributes most seen in reality were: self-sufficient decision maker, strong-willed, ambitious, energetic and motivated by power. Unfortunately there was no relationship given in the study between the CEO characteristics and the success of the enterprise. Studies of chief executives are popular, but of limited help because the characteristics we want to develop are unique to our organization and its needs. One such internal study is summarized in Table 3.4 – this gives a specification of the skills and experience for a general manager in the information technology industry for the mid–1990s. It was drawn up by a group of specialists brainstorming the requirements and then carefully checked with the directors of the organization.

When one analyses the portfolio of knowledge, skills, values and experience required of a general manager and of other senior managers they are not so different. This is because top functional managers need to participate in senior teams and to wear two hats – their professional/technical leadership hat and the hat that shares the problems of colleagues and general manager for the good of the organization as a whole. Is the finance director going to be more effective if he or she understands the markets the organization is involved with? Undoubtedly so. Indeed, is it not a distinguishing marker of the effectiveness of those functional leaders who wear the two hats comfortably?

The general manager will have majored in a particular function – his or her task is to know how to use all the knowledge, skills, attitudes and experience in the team.

Table 3.4 Skills and experience for general management in the 1990s

EXPERIENCE	
E1	Line management accountability for specific deliverables relating to the business results.
E2	Significant P&L financial accountability.
E3	Significant man management accountability through at least two levels of subordinate management.
E4	Commercial experience – personal involvement in customer or supply negotiations.
E5	International experience – preferably through physically working outside the home country or extensive involvement in working with overseas countries.
E6	Staff appointment – responsible for helping influence line managers to perform better in a particular function of their role.
E7	Has operated within more than one division in this organization or in other companies.
SKILLS	
S1	A good team leader, able to weld together and use complementary knowledge and skills towards common objectives.
S2	A good strong people-manager; fair/firm, balancing task/team/individual needs; known for developing staff.

S3 Able to delegate accountability.

S4 A strategic thinker – demonstrates wisdom, sees the overall company as well as local need, formulates tactics within an articulated strategy.

S5 One who sees and seizes opportunities within agreed strategies.

S6 Able to multiprogramme a large number of issues at any given time, and keep all major accountabilities in progress.

S7 Able to balance long term requirements against short term objectives.

S8 Able to manage conflict constructively, with peers or peer groups.

S9 Able to adapt management style to different needs.

S10 Skilled at communication, especially verbally.

S11 A good probing relevant questioner, and a good listener.

S12 Ready to take necessary decisions at the right time.

S13 Able to cope with stress without loss of performance.

S14 A controlled risk taker.

S15 Has a personal presence that can command respect internally and externally.

S16 Personal ambition – desire and drive to take senior accountability.

PEOPLE AND JOBS

A systematic approach calls for a link between the characteristics of people and jobs, using the common language that is decided upon and that can be related to development actions. Figure 3.5 illustrates this matching process.

Measuring the status of personal growth

If you go to the garden centre you pay a lot more for tomato plants than you do for seeds, or for a good mature shrub com-

POSITIONS	PERSON SPECIFICATION		PERSONAL PROFILE
Short term specific	**Relevant**	**C a r e e r**	**Current** knowledge, skills, attitudes, experience
Short term generic	knowledge		
	skills		
Long term specific	attitudes	**p l a n**	**Current** perception of potential
Long term generic	experience		

Figure 3.5 Matching people and posts

pared to a rooted cutting. Growth has value and growth is dependent on the passage of time. There is no direct relationship between a person's 'Personal Growth Profile' (PGP) and age – and few modern organizations in western countries today promote on time served. (This is still prevalent in, for example, Japan, albeit changing slowly.) But it is suggested that PGP is a function of the following, and age only comes into it in the sense that it takes time to acquire some of the components:

$$PGP = f\ (\text{knowledge, skills, attitudes, experience})$$

The PGP measures the ability of an individual to do a job today.

In its fullest sense it is an accumulation over all the years to date and maybe from different organizations. Not all are relevant to career and personal growth in the current organization, so a selection may be made appropriately. An example is shown in Table 3.5. Note that it is a profile of expertise – it requires some qualification of that expertise and the example shown uses three levels.

This is of much more value than the traditional CV which may give job titles and responsibilities, and the writer's version of achievement. It does not tell the reader much about the new knowledge gained from a position, the new skills developed, the specific areas of real experience, the lessons learned from mistakes. These have to be prised out by the skilled interviewer. (The biographical CV has its place alongside the profile to complete the picture.)

We do not include qualifications. In France and some other European countries they have significant importance and are often an entry point to a recruitment or development discussion about someone. In some less developed countries, a qualification is a passport to jobs far beyond a person's current capability. Organizations that have looked upon an MBA in the same way have learned quickly from their mistake! Training for qualifications is a means to an end – it provides certain kinds of knowledge, may give a guide to intellectual strength, and in some cases can provide certain skills. But qualifications are not a key to career growth in organizations.

In the same way that we can describe the value of an individual, we can write down a similar list for a job or type of job in the organization usually known as the person specification. It is useful here to distinguish between the essential requirements necessary for entry to the job, and the desirable ones that represent full capability. The essential list provides us with a basis of matching for career development purposes – in the context of developing people, we would not expect a person to go into a new job with *all* the necessary attributes for that job already present; some are to be learned as a result of the job experience.

In drawing up a person specification for career development or recruitment purposes, therefore, we need simply four

Table 3.5 Example of a personal growth profile

Name: Jane Smith	**Current job:** Team leader, Internal Systems
Grade/level: 10 **Date to current job:** 5/91	**Age:** 38
Knowledge:	Qualified accountant, specializing in cost accounting Project management methodologies (3) Systems analysis (2) Programming in COBOL and ADA (2) UNIX application environments (2) Company organization and operations (3) External packages available in the F&A area (2)
Skills:	Project planning Team creation/motivation Documentation and report writing Personal use of IT Objective setting and control Influencing Resource scheduling Presentations Project costing Coaching of staff Work relationships
Attitudes:	High work commitment Care for development of staff High work standards – second best will not do Meeting timescales and commitments to 'customers' Belief that controlling costs is important Importance of personal image
Experience:	General financial training, all functions (4 years) Specialist cost accountant (2 years) Systems analysis and programming (5 years) Team leadership (2 years) Accounting and order processing systems (4 years) Involvement with international operations (3 years) UNIX based applications (2 years)
Last updated:	
Expertise key: 1=Working knowledge; 2=Fully competent; 3=Known expert	

headings – an example is given in Table 3.6. There is a lot of commonality in the skills and attitudes specifications between different jobs from a similar family. Thus there is a basic set of management skills that applies to all management jobs; others may be added depending on seniority or for special circumstances such as operating internationally.

One important thing to remember in writing such specifications is whether they are being written for today or tomorrow. Recruiting or promoting someone today reflects the needs of the job today. But if the profile is for the purposes of setting goals for development, then we are aiming at a specification of what the job will require some years ahead. That is achieved by a careful analysis of the requirements of the organizational long range plan – as discussed in Chapter 1.

Just as in job evaluation a series of benchmarks provides a framework for valuing jobs in the organization, so one can do the same thing for the person specifications for a particular job. There is a good case for ceasing to value jobs in the traditional job evaluation sense above a certain level, where the accumulated PGP of an individual transcends the job that is currently being performed. Besides, there are a number of organization cultures where the grade and its associated status symbols dominate a person's career decision in a counter-productive way, whereas he or she should be asking questions about what the move would do to their PGP.

If the PGP and the essential requirements of the person specification of a job match, then we have a potential move. But not quite . . . there is always a personality factor, a chemistry factor to do with human interaction which is critical. The ultra analytical HR professional should never forget this 'fit factor' – it is not just with the organizational culture but with the boss and his or her team. It's impossible to analyse as it is dependent on a given set of players; but many a succession plan or logical career move has failed because of the fit factor.

Table 3.6 Example of a person specification

<table>
<tr><td colspan="3">Job name: Country general manager Grade/level: 14</td></tr>
<tr><td colspan="3">Expertise Key: 1=Working knowledge; 2=Fully competent; 3=Known expert E=Essential; D=Desirable</td></tr>
<tr><td>Knowledge</td><td>E:</td><td>Products and services (2)
Financial analysis and control (2)
Company strategies and processes (2)
Competitive strategies (3)</td></tr>
<tr><td></td><td>D:</td><td>External environment (1)
Commercial legislation (1)
High level personal contacts (1)</td></tr>
<tr><td>Skills</td><td>E:</td><td>Creation of balanced teams
Selection of subordinates
Helicopter vision
Presentation/communication
Political awareness
People development
Planning and Control
Local language speaking/understanding
Team leadership
Effective delegation
Strategy creation
Multiprogramming
Priority setting
Conflict management
Breadth of management attention</td></tr>
<tr><td></td><td>D:</td><td>Financial forecasting
Risk taking</td></tr>
<tr><td>Attitudes</td><td>E:</td><td>Profit motivation
Inherent integrity
People, customers and quality first
Commitment to company goals
Flexible working hours
Perseverance to achieve objectives
Resilient against setbacks
Unprejudiced; good listener</td></tr>
<tr><td></td><td>D:</td><td>Entrepreneurial
Cultural sensitivity
Value on personal use of information technology
Personal image and impact</td></tr>
<tr><td>Experience</td><td>E:</td><td>of another function than individual's base (2 years)
of managing managers (2 years)
of profit and loss accountability (3 years)
of a multinational environment (5 years)
of consistent achievement (5 years)
of the industry sector (8 years)</td></tr>
<tr><td></td><td>D:</td><td>of integrating acquisitions
of large account management
of growing a successor
of a business of minimum 80 employees/£80m revenue</td></tr>
<tr><td colspan="3">LAST UPDATED: BY:</td></tr>
</table>

KEY ISSUES OF IMPLEMENTATION IN CAREER MANAGEMENT

How can an organization plan and manage careers when the concept of cradle to grave employment is no longer the norm in most western countries?
Life would be much easier if we knew, barring accidents, that each new member of our organization would be with us for 40 years, and we could model our manpower flows and careers to match them accordingly. An illusion, because even if that were so the changing environment would not allow such stability. Every organizational situation is dynamic and the timespan of forecasting with any precision in today's world probably has its extreme at five years, and for many will be not more than six months. The aim will always be to keep the best people for as long as possible. Each organization must, therefore, develop its own framework, recognizing its own speed of change and range of opportunities, to achieve this aim. Sometimes, helping people to leave the organization should be part of that framework. But the fact that some people do not stay for long and see their stay with the organization as but one step in their personal career plan is, therefore, a red herring. Every organization has as a primary aim: the attraction and particularly the retention of the best people.

Mobility between employers has increased over the years from a situation in the 1960s where about one third of all managers would have one employer only to a figure of about one in ten today. Readers are referred to one of the more interesting research studies of recent years concerning managerial job change.[15] In this survey of 2300 managers across all UK sectors of employment, about 40% experienced a job change in the 15 month period of the study. Looking at all job changes the sample had experienced over a five year period some 57% were changes of employer and 80% were promotional moves. The authors coined the term 'spiralling' to indicate upward moves involving a functional change and found over half the job changes were of this type. A study referred to earlier – jointly between KPMG Management Consultants and the Institute of Personnel Management[5] – surveyed 2800 managers over 40, and found that only 15% had changed employer in the last five years. The probability of leaving an organization decreases with the years of service and someone with more than 25 years' service is usually only going to leave involuntarily or through acute mid-career frustration. Some factors which affect this are: discrimination against age in securing a new job, achievement of a level of synergy and compatibility with an organization, concerns about pension rights, and personal constraining factors such as children's education.

Each organization has different manpower flows and many report loss rates at managerial level of less than 5%. However, it is always in the organization's interest to keep and grow the good people and to lose them is a significant cost – whatever the stability rate, the case for effective career management is strong.

Career management is fine for organizations with plenty of movement but is it worthwhile for those that are relatively static?

Without doubt, organizations vary in the range of career opportunities they can offer. They vary in their rates of turnover of staff, in their degree of turbulence and so on. It does not follow that high rates of turbulence make career management easier, despite the apparently increased opportunities. Fundamental is a belief in the importance of investing in people growth, and this, together with some creativity, can lead to an appropriate framework for all organizations.

Smaller companies will find life much simpler, and often people trade frequent steps in career development for the level of early responsibility and lack of constraints that they can achieve outside the large organization.

Is there such a thing nowadays as 'one career'?

We need to think of careers as an abbreviation for 'people growth through experience'. If our framework is flexible enough we shall be able to recognize a variety of possible paths. It is not the thesis of this book that a career should be restricted to one arena of work. The task for the organization is to understand all the career options it has to offer, the interests and abilities of its people, the needs and objectives of the organization in the short and long term – and see what this means for individuals.

In the study referred to earlier, 80% of the moves that were examined were changes of 'function'. So the use of the word career is not in the traditional sense of one vocation exclusively; rather it is the set of work experiences that provides people growth over time.

Are not expediency and opportunism as effective in practice as systematic planning?

Perhaps the greatest conflict in making integrated career management policies work well is the conflict most organizations face between the immediate needs of expediency and the longer term investment. So the carefully prepared multi-colour succession plan is hardly consulted in the choice of a candidate whom the MD feels is right at the time; the great development opportunity is filled with the obvious candidate with the most relevant experience, instead of asking whether this is a chance for the person with potential needing a broadening experience; the international experience or special training course is put off in the interests of the short term business priorities – and so on.

Career planning must span a long period of time. Just as discounted cash flow and rate of return calculations are done on a financial investment, so we should regard the investment in people growth as one that yields future returns. But we need to find a balance between the short and long term in a sensible and realistic way. This means firstly getting the maximum buy-in from senior line management to the career management policies in such a way that they feel as much ownership of them as any personnel specialist. Secondly it requires designing the set of processes in a way that the reality of line management accountability is recognized and the areas of possible override on, for instance, a placement decision are both limited and understood.

This will ensure the specialist does not regularly tear his or her hair out in frustration at the disowning of carefully thought through plans, and furthermore that the top manager does not fire the specialist for being out of touch with the realities of the business.

Issues in the career development of women

Everything described in this book should apply equally to men and women. The proportion of women in the UK workforce is around 40%,[16,17] one of the highest in Europe, but 45% of these work part-time. The proportion of women managers is estimated at around 20%, and they predominate in certain sectors. Less than 5% of middle and senior managers are women. Two aspects of this should concern us – first that our career management processes do take due account of the special needs of women needing a career break and needing to make provision for childcare for periods of time, and secondly the cultural issues of the reality of equal opportunities.

Wendy Hirsh[16] summarizes the hurdles that need to be overcome for women to succeed. She concentrates on the achievement of management levels (although there are equally satisfying careers in specialist and technical roles). The hurdles are divided into two groups – 'career' and 'domestic'. In the former, she lists qualifications, early career choice and promotion. In the 'domestic' group are included mobility; re-entry; flexible working; childcare and career breaks. Hirsh makes the point that a lot is expected of any successful ambitious person today – working long hours, full time, anywhere; being noticed, being at the right meetings, taking the right opportunities. In addition, the prejudices concerning age work against women who take a break. Traditional frameworks of career management are not built to cope with periods of leave, part time working, job sharing and other practices helpful to the woman who wants a family life.

There must be very few organizations which can afford to neglect the talent of women employees, however. Not only is this so because of the demographic demands of the coming years, but women entrants receive the same investment in early training and development as men. A career management framework is, therefore, incomplete without consideration of the needs of personal growth for women.

Many male-dominated organizations have deeply ingrained prejudices regarding the real ambitions and capability of women to manage. Some women succeed by playing the same games and operating in the same style as the successful men. Each organization has its own characteristics for success anyway and if men do not show them they will not rise either, but it is more subtle than that. Hofstede (see Chapter 2) makes one of his major discriminators between national cultures a 'masculinity/ femininity/ spectrum, recognizing the different sexual characteristics. In management particularly, whereas men emphasize tasks, individualism and competition, women are more interested in collaboration and managing through relationships. Mumford[18] lists some of the kinds of adaptation that women may have to go through to reach acceptance as:

- Coping with competition,
- Adopting at least some of the behaviour of male clubs,
- The use of personal and role power,
- Developing individual self-awareness,
- Acquiring a positive self-image:
  - self-confidence and assertiveness,
  - dealing with stress.

In specialist roles, there is even less logic in not having a proportionate number of senior women. Human resources is an area where women have been particularly successful, and more and more women are rising to the top of such a function in both management and specialist roles.

In career terms the traditions of a woman's job being subservient to the husband's – who was the one deemed to have the career – are changing. In the case of a dual career family where a move is offered to one party it is considered by the couple in the light of both careers. I have seen several cases of decisions made such that the man will follow the woman in a career move for her. Studies show, however, that a considerably higher percentage (four to five times as high) of women in senior positions are single, divorced or widowed compared to men.[13] Being married and having a family unquestionably makes it more difficult for those with ambition. We must conclude, therefore, that if we wish to maximize the growth potential of those women employees who wish to take time off for family reasons but still wish to pursue a career, some special consideration is needed. We come back to this in later chapters.

SUMMARY

Career management encompasses a range of processes and activities in an organization that are concerned with people growth. Much emphasis has been placed on the self-development and manage-your-own career aspects, but the total spectrum needs to be integrated within an organizational context and in harmony with a philosophy of caring about the continued growth of employees.

Whatever the type, the size, the turbulence of an organization, some framework of these processes is essential to realize the tremendous untapped potential of the employees. Even though careers may be complex and may not be confined at all to one organization, the need to manage them remains. It cannot happen effectively throughout an organization by leaving it to a multitude of individual managers to do their best; some specialist person or people who draw it all together in a consistent and coordinated way is needed. We called this person the careers manager, although a number of other titles might embrace the same responsibility, particularly in small and medium sized organizations.

The interaction between work and other areas of life must not be ignored, and we looked at three career phases – discovery, consolidation and maturity. The needs of each are different, and processes need to take account of this. We could argue that most care needs to be taken with the individual in the discovery phase, and that the organization needs to be the most creative and flexible in the latter phases. Decisions made to enhance the performance of the organization often appear to mitigate against people growth – such as flatter organizations – but the effective careers manager takes this as a challenge to find new ways of developing individuals.

One of the problems in this field is language. We argue the logic of a common way of describing people and jobs – and propose the elements of knowledge, skills, attitudes and experience. All change is to do with closing some kind of gap between where one is today and where one would like to be. Equally in career management, a gap in knowledge, skills, attitudes and experience has to be closed to make people ready for a target job at some time in the future. Rather than let this happen by accident – or, as is often the case, not happen at all with the result that people fall into jobs ill-equipped – we argue that systematic planning, however difficult and imperfect, is better than opportunism and expediency.

Finally, no career management framework is complete without ensuring that the personal growth of women employees is assured, and that the processes used throughout the organization are applied equally and fairly to them.

PLANNING FOR ACTION

Problems of reality

1. Most managers and their staff may go through a once off exercise to write their personal growth profiles, and job specifications, but the ongoing discipline to keep everything up to date is a real problem.

It is difficult keeping all systems up to date. People are motivated to do so when they see it as important and beneficial, not because they like filling in forms. Growth profiles will become important to individuals if they see them really being used in job matching and career planning. It is not an easy intellectual exercise preparing them for the first time, but updating is not so difficult. So the real hurdle to cross is seeing the value of the initial exercise. That comes through understanding how it fits in the total career management framework.

2. Creating one language is easier said than done. Processes are not all introduced or modified at one time: different parts of the organization take different initiatives and have different histories. Few start with a clean piece of paper.

There comes a point where somebody needs to survey best practice and look at all the languages that are being used in order to see those that are clearly effective, established and understood; that are adding value to the organization through their use; and that could provide a foundation for extension across boundaries.

However, the 'clean start' is not to be dismissed – for a period some translation may be necessary from old to new but people eventually get used to the new terminology.

In a large and complex organization innovative people will constantly try and bring in new ideas and concepts. This healthy trait needs to be channelled into new areas of effective implementation of personal growth rather than changing concepts and language too frequently. Some things need safeguarding!

Indicators of success that might be applied to the matters discussed here are given in Table 3.7 below.

Table 3.7 Indicators of success checklist

Career phases	1. The processes and practices of career management (reference Chapters 4–7) recognize the needs of particular phases of personal growth, and are flexible as needed.
Language for describing personal capability	2. A common language is generally understood in the organization for describing elements of personal growth and capability, and this has been standardized.
Personal growth profiles	3. All employees are encouraged to maintain and update their personal growth profile and to use it in development planning.
Person specifications	4. Each job or group of jobs has a specification described in a language that is consistent with other human resources processes.

Action for those responsible for career management

1. Draw up Figure 3.1 for the organization. If you also did some of the actions from Chapters 1 and 2, what can be concluded about any processes that are missing?
2. What career phases can be recognized in the organization? List any conscious activities specific to people in each of the phases, and ways in which these could be enhanced or added to in the interests of more effective career management.
3. If the idea of a personal growth profile is new, try one out on yourself. If convinced of its usefulness, plan how it might be introduced into the organization.
4. Draw up a version of Table 3.1 for your organization and note in the right hand column the formats and language that are used. How consistent is it? What plan could be made to achieve more commonality?

REFERENCES

1 Hall D. T. and Associates, *Career Management in Organisations*, 1976

2 Schein, E., *Career Dynamics – Matching Organisational and Individual Needs*, Addison Wesley, 1978

3 Hunt, J. W., *Developing Middle Managers in Shrinking Organisations*, Journal of Management Development Vol 1 No 2, 1983

4 Hall D. T, and Goodale J. G., *Human Resource Management – Strategy, Design and Implementation*, Scott Foresman, 1986

5 Institute of Personnel Management, *Age and Employment*, IPM, 1991

6 KPMG Peat Marwick Management Consultants/Institute of Personnel Management, *Age . . . has its compensations*, 1990

7 Mintzberg, M., *The Nature of Managerial Work*, Harper and Row, 1983

8 Stewart, R., *Choices for the Manager*, McGraw Hill, 1982

9 Hirsh, W., and Bevan, S. M., *What Makes a Manager – in Search of a Language for Managerial Skills*, Institute of Manpower Studies Report 144, 1988

10 Hirsh, W., *Defining Managerial Skills*, Institute of Manpower Studies, Report 185, 1989

11 Handy, C., *The Making of Managers*, HMSO, 1987 and Constable, J. and McCormick, R., *The Making of British Managers*, BIM/NEDO, 1987

12 Philipson, *Career development and Job Templating*, International Journal of Career Management, 1990

13 Stewart, A., and Stewart, V., *Tomorrow's Men Today*, IPM 1976

14 Mainguy, W., *Leadership Qualities; Europe's CEO's Are Surveyed by Management Centre Europe*, European Management Journal, Vol 6 No 3, 1988

15 Nicholson, N. and West, M., *Managerial Job Change – Men and Women in Transition*, 1988

16 Hirsh, W. and Jackson, C., *Women into Management: Issues influencing the entry of women into management jobs*, Institute of Manpower Studies Paper 158, 1991

and Hirsh, W., *Women into Management: jumping the hurdles . . . or knocking them down*, Coutts Career Counsellors Occasional Papers, 1991

17 Pearson, R., Andreutti F., and Holly, S., *The European Labour Market Review: The Key Indicators*, Institute of Manpower Studies Report 191, 1991

18 Mumford, A., *Management Development Strategies for Action*, IPM, 1990

4. CAREERS IN AN ORGANIZATION

CAREER ANCHORS

In Ed Schein's book,[1] he introduces the concept of career anchors, a term that others have taken up in later works. Through successive job experiences the individual develops a self-concept of:

- Talents and abilities – what the individual discovers he/she is good at, and also not so good at,
- Motives and needs – what is important to the individual as goals (money, status, challenge, travel, etc)
- Attitudes and values – what kind of organization he/she feels comfortable working with.

These comprise his or her eventual career anchor. This is based on experience and not on psychological tests. Once formed it provides a means of matching to an appropriate 'career direction' and in the making of choices along the road. Its formation takes a few years but it is then likely to be reasonably stable. The idea of an anchor is that of a 'root' – it does not mean an individual will be permanently doing work that matches it but there will always be the tendency to return to it in situations of free choice. For instance, when someone describes work as 'not really me' it means that the current occupation is not in harmony with their career anchor.

Working closely with the development of young people shows the formation of these self-concepts clearly – the engineering graduate who thought he would always be an engineer recognizing his ability to motivate teams of people; the once ambitious newly qualified accountant settling into a comfortable and secure role; the languages graduate who thought her last career option in the world would be selling becoming a star salesperson; the ambitious MBA whose dream of being a CEO fades when he understands the demands such a position makes on the balance of his life . . . and so on. When people start work they have relatively little information about themselves and their capabilities; they may have been subject to various influences – parents, friends, university staff – seeking to guide them but have lacked the necessary benefit of self-discovery. The real world of work usually turns out to be quite different from the hazy concept they held previously. As life develops the individual is faced with more and more choices and forced to evaluate and reevaluate the three components outlined above.

Based on studies of 44 alumni of the Sloan School over a period of about ten years, the two major career anchors that Schein found were (not surprisingly) technical/functional competence and managerial competence. At the end of the study people were pretty firm in their understanding and commitment to the direction they felt was best for them to follow. 'Managerial competence' is a broad term and Schein outlined some of its components back in 1978 – predating the work that has become popular in the UK in the late 1980s and early 1990s in connection with more systematic ways of developing managers. The distinguishing features of this anchor are the desire to manage resources – human, financial and often capital; analyzing and solving multidimensional problems; making decisions; taking responsibility; exerting authority; breadth of interest and freedom and variety in managing the workday. The 'technical/-functional' competence on the other hand is concerned with expertise, the modern version of the craftsman, having a skill that can usually be applied in other organizations. Such people do have to be managed within the organization and one of the frequent conflicts of values that can happen is that either a) they are managed by someone with a similar anchor whose fundamental interest is not in managing at all or b) they are managed by a manager who lacks understanding of their fundamental motivations and priorities. Functional/technical management is a major issue in career management, as discussed below. How often is the best salesman (often unwillingly) promoted to sales manager, the most talented engineer to engineering manager with the career and self-esteem of the individual being ruined in the process?

Schein discussed three more anchors: security, autonomy and creativity and, having explored the concept with several organizations, added in a later paper service/dedication to a cause. The security-conscious value stability and security, and this is an overriding concern for them. They are not driven by particular ambitions of personal competence but are happy to be dependent on the organization for any career progression. They may still perform conscientiously and be loyal and dedicated but they may be unwilling to take risks either functionally or in terms of location. All organizations have people like this, whose thrust and ambition has become low in their hierarchy of values and it is probably still true that government and civil service type organizations tend to attract security minded people. Such people do not usually go through the 'mid career crisis' (although American writers seem to think everyone automatically does) – by that time they are wondering how early they will be able to retire with a satisfactory pension.

The autonomy anchor is for those who have no particular desire to rise up a corporate hierarchy for its own sake but want to be accountable for their own success and failure. This is not the same as the managerial competence anchor. Many organizational managers are content to have the surroundings of rules and procedures to guide them in their jobs. This type of person, however, has no time for bureaucracy and complex decision taking routines. Most of these people, who typically become entrepreneurs, free-lancers and consultants, do not fit well in organizations except perhaps in a few special roles or in running operations remote from the centre (as, for instance, in a third world country).

The creativity anchor is similar to the last in some ways but includes an overriding desire to build something – a product, an idea, a company. Sometimes this urge is fulfilled outside work – building a boat, or writing a book for example. The word entrepreneurship fits most closely in this area – the obsessive desire to break out and do something one can call one's own. Studies have shown that most successful entrepreneurs broke out relatively early in life, unless they were able to have a satisfying niche within an organization. Senior executives say sometimes 'what we need around here is some real entrepreneurs'. Is that what they really need? People who can create new businesses and run them with minimum interference? If so then the organization has to have procedures of management and control that are consistent with that desire.

The service/cause dedication anchor applies mostly to the helping professions – such as teaching, social work, religions, charities and so on. It should not be confused with those people whose prime motivation is technical/professional excellence (like many in the medical profession), and it is of interest mainly to note that some young recruits discover that this is for them and leave an organization early on to take up a vocation in this area.

Once formed career anchors are usually permanent but sometimes, at the end of a career or on retirement, people do start something completely different, having fulfilled their main life motivation.

A number of instruments have been designed by Schein[2] and others to help individuals determine their personal anchor.

CAREER DIRECTIONS IN ORGANIZATIONS

Within the context of organizations Schein's framework can be used in a practical way and, although all organizations are different, we can assume four main career directions. This is not meant to be an alternative nomenclature to Schein's career anchors but complementary – understanding the anchor gives a foundation for career counselling and in determining the direction the career will follow in the organization. The four are:

- Manual skill, clerical, administrative
- Technical or professional specialism
- Functional management
- General management

The characteristics of these 'ladders' may typically be as shown in Table 4.1.

Manual, clerical and administrative

This group involves a wide range of occupations with common characteristics in terms of entry and progression. Education is normally at pre-graduate level, although when and where there is an excess of graduates for the labour market to absorb some may join this group to get a job. This has been the case in India for example, and there are many graduates in secretarial and administrative roles in Europe. However, the majority have come direct from school on to a trainee programme – which may be combined with off-the-job studies, or from college having obtained a vocational qualification. The highest level is either some kind of supervision or the achievement of a recognized level of expertise. A chairman's secretary, for instance, is at the top of the tree for secretaries and this job frequently involves supervising one or two junior staff. Career structures or ladders are discussed in detail in the next section but apply equally for this group.

Careers can lead to the top of this ladder at a relatively early age and, whereas many are content to stay, others seek opportunities to move across to another career stream. We look later on in this chapter at the bridges that can be built. However, the cases of working up from the shop floor to the Board are becoming fewer and fewer (and studies of those who have done so less and less helpful). This is not because organizations have cut off opportunities in their development processes, but because it is rare today for really capable people not to seek and achieve a college education, and secondly the demands of more and more modern jobs require a significant level of intellectual development.

Technical/professional career structures

Whatever business or service the organization is in, it wants to have the best in its field of activity. Whereas the prime motivation of technical and professional people is their expertise, they are not immune from the general issues of rewards and recognition. An organization should not give the message that only by moving to management can one achieve a high level of

Table 4.1 Characteristics of main career directions

	Manual, clerical, admin (MCA)	Tech/prof specialism (TPS)	Functional management (FM)	General Management (GM)
Entry point	School/vocational college	Graduate *or* progression from MCA *or* external entry.	External entry *or* progression from TPS. Some progression from MCA possible.	External entry *or* promotion from FM *or* planned graduate development scheme.
Highest point	Maximum skill level or supervisor	Senior consultant *or* equivalent 'Fellows'	Functional director	Managing director/CEO or equivalent
Typical time to reach highest point from entry	10 yrs	20 yrs	20 yrs	25 yrs
Progression options	To TPS or FM	To FM or GM	To GM	

recognition. So we must ask how well we are rewarding the best in their field. Do they have the same status as senior managers? They are certainly worth as much. Are younger professionals encouraged to aspire to being the best? It is important to show visibly that the organization recognizes careers for these groups of people and does not just provide a process of moving up grades with the passage of time.

Many organizations today have formal, systematic structures for professionals, showing progression from graduate trainee to a senior level, which are parallel to management progression ladders after a certain point. This gives the well known concept of the 'Y' structure. The most senior level of the technical arm should be on a par with managerial executives in the organization. Some large, technically orientated organizations have created a super level of expertise known as 'Fellows', who work both internally and externally with universities and other research bodies. A specialist can, in some cases, be working for a lower graded and lower paid manager. This may require some cultural acceptance when first introduced, and is less common in hierarchical environments such as France.

Whereas the majority of entrants to these structures are graduates, a number of bridges can be built into these streams for people who started with a lower education level. For example, it is not uncommon for the bright and capable secretary to move to a professional career in personnel, bridging via an administrative role, and to supplement suitable work opportunities with professional study which is equivalent to degree level.

In a business organization there may be career structures for the following functions:

- Personnel
- Marketing
- Professional sales
- Design and development
- Production engineering
- Finance
- Information systems
- Customer service
- Purchasing
- Business consultants

Career structures can remove the need to evaluate jobs in the organization. By laying down comprehensive and thorough entry criteria for each rung on the ladder, they effectively place a value more on the person's knowledge, skills and experience – the nature of the job changing only marginally as people progress up the ladder.

What are the characteristics of a good career structure (sometimes known as career ladders)?

- It has steps consistent with the general value of jobs (as evaluated in the organization) and with other career structures,
- It makes clear that getting to the top of the structure is not a right but is based on merit and capability,
- The entry requirements for each step are clear,
- There is a formal assessment procedure in order to progress from one step to another (this may vary from a written report justifying the promotion at more junior levels to expert panel assessments at higher levels),
- The time spent between grades is consistent with the overall timespan of growth in the organization, and varies with different performance levels,
- The structure is published and everyone has a copy and understands it,
- It is controlled and implemented with integrity,
- It links with the development review part of appraisals,
- It shows clearly the bridges that can be made into other career structures to gain broader experience.

Table 4.2 and Figure 4.1 show examples for career structures for a clerical, secretarial and administrative stream, and for a sales support stream. Both are reproduced by kind permission of ICL and are extracts from descriptive booklets.

Career structures of this kind make career management and development planning for people who wish to stay with this career direction relatively easy. However, there is a danger that they may focus too strongly on a narrow path of development, resulting in a limited comprehension of the overall activity and objectives of the organization. It is also important to give people opportunities to 'break out' at a relatively young age – and to broaden their experience to enhance their understanding of both the internal and external environments that they will contribute to.

Table 4.2 Career structure for clerical, secretarial and administrative staff

Career Structure Level	SKILLS, KNOWLEDGE and EXPERIENCE GUIDELINES (Each level assumes competence at previous level)	Attitudes	Examples of accountability
5	Competent ■ to provide documentation, reports and service to management executive. ■ to deal with management executive level confidential information. ■ to produce complex statistical reports. ■ to organize special events and conferences with minimal supervision. ■ to communicate with executive level personnel and their equivalents in suppliers and customers.	As below	■ Accountable for management executive level documentation, reports, service. ■ Accountable for management executive level confidential information ■ Impact of errors major.
6	Competent ■ to provide service, reports and documentation to division or operations level. ■ to handle strategic information and exercise a high degree of discretion in revealing that information to others. ■ to carry out one-off research and other projects to completion with minimal recourse to Director. ■ to undertake administrative duties associated with a similar level in related career structures. ■ to supervise junior staff. ■ to manage cash and resources. ■ to communicate across major divisions and multiple interfaces at senior director level.	As below and showing high levels of interpersonal skill, discretion, tact, and diplomacy, as well as being mature, trustworthy, reliable and creative.	■ Accountable for division or operations level documentation, reports and service. ■ Accountable for working with a high degree of autonomy. ■ Impact of errors substantial. ■ Accountable for many one-off projects and research exercises. ■ Accountable as senior secretary/administrator in major division. ■ Accountable for cross-division communications and multiple interfaces at senior director level.

Table 4.2 Career structure for clerical, secretarial and administrative staff *(continued)*

Career Structure Level	SKILLS, KNOWLEDGE and EXPERIENCE GUIDELINES (Each level assumes competence at previous level)	Attitudes	Examples of accountability
7	Competent ■ to provide service, reports and administration normally to at least a direct report to director. ■ to produce outputs of small projects, collating reports, supervising junior staff. ■ to maintain confidentiality of strategic level information. ■ to communicate internally and externally at senior manager/director level. ■ to produce presentation material for internal or external use, often using advanced office-automation equipment to do so.	As below grades plus: flexibility, maturity and leadership. Also self-confidence, self-presentation, confidentiality, tact and interpersonal skills. Evidence of approach to work which moves outside the formal minimum job requirements, eg. responsive to deadlines and peak workload.	■ Accountable for documentation, reports and service normally to at least direct report to director level. ■ Accountable for maintaining confidentiality of information, possibly at strategic level. ■ May be accountable for supervision of junior secretaries.
8	■ Advanced word processing competence or advanced knowledge and ability in clerical/administration operations. ■ Competent to operate, communicate and interface at major department manager level. ■ Able to provide full manager/department support in secretarial or clerical/administration function. ■ Able to advise on ICL procedures/policies. ■ Able to co-ordinate exercise within/outside department. ■ Able to initiate draft documents/reports.	As below, but demonstrating greater flexibility, reliability, initiative, co-operation and general maturity of approach. Stress tolerance a consideration from this level upwards. Uses initiative to solve problems.	■ Accountable for documentation, reports and service to senior management level. ■ Increasing responsibility for handling exercises of communications, information gathering, analysis and presentation without reference to supervision. ■ Accountable for more varied or changing routines and for higher level internal and external contacts than lower levels.

Table 4.2 Career structure for clerical, secretarial and administrative staff *(continued)*

Career Structure Level	SKILLS, KNOWLEDGE and EXPERIENCE GUIDELINES (Each level assumes competence at previous level)	Attitudes	Examples of accountability
9/10	■ Competent in use of all office equipment necessary for job, eg. word processor (intermediate), keyboard, systems, databases, spreadsheets, filing, fax, copiers, mail, diary etc. ■ Basic secretarial training or training for clerical administrative role. ■ Sound knowledge of grammar, spelling, vocabulary, punctuation, correspondence. ■ Competent to maintain accurate record systems (manual and IT).	Expected to show a positive approach to quality and use of resources and make suggestions and innovations related to work responsibilities. Image and interpersonal skills of increasing importance. Great flexibility expected.	■ Accountable for documentation, reports, services and administration for an office or team. ■ Accountable for performance of mainly routine work but able to handle some complexity and varied sources of information.
SCHOOL LEAVER ENTRY	■ GCSE in maths and English or equivalent. ■ Basic training, secretarial, keyboard, VDU. ■ RSA 1 typing/shorthand or basic office administration.	Expected to be co-operative, tactful, courteous, polite, industrious and trustworthy. Requires interpersonal skills to perform in the team.	■ Job contains work largely requested by immediate supervision and checked before release. ■ Limited degree of initiative and independent action required. ■ Accountable for routine work where consideration is required over the correct applications of procedures and information.

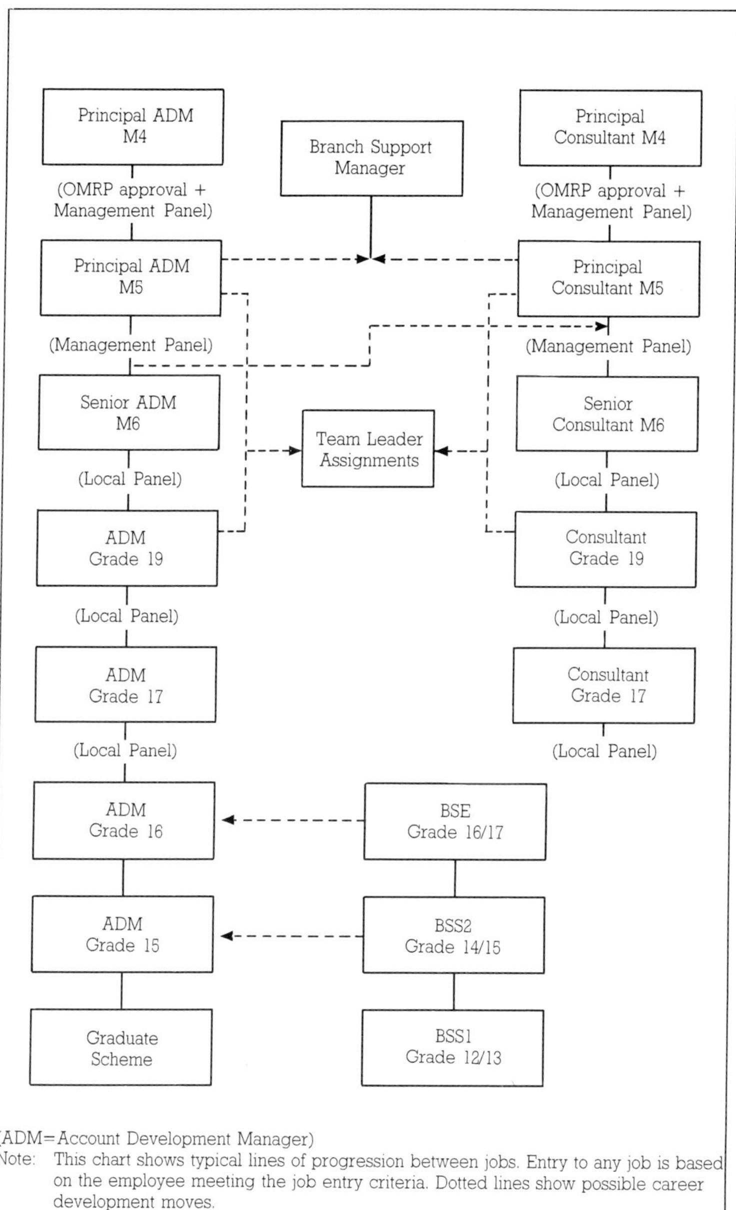

(ADM=Account Development Manager)

Note: This chart shows typical lines of progression between jobs. Entry to any job is based on the employee meeting the job entry criteria. Dotted lines show possible career development moves.

Figure 4.1 Career structure for sales support staff

Functional management

A natural career decision to be made at some point by every specialist/professional is whether or not to become a manager. The first observation of managerial functions is of one's own functional manager, and if a person's career anchor is going to lie in managerial work it becomes apparent in the earlier years. We will look in Chapter 5 at how to make realistic and mutual assessments of the capability to make this significant change.

Technical and professional career structures usually show a branch into management at a certain point – typically after the second or third rung – giving rise to the 'Y' structure.

The availability of management positions depends on several organizational factors. Supporting functions such as personnel and finance are normally structured around the organizational business units (or equivalents), which change as organizations evolve. In addition there are usually one or more HQ departments. In research and development (usually a more free-standing function) the number of posts depends more on the distribution of projects and the desired span of control.

Managers can always revert to their professional or technical expertise if management does not work out, but it becomes more and more difficult to break into management as people get older.

General management

The aim of many a young person is to be a general manager. Sometimes what they really mean is that they want to run a business – and the two (as we have seen above) are not necessarily the same thing. This is particularly true of many MBAs who are led to believe by some academics that what organizations want is more and more budding general managers. They are educated to understand the complex issues surrounding top level decisions and naturally find them challenging and exciting. Their application of this body of knowledge may, however, be a long way into the future.

What is a general manager? The following simple definition is suggested:

- Accountable for a freestanding profit and loss and balance sheet,

- Managing at least a set of functions that includes product development; sales and marketing; production or product procurement; and customer service (or the equivalent breadth in a non-industrial organization which includes customer interfaces).

The reality is that most organizations have few such positions, even though they may use the title quite freely. So the term is often used for positions where accountability for profit is combined with a span of responsibility over three or more functions. There is nothing wrong with this, for we need a distinction between the skills needed for breadth and those needed for the single function manager.

Changing career direction

Figure 4.2 shows how movement between these ladders typically occurs. The top of the MCA ladder may be a supervisor, a senior secretary, an administrator; these may bridge to the TPS structure at, say, the level above the graduate trainee who would be the normal entrant to that structure. Some additional professional training would be undertaken, and study leading to membership of the appropriate professional body. People progress this way into (for example) personnel, finance and administration, public relations, or selling.

In certain situations – from, for instance, a factory supervisory role – possibilities to progress directly up the management grades exist. However, the competition from entrants of higher education make it less easy for those who do to climb quickly up the functional management ladder.

TPS starters are usually considered for a management option after two or three steps on the specialist ladder. They may be well advised to ensure they have achieved the relevant professional status before doing so, as this always helps. For some this could be four to five years after entry. In some organizations the option to move on to a general management track through a high-flier scheme may also exist around this point. The bridge across to management becomes increasingly difficult to cross as people move higher up the TPS ladder.

Functional management may take direct trainees at the bottom but it is more common to move into this from the

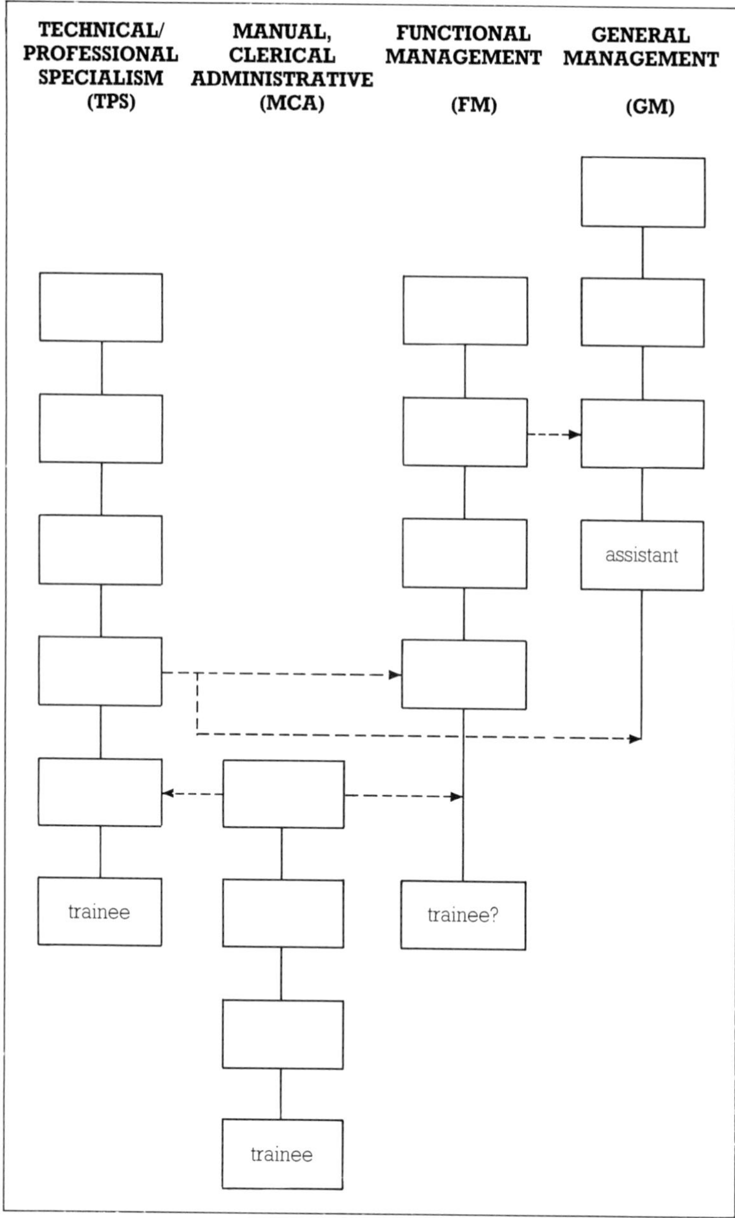

Figure 4.2 Changing career direction

other streams as a natural part of progression, subject to some assessment of capability.

The pros and cons of direct entry general management schemes are covered in the next section. This ladder (it may only be one or two levels in smaller companies) is usually reached from a position of success in functional management.

GETTING STARTED – ENTRY TO THE ORGANIZATION

There are three main types of entry into an organization, as shown in Table 4.3.

Most large organizations have all three types of entry, although some well known and respected ones have few mature entrants of any seniority. This group includes IBM, Proctor and Gamble and many oil companies which have policies designed for lifetime employment and, therefore, focus on processes of internal development. Other organizations are totally pragmatic when it comes to filling a vacancy – normally searching succession plans (if in existence) or advertising internally first and then, if no candidate is forthcoming, looking externally. Some prefer to go for 'bringing in new blood' – at least for a while when the CEO or personnel director is convinced that the world outside is full of better people. (In reality the world is full of people about whom you know a lot less than you know of your own people!) A good ratio between internal and external sourcing is, however, an important policy decision because of its effect on the size and nature of career management requirements, and in calculating the numbers of young entrants. This topic is examined in a discussion on manpower planning in Chapter 7.

The mature recruit

Mature recruits arrive through the processes of recruitment and selection. As part of the recruitment documentation, the person specification should state the knowledge, skills, attitudes and experience required of the position. Are we only recruiting with the current position in mind or are we looking for potential as well? In which case the person specification may need modification. So when we have, for example, a shortage of capable

Table 4.3 Characteristics of different types of entry

Type of entry	Characteristics	Examples
Mature recruit	– Most likely recruited for a specific job within a career structure; may or may not be recruited for future potential. – Such entries do not exist in many large organizations. – Such people may find difficulty in getting credit for pre-joining experience.	Sales manager Contracts adviser Technical group leader Marketing consultant
Post-school	– Vocational training perhaps plus academic study. – Primary objective skill acquisition and early reward/recognition for it. – Upwards penetration in organization increasingly limited.	Engineering apprentices Secretarial Retail store management/buying Banking and other finance services
Graduate or equivalent	– Training scheme geared to professional knowledge or to management. – Wide range of career options available. – Professional effort in recruitment/selection likely to be high. – Recruitment most likely to have future potential in mind.	Chartered engineers Accountancy Personnel Civil Service

first line managers or supervisors, in the recruitment of those with the right technical expertise to do the vacant job we should look also for evidence of managerial capability.

In some countries (such as Italy) a probationary period before a firm contract is required and this has much to recommend it in ensuring a sound mutual understanding exists before final commitment.

The mature recruit arrives at a certain level on the existing career ladders, usually with expectations about progression, having asked the appropriate question at the interview. If their ambitions are thwarted or delayed, such people lack the loyalty and social/cultural cohesion of the longer serving employees and may decide to change jobs again. Unless recruited because of specific past experience they can be frustrated by little account being taken of their pre-joining experience and achievements, or of qualifications that to them are important. (People are judged primarily by the first hand experience obtained through working with them.) So an organization must integrate new recruits speedily into the career management processes and ensure that their full personal value is both recognized and used. The concept of the personal growth profile (see Chapter 3) should capture both pre- and post-entry expertise. An example of an induction format appropriate for mature recruits is outlined in Chapter 7.

Post-school recruits

Practices vary in different countries regarding post-school continuing education other than universities or equivalent courses. The UK has the lowest proportion of 18 year olds in full-time or part-time education, 42% in 1988 compared with 80% in Germany (Institute of Manpower Studies).[3] The UK has had numerous initiatives over the years by successive governments to try and correct this problem. The National Council for Vocational Qualifications (NCVQ) sets standards at various levels of competence in an increasing range of vocations and sectors (but not yet over all industry and commerce). These standards are transferable and generally recognized. As the European Economic Community moves to common recognition of a wide range of qualifications we are likely to see significant movement towards a common approach to vocational training. The German system, which has served extremely well, involves a three or more year apprenticeship inside an organization, with one or two days a week studying the background to their chosen career at school. They are paid very little, but their qualification at the end has some status. The firing of apprentices in hard times would be extremely rare in Germany.

The shortage of graduates, particularly in engineering, and the predictions regarding demographic downturns in the 1990s have led organizations to put much more effort in the UK into the relationships with schools and with 16–18 year olds – both in educating them in respect of their sector and in systems of sponsorship through university courses. A large proportion of engineering undergraduates are now sponsored by firms – given a modest bursary and guaranteed vacation work each year. The relationships that result provide an excellent basis for final recruitment, and firms experience a high loyalty rate if the trainee's working experience has been well managed. As a selection method it cannot be beaten.

Whatever the method of entry a well documented and well managed trainee scheme, involving a local educational institution, should exist for the various career streams involved. Effectiveness is more likely if there is someone personally responsible for the schemes, with clear measures of success to work towards.

Graduate entrants

The most significant entry group for most organizations today is the graduate entrant – although that loose term spans a great range of academic experience and quality. Some organizations (eg, computer companies, oil industry, the higher civil service) have a long standing graduate culture. Today, however, a majority see graduates as a necessary source of competitiveness and of longer term management capability. This is true also of those parts of organizations which traditionally may have promoted people from other entry sources – such as factory supervision and sales. Jobs like these now have complexities that require a level of expertise and skills quite different from before. Organizations find benefits from the graduate over and above academic knowledge – the broader education in life skills, personal adaptability, less narrow value systems and so on.

The demand for graduates grows each year and most European countries experience and anticipate shortages of those with key disciplines. Graduate recruitment must be seen by organizations as a marketing exercise – first selling the organization as a desirable employer – and then using increasingly sophisticated methods of selection. The Institute of Manpower Studies estimates that graduate demand has increased by about 35% in the 1980s with higher increases in the finance, retail and high tech sectors. In the 1990s a further 30% growth is expected, and although the supply nominally will – in the UK – match this, the quality graduate population is always limited and sought after. Of particular concern in the UK and France is the lack of engineering and technical graduates; the popular subjects are those I would describe as the soft options – conglomerate subjects and those that lack real discipline and depth. Although in the UK women now represent 40% of the intake they are still poorly represented in the technical subjects. This shortage of technical graduates, together with the freedom of movement in the European Community and the mutual recognition of qualifications, has already led to cross-border recruitment. ICL, for example, started to target in 1990 10% of its graduate intake for UK work to be from other countries in the Community. One of the effects of the shortage has been for organizations to go further back in their marketing activity – to spend effort on schools in order to sell their industry, and to review their entry policies for post-school young people.

Recruitment and selection methodologies are of crucial importance and have been well covered by other authors. Graduate recruitment is not a task for junior personnel officers. This is a job for men and women of stature in the organization – who understand and care about the type of people the organization needs for its future. Line management should always be involved at the last stages, and preferably throughout. An organization should not recruit for the requirements of the immediate job that the graduate will do. The graduate entry group must be recruited with both the potential for the future management of the organization and the need for top specialists or technical people in mind. So some understanding of the personal characteristics that lead to success within the particular organization must be present – and selection techniques that can measure them must be used. Many organizations are experienced in doing this and there are many consultants available to help.

One sometimes hears the statement: 'We don't want too

many (or any) high flyers in our organization – we couldn't keep them happy and they'd cause trouble . . .'. I find it amazing that any organization could say it did not need the best people it could manage to attract. Such statements are often, sadly, true – they do not know how to keep high flyers happy, they do not know how to manage their careers, and they often experience premature losses which sour their perceptions of graduate intakes. An IMS study in the UK in 1987[4] found that 50% of graduates had moved on within five years – 20% within two years – but wide variations exist between sectors and occupations.

Graduates are most likely to be attracted by an organization's training and development schemes, its public image as an employer, and empathy with the people they meet, the location, and the link between their degree and the work that is offered. The best salespeople for a graduate trainee scheme are always previous graduates of the same institution or any friends of the candidate. But their perceptions of life, their maturity and their expectations change rapidly in the first year as they understand more of organizational life. Disillusion is an endemic disease which needs to be positively countered with an investment of time and effort. It is worth while listing some of the causes of dissatisfaction and their remedies (see Table 4.4).

One of the characteristics of British and American tertiary education that distinguishes it from most continental European countries is that the acquisition of a first degree is an end in itself, and with a few exceptions is not an automatic route to a related career. In the US a figure of some 25% was quoted in 1991, however, as the number of entrants to business who had either a first or second degree in business related studies. On the continent people study longer and with a narrowing focus to equip themselves for their career. The UK gives more emphasis to experiential training within the organization in the early years.

The graduate market in Europe is crossing boundaries: more and more study in another country as part of their curriculum, encouraged and aided by various funds from the European Community. In continental Europe all countries have a period of military service for men, ranging from nine to 15 months, and courses are longer than in the UK and Ireland. New

Table 4.4 Causes of disillusionment among young graduates

Causes	Sources of remedy
Lack of challenge and responsibility; ignored; left to read manual	Review design and content of graduate trainee assignments; ensure early responsibility given; reinforce immediate manager role.
Lack of attention from immediate manager	Lay down clear guidelines for managers in training and coaching; train them to do it well and monitor at appraisals.
Constant change of manager through reorganization etc	Ensure there is a mentoring system that has some constancy and overrides local changes.
Lack of feedback and interest in performance	Insist on six monthly appraisals of graduates.
Resentment on the part of other employees	Communicating to all how graduate entrants fit into the scheme of things and taking steps to maintain the self-esteem of other groups of staff.
Manager prevents attendance at training courses (or similar) due to local work pressures	Make majority of intial training mandatory and budgeted centrally; target managers with meeting trainee scheme requirements.
Disillusionment with organizational fighting/politics	Focus on job satisfaction and achievement and individual growth.
Lack of career guidance – left to fend for oneself	Review career management systems and processes; career counselling especially towards end of formal training period.
Underuse of ability	Review of each job and its requirements; better matching.
	Consider a 'technician' type of entry point for some kinds of supporting work.

Note: an interesting study of this issue in an American context is contained in Ed Schein's book referred to earlier: *Socialisation and learning to work*[1] (Chap. 8).

entrants start later on their careers, albeit with better initial preparation for them. Recruitment ages are typically 25 or 26 and may be up to 29 after some courses in Germany.

An excellent summary of the secondary education system and the management education framework in each country is contained in the ILO publication *European Management Education*.[5] Another useful reference is *The European Labour Market Review*[3] which shows the systems of the main countries in diagrammatic form.

There is less emphasis on the degree subject and level of achievement in the UK, and more on the personality and fit of the individual. Recruiters are conscious that the educational experience from different institutions varies considerably, and that degree disciplines vary enormously in the effective training of the mind. But considerable effort is now given to assessing personal skills and in a survey of 19 major firms done by the Institute of Manpower Studies in 1990[6] all were using assessment centre techniques in their selection.

In France, competition to get into a prestigious Grande Ecole is intense but, once there, desirability to employers is guaranteed. The hierarchy of educational institutions is regularly measured on various parameters – one of which is the salary commanded by their graduates for the first job. The link between degree discipline and first job is much stronger than in the UK. In Germany, where professionalism is the highest value, that link is very strong indeed.

GRADUATE TRAINEE SCHEMES

In many organizations the graduate group is the starting point for serious career management, and for focused development planning.

Most new graduates have only a hazy idea of how careers really develop in organizations, and that which they have is conditioned by parents, friends or older siblings. I have lost count of those who have said at an interview: 'My main objective is to use my degree that I have worked so hard for'. The decision may be based more on the interest and credibility of the initial training offered than with the longer term in mind.

However, although they appreciate it little at the time, the kind of development scheme on which they are placed shapes their early career towards a particular stream. When that way becomes uncomfortable the only solution may be to leave unless there are appropriate processes which enable discussion and action on a change of direction.

The new graduate wants a feeling of being in a real job as quickly as possible, so the Cooks tour of learning about a wide range of functions over a period of time is usually frustrating and dissatisfying. The questions on direct job entry are how long the individual stays in it, what development experiences are given over the same period in parallel, and how well this crucial first period is managed.

A common approach is to have a training/project period of six to 12 months before the first formal job placement. This has the potential advantage of common standards being applied and consistent management of each individual. Direct job entry places a responsibility on the manager of that young entrant for creating and managing a personal induction and growth plan. If the managers who are given this responsibility are chosen carefully and there is also a central mentoring activity (from, for instance, a graduate development manager), then the scheme has many benefits. The choice must finally depend on the needs of the organization and the target jobs for the young entrants.

The choice of assignments to gain experience is key in the design and management of trainee schemes. Some professional institutions – such as the engineering institutions – provide guidelines for employers about the content and duration of certain types of experience within an overall scheme. Types of assignments may be, for example: being a member of a project team; undertaking one or more special projects as part of a busy department; assisting a senior manager by shadowing and taking some of his/her routine work.

A second or third assignment should add value in knowledge, skills and experience to the previous ones and have the requirements of the transition point to the permanent job always in mind. The capability of the assignee's manager in young people development should always be a factor in the choice. Managers do vary in this capability and it is a mistake to hide behind the understandable reactions 'well he/she *ought* to act responsibly . . .'

In the case of professional staff functions such as finance and personnel it is normal to have common professional entrant schemes – which may be managed from the centre. For example ICL has a personnel graduate trainee scheme managed by the central human resources department over a period of 18 months. It determines the number to be recruited each year (based on manpower planning techniques); arranges the selection process, using personnel managers from around the organization; inducts and organizes common professional training events; organizes secondments of about six months each with willing divisions (which pay the basic costs themselves); acts as mentor and adviser to the individuals, and organizes the eventual full time placement.

However, the selection and definition of detailed schemes for general entrants can be left to particular divisions or subsidiary companies. What is important is that within each subset of the organization someone has the responsibility to monitor what is happening to the trainees, overviewing their progress, mentoring them and ensuring that all the requisite components of the scheme happen.

Some of the questions that need to be asked by an organization are as follows:

Should there be a high flyer scheme for those graduates who are perceived to be outstanding to allow them rapid progress to senior management?

The assumption here is that the organization has sufficiently good selection methods to cream off a percentage, with minimum work experience as a guide, to create an elite. Some significant organizations do take this approach – Shell and NatWest Bank for example. A small number of candidates do stand out in selection events but even with the most sophisticated assessment techniques it is asking a lot to predict long term potential at this stage. The approach also has other problems. The organization has visibly created division in the way people are treated and the opportunities given. A high level of expectation is placed on the individuals and on the managers who are asked to have them – a level of pressure that can be counterproductive. Those who do not meet the expectations may quietly fall into dead ends of the organization with an early sense of failure. Assignments may lack real responsibility and the opportunity to take the time to achieve results – in the effort to rotate round the organization (typically having a new assignment every nine to 12 months). The IMS study referred to earlier found three such schemes, with a four year lead up to the first real accountable job. Schemes of this kind are usually managed and funded centrally by an organization (as would be normal for schemes considered to be strategically important for the organization as a whole) – a potential problem is the real value that is placed on 'free gifts'.

There are many excellent products of such schemes – people who were the right choices, and who responded well to all the challenges given. However, on balance this author favours a more considered assessment of potential after a period of real work and observation in the organization.

Should there be a graduate scheme for management direct from entry?

We are not referring necessarily to general management but to schemes targeted at early functional management, particularly in manufacturing or retail. This would be quite normal in the USA, particularly for those who have taken a business management degree or postgraduate qualification (some 70,000 in 1987). In the UK it is not so common, although there are some well known examples such as the Unilever Management Development Scheme which has many famous 'graduates' now spread through industry.

I joined such a scheme in the manufacturing division of Procter and Gamble. As a new graduate in chemical engineering I chose P&G as they were the only organization of 12 I contacted (one exception – the Atomic Energy Authority of Canada) which was prepared to train me immediately for management responsibility. I trained for five months alongside a graduate of the previous year whose job I was to take, with regular inputs and mentoring from my manager who looked after five or so departments. There came that magical day when, aged 22, I made all the decisions as the appointed manager for my department of 12 people producing household name products and working around the clock. After 15 months I moved to a much larger production facility, a challenging assignment, and then later to an industrial engineering staff role and to a personnel role. The same pattern of mixing staff and line roles, having real responsibility together with complementary training and a strong coaching role from senior managers, was applied to all new graduates. Many of my university colleagues in similar organizations spent their time as junior engineers, then project engineers and so on – and by 30, maybe, moved to production management.

In retrospect, I would not have chosen any other scheme – but it was only some years later that I realized the low place in the British hierarchy enjoyed by production manufacturing (a great contrast with Germany and Japan). It was a long way from the realities of commercial decisions and customers, and few made the bridge into managing other functions or into general management.

The answer to our question lies for each organization in the nature of the profile of knowledge, skills, attitudes and experience that senior jobs require. If it is important for managers to have a technical or professional base of knowledge and experience then this must be acquired on the ground in the early part of their careers. Thus computer and engineering companies normally do not have direct entry management career streams – whereas retail and consumer goods companies do.

What happens at the end of the trainee scheme?

At the end of the scheme the graduates should be ready for an established post, of a type for which the scheme has prepared them. These should be natural bridges in the career structures of the organization, and planned in advance. The graduate trainees will be making the transition into the normal career structure of the organization. In some cases more than one option for a career stream may be possible: for example it is not uncommon in computer systems companies for graduates to be given the option of being assessed for a sales role at this point – sales being a prestigious occupation in such organizations. Normally, however, the movement is to a post which directly consolidates the knowledge gained.

The systems that exist and the methods of progression should be well explained to the graduate trainees. Many become frustrated through not knowing how future progress is obtained in the organization. Counselling as a part of the appraisal discussions should be normal – some organizations offer career direction/guidance sessions specifically to enable the graduate to make choices. However, these may be a little premature if graduates have been prepared for a particular stream up to this point. If the organization has no structure of careers and progression to explain to the emerging trainees, then it needs a book like this!

What about recruitment of postgraduates and MBAs?

Few organizations have separate trainee schemes for postgraduate entrants. Although they may pay a somewhat higher salary, the individual is likely to enter on a trainee scheme at the same point as the first degree graduate. This is entirely logical. The exceptions are research oriented organizations that may focus on some specialized PhDs or operate a 'teaching company scheme' where a Master's degree can be obtained through in-company work and may lead to future employment.

MBAs are different in the sense that they have normally had some years' work experience. Those who do not, despite their glamorous second degree, are little different from a first degree graduate, and all the best management schools insist on a minimum period of work before the course. Organizations differ widely in their view on MBAs; whereas they are a normal entry requirement for firms of management consultants and some financial institutions, general commerce and industry are more cautious, particularly in the UK. In the USA there are some 70,000 produced each year and they are much more accepted if not universally appreciated. In France it is not a valued qualification compared to one of the Commercial Grandes Ecoles; in Germany it is not valued at all.

Why the caution? Two basic reasons – firstly, the high self-opinion that many (although not all) MBAs appear to hold and secondly, the difficulty organizations have in fitting into their structures people in their late 20s with high expectations of their worth. This is a serious problem. Few organizations sponsor their own employees to do an MBA full time because of the problem of post-course expectations: it is unwise – at least where it involves residential full time commitment away from the organization.

The label MBA may be the qualification from a wide range of courses today and we discuss some of these in Chapter 7 in the context of managed development. At this point we are referring to those who are in full time study and available for recruitment. But the problem of fitting MBAs into the structure is worth trying to overcome. It is not that the educational experience is so overwhelmingly valuable – most MBAs teach skills and concepts that are appropriate to a few people at the top of an organization and a few strategists – but that many able young people today see the MBA as their final piece of equipment for a successful future and, therefore, it is a key recruiting ground for good people. A place like Insead in Fontainebleau, France (which is totally divorced from the French system of education and is like an international island) brings together first class people from a multitude of nationalities and gives them a truly international outlook.

So it is worthwhile looking for MBA entry points in the career framework – defined as 'positions which carry the grade and salary levels that will attract MBAs from the best schools, provide real responsibility, and yet be posts that an outsider can pick up and be competent in fairly quickly'. Such positions may be in business and strategic planning; mergers and acquisition analysis; financial analysis, human resource development, production management, etc. Unless the career management system is well developed MBAs can find it hard to escape from the analytical staff jobs, even though their ambition is more towards management, so – as always when recruiting – one should be thinking of the next job as well as the immediate one. The label MBA has to be shed as the individual is absorbed into the normal systems of the organization – a standard answer to those who ask what career paths you offer to MBAs in your organization. It is a common complaint of MBAs that so much is expected of them when they join that often nobody takes the trouble to understand their induction needs – they need a personal induction programme in the same way that all new recruits do.

In several years of recruiting MBAs on behalf of two companies in quite different fields I tried for a period to focus very hard on the European students studying in the US – at Harvard, MIT and Columbia. It is easy to establish personal contact with students using the excellent job placement services but, however professional my recruitment method, I found I could never attract on a competitive salary level compared with the options in the US or with the major management consulting firms in the UK which offered significant joining incentives. So I retreated to the European schools.

COMPLETING THE FRAMEWORK FOR MANAGING CAREERS

The needs of each career direction

Manual, clerical and administrative This group deserves formal career structures just as much as the technical and professional group, although it can be sadly neglected. National Vocational Qualifications (NVQ) in the UK (still being developed at the time of writing) should provide a basis for continuing learning and standards of capability linked to steps in the structure. An article by Penny Cole and Margery Povall[7] describes a cooperative venture between British Airways, Reed Employment, W H Smith and the Training Agency in creating a career structure for secretaries, with assessments based on the relevant NVQ levels. In addition to the structures themselves, the bridges to other career streams need to be evaluated and defined.

Technical and specialist staff Managing the careers of technical and specialist staff is the easiest of our tasks in that the main aim is to encourage them to develop their specialism; and to provide opportunities reasonably early on to come to a decision regarding the management option – taking the right branch of the 'Y'. However, it is important to recognize that many such people will be more effective as a result of some broadening experience, particularly in understanding customers and suppliers and the interface between them and the organization. This lateral development is less likely to be in an actual horizontal job change as in some planned learning experiences such as are described in Chapter 7.

If we consider the concept of the personal growth profile, knowledge and experience deepen naturally with time. As one progresses, the development of additional skills – communications or interpersonal skills for example – may require formal training. Some skills seem to be more naturally present and just need developing – planning and organizing, team leadership, for instance, while others need to be grown from the ground floor.

Functional management Moving into management of a function represents a steep change in the skills element. One has to learn the basic skills and competencies of management; and one has to learn to balance the professional or technical interest with wider participation in the business team (or equivalent). At a senior level the original technical or specialist knowledge may cease to deepen in itself as managerial and internal political priorities absorb the working life. For the individual with potential to reach the higher levels a horizontal move into another function for a period is highly desirable to provide a broadening experience. The synergy resulting from such experiences may vary – one can draw up a table for each organization showing the most desirable additional experiences (see Table 4.5 which gives some examples).

Table 4.5 Functional management development

Function	Desirable broadening experience: horizontal moves
Marketing	Product planning
Personnel	Finance, production
Contracts control	Marketing
Business planning	Marketing, finance

General management Managing the growth of those who are to become future general managers presents the organization with the most difficult problem in career management – even though the requirement may be relatively low in numbers it is extremely high in importance. Growing people up vertical professional trees is much easier and much more natural; even progressing in functional management is relatively simple to manage – but to avoid a career jump that demands too much in its profile of knowledge, skills, attitudes and experience we need to plan the growth of general management capability.

In defining a general manager earlier we delineated it simply as focusing on profit accountability and with a breadth of span of control. Organizations have traditions about their routes to the top. For many British companies it used to be via a pure engineering career, often with sad results as markets became worldwide, and fortunately this has received much attention in the 1980s. For some consumer goods companies it is through advertising, in computer companies it tends to be via sales (graduate salespeople have been the norm for 25 years), in chemical companies through manufacturing. In some organizations requirements are laid down for the path en route – for example in Shell no one can make it to senior management without international experience. These norms are not easily transgressed nor changed. Nevertheless, most would not argue with the statement that general managers would be the better for having had a broader experience than many receive.

The career direction decision

Along the way choices have to be made regarding an individual's career direction. Even if a person has started organizational life on a management trainee scheme a choice has to be made about continuing in that direction. How and when should these choices be made? It is a common approach today to leave this to the individual, while providing information and resources to help him or her decide.

The organization, however, which believes in a more proactive role in managing people growth has policies and practices that help individuals answer such questions in a systematic and mutually satisfactory way. Figure 4.3 shows a suggested map of decision points based on a graduate entry, and similar maps can be made based on other entry points and other possible points requiring choice.

In preparing such a picture for each particular organization we must answer the question as to when is the latest time for us to commit positively to a plan for developing a person as a senior manager. It is reasonable to assume that on average (depending on experience) we need three jobs of say two to

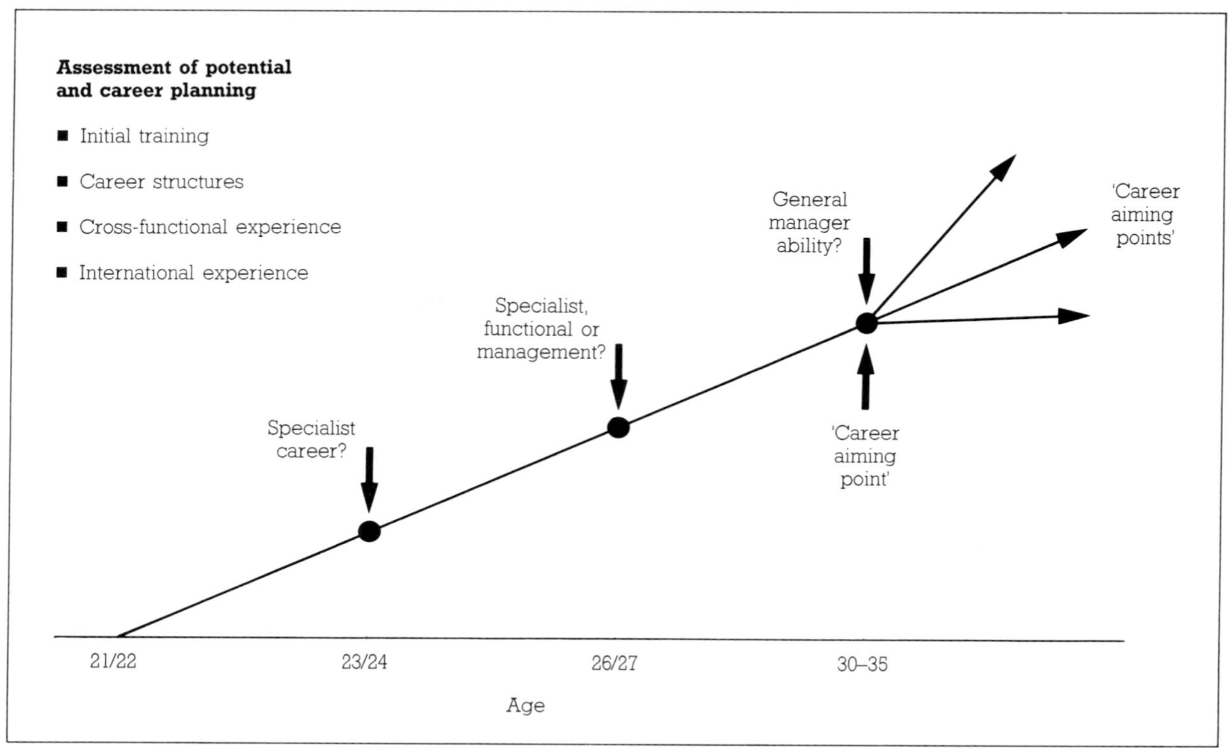

Figure 4.3 Career direction decision points

three years each from the time of decision to reaching a general management position – say eight years. The typical entry age for this senior level might be 40 years (in some organizations it may be early 30s; in others it may be 50), and so we could say the latest date for a decision would be around 32 years old. To expect people to choose their preferred career direction by that time is reasonable – they will have had (at least in the UK or America) ten years of experience and their personal career 'anchor' should be well formed. They may need some help and guidance in making the choice (see Chapter 5).

But they may be able to make the choice earlier than that.

- Clearly the graduate trainee scheme into which the individual is placed sets him or her in a particular direction – unless it is the aimless Cooks tour that is not recommended. Understanding and acclimatizing to the world of work, linked with the opportunity to achieve something, provides a base for making a much more intelligent and informed decision than is possible on entry. Nevertheless, most trainees will progress 'vertically' in the line they have chosen or been placed.
- Two or three years into the organization is a good time to provide the first change opportunity (although this needs to be longer if the completion of a professional qualification requires it). It is a time of high risk in graduate attrition and some will already have formed a wish to change. Both parties have got to know each other well and there is now plenty of behavioural evidence of capability. This is probably the earliest time when one can make an assessment of managerial capability.
- Five or six years on – by this time the young person is in his or her late 20s and should have firmly established some achievement. His or her potential should be fairly visible and the specialist-professional versus management decision should be made without too much difficulty. It is not the latest time to make a positive decision regarding a management career – but the earlier the better because of the new skills that need to be built up. Such a commitment means that detailed functional specialism and knowledge – while remaining an interest – is going to be subservient to managing others effectively.

- After eight to 12 years, we should be able to assess whether 'this is a person to career-manage for senior management'. We will have been able to observe the individual in one or two management positions, and know how strong the basic set of management competences are. Using appropriate assessment techniques (see Chapter 5), we can assess the basis of the requirements of a general manager position.

Career aiming points

All too often a career conversation between an individual and his or her manager is built around the words 'what next?' But the essence of managing careers is that you cannot answer this question until you know where you are heading for. At 30 I set myself an objective that I would be a personnel director of at least a medium sized company by the age of 40. This sense of a target to aim for I found extremely helpful – and, even though I deviated from the functional personnel path en route, every career decision was taken in the light of the desired end point.

Given that we have determined with the individual the most appropriate career direction, how far ahead can we sensibly aim for? As Cheshire cat said to Alice, 'it doesn't matter which path you follow if you don't know where you want to end up'. Can we be more precise than, for example, 'a high level position in finance'? We need to fix an aiming point which is a particular type of position that we believe is a reasonable target. The young person who starts with the ambition of becoming managing director is more in the realm of dreaming than planning – although it is surprising how few do have such ambitions, and the number decreases with age. The level of the aiming point is tied up with the assessment of potential. It is not enough to take just the individual's perception of the heights to which they could rise – it needs to be a joint and agreed assessment.

Five to ten years ahead is probably the most that one can sensibly plan for. It is not the ultimate that we are trying to define here, but a position in time. A mistake that is often made is to try and guess a final level of which the individual is capable – none of us can predict the result of so many variables at once. If the person is young and in phase 1, we may set an aiming point over a shorter period as we may still be working out the right career direction to follow. By the time we are in phase 2, we should know at least our penultimate realistic aiming level – reached typically around age 40 – and beyond that our aiming points may be to have a particular post or to gain particular experience. Phase 3 will be similar – the concept is less important here.

The career aiming point is fundamental to the practice of personal growth through career development in our framework. Figure 4.4 shows its importance in enabling us to create a meaningful career plan with purposeful learning experiences designed to enhance the elements of the personal growth profile.

Fixing the aiming point is not easy in a turbulent environment – in trying to put into practice my own thoughts on career management for others I find it one of the hardest things to do. One has to lay out the scheme of careers in the organization and take people through the choices and options steadily, and get their minds thinking beyond the next step. To those who say – well, I'll just take my chances and trust to luck and keeping good contacts – the answer is that this is not good enough. We do not want people drifting aimlessly, even if it is upwards. The organization needs to *manage* the person's development in an informed and intelligent way to meet its future requirements. This means managing experience and the acquisition of further knowledge and skills.

We look at the subject of individual career counselling and career planning in the next chapter.

Career bridges

Gaining experience by moving from one function to another has increasing importance in the different career directions as we move closer to general management. The greatest weakness of the self-development approach, I believe, is that it is very difficult to make such cross-functional moves (either internally or externally) from the standpoint of individual initiative. Some will and cooperation is needed from the organization, and some systematic approach as to how it can happen.

Developing one's career to move up a ladder is relatively simple to make happen – and even without written career structures or formalized processes a natural progression of upwards movement is likely for the most able. But what we need to find

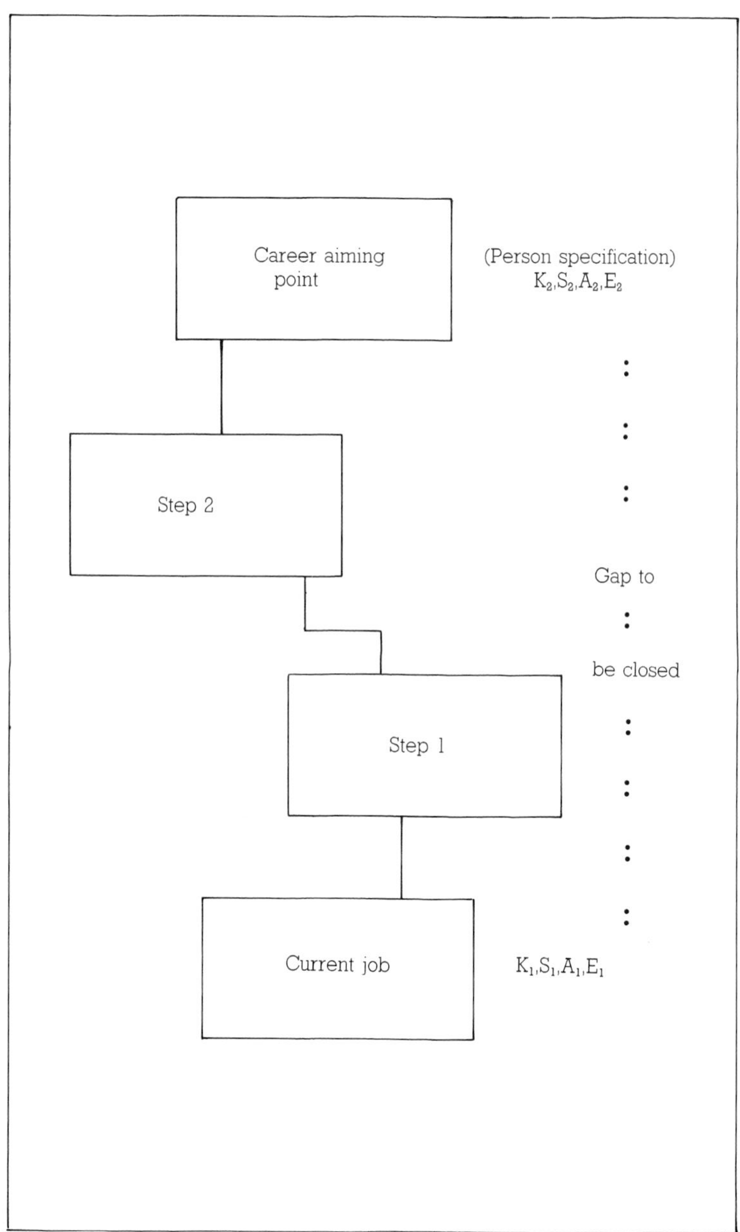

Figure 4.4 Determining the development gap

are the bridges that enable a person to cross from one ladder to another.

Career bridges then are career changes which move the individual into new areas of experience and build on aspects of the personal growth profile already there. So often someone in their late 30s or early 40s has achieved a senior functional position but wants to get into general management. They know certain aspects of the business well, but always in a staff role. They have never managed a significant number of people, and almost certainly never managed managers. Although they may have the ability it can sometimes be too late to make the necessary bridges to fill in gaps of experience. How late it is depends on the 'progression versus age' patterns (see Figure 3.2) in the organization. But if an individual has reached too high a level in his or her function, crossing over may need some downsteps to achieve the desired learning experiences. It is important to have an environment that accepts this in the context of job grades and status, so that personal growth is not subservient to a bureaucratic inflexible rewards system. However, an effective career management system takes care of the right bridge-crossing early in a career rather than later.

In a non-directive career culture it is particularly difficult, as few managers are prepared to take risks with the unknown and untried candidate for a job. I am particularly grateful to a director in ICL who, in a major reorganization, was prepared to move me from a position of personnel manager to that of one of several industry marketing managers responsible for the production and marketing of software to the hospitality and leisure industry. My personal growth profile increased in leaps and bounds in the next two years on every front as I learned about customer requirements, software development, negotiation of deals, international markets and internal politics. But a small price had to be paid – I had to step down a level hierarchically.

Although each individual has his or her own set of bridges, a map can be drawn up of natural bridges in the organization and this is a key activity in good career management. First we should draw up a matrix of levels and functions in the organization. We can then do three things:

1. Define the bridges that sit comfortably in the organization and historically have been known to work well. We look for

similarities in the specifications of knowledge, skills, attitudes, experience, where we could expect that a person doing Job A will have acquired some of the components of the specification needed for Job B. Thus to move from sales to marketing, though requiring different skills, is relatively easy. To move between personnel and production management is more difficult in either direction.

By a simple study of the last ten years of a number of people – including particularly some of those who are now general managers – or of all the moves in say the last two years, one can easily get a feel for what the natural bridges are. A bridging map can be drawn up which helps employees see clearly where movements can be made – allowing for the exceptional moves that may not be on the map.

An example of a bridging map is shown in Figure 4.5, and a matrix of possible bridges for people currently in a clerical, secretarial and administrative role in Table 4.6. This matches Table 4.2 and is taken from the same booklet.

2. Mark those positions which offer particularly strong opportunities for key types of experience. Thus this might include such experiences as:

Commercial interfaces	Significant man-management
P&L accountability	Managing managers
Strategic importance	International exposure
Government relations	Large project management
Responsibility for trainees	Policy development

As each organization completes the experience requirements for the key job person specifications, a list can be made of what amount to ten to 20 areas of experience such as those illustrated above.

3. Identify specific positions which could be described as development positions. These are defined as those positions where (a) the person with potential and sound basic skills can make a contribution within three months without prior specialist knowledge and (b) the department concerned will not be unduly disrupted by frequent changes. These positions should never be blocked but be carefully monitored as 'the oil of career management'. It is an interesting and often surprising exercise

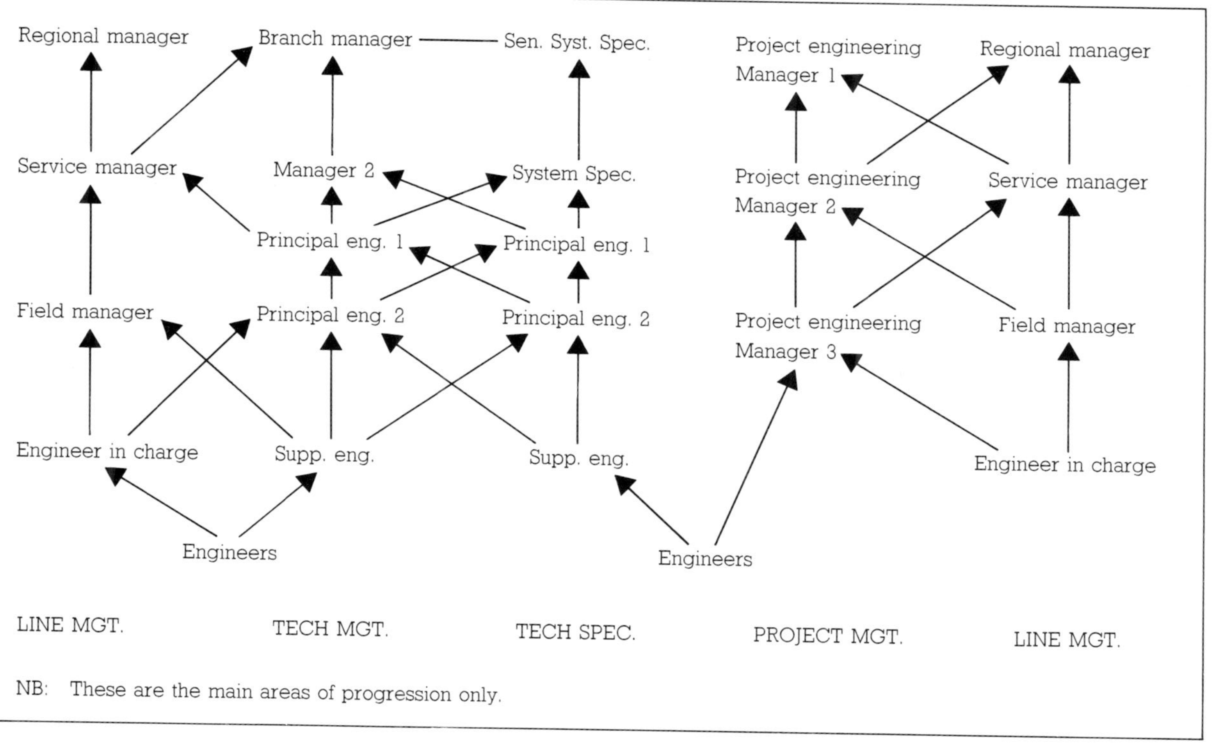

NB: These are the main areas of progression only.

Figure 4.5 Example of a career bridging map

Table 4.6 Career planning guide – clerical, secretarial and administrative

Career Structure Level	Clerical, secretarial, administrative	Personnel	Finance	Marketing and Support			Technical		Materials		
	Refer to Clerical Secretarial and Departmental Administrative Career Structure	Refer to Personnel Career Structure	Refer to Finance Career Structure	Refer to Marketing Career Structure	Refer to Sales Support Career Structure	Refer to Customer Service Career Structures	Refer to Systems Software Support Career Structure	Refer to Technical Author Career Structure	Refer to Materials Management Career Structure		
5	Senior Executive Secretary	Personnel Officer or Personnel Admin Officer	Financial Analyst	Marketing Officer	Technical Presenter	Support Executive or Product Specialist	Systems Software Support Specialist	Author		Materials Controller 1	Purchasing Officer 1
6	Executive Secretary Senior Administrator	Assistant Personnel Officer or Personnel/Training Admin Officer	Financial Analyst or Financial Assistant	Marketing Officer	Technical Presenter	Support Executive or Product Specialist	Systems Software Support Specialist	Junior Author		Materials Controller 2	Purchasing Officer 2
7	Senior Secretary Administrator	Assistant Personnel Officer or Personnel/ Training Admin. Officer	Financial Assistant	Marketing Assistant	Demonstrator	Customer Service Represent-ative	Systems Software Support Specialist	Trainee Author	Senior Distribution Operator	Materials Assistant	Stock Integrity Analyst
8	Secretary		Accounting Assistant						Flexible Distribution Operator		Order Processing Operator

to define these positions. The higher the level in the organization the fewer we will find, and at the bottom end of the structure most positions – other than those requiring highly technical or specialized training – would count. An example of what a matrix of such positions might look like is shown in Table 4.7; this is taken from a real study of such positions in the customer service organization of a manufacturing organization.

Table 4.7 Development positions

FUNCTION	JUNIOR	LOWER MIDDLE	UPPER MIDDLE
Service line management	Control centre supervisor	Service manager	
Technical management	Planning and Control engineers	Performance improvement manager	Manager, planning & control
Project management (professional)	Project accountant	Customer engineering project manager grade 2	Special projects manager
Finance and administration	Cost accountant; Performance standards engineer	Spares investment controller; Manager, site service	Business planning manager
Personnel and training	Recruitment or communications officer; Manager of trainee programmes	Recruitment manager; Senior personnel officer	Training manager; Internal communications manager
Supply and distribution	Procedure controller; Inventory planner; Spares analyst; Factory liaison officer	Traffic manager; Business planning manager	Inventory manager; Warehouse manager

Can the good manager manage anything? Can the high flyer cope with any challenge thrown at him or her? I do not believe the evidence supports this approach and successful organizations place a premium on knowing the business. Conglomerates do not usually find that the successful manager in one business can automatically succeed in an unrelated one, except perhaps at the highest level where the need for detail is limited. Effective career management therefore looks for solid bridges rather than leaps into the darkness in the hope of hitting land on the other side – bridges which are systematic steps in a career plan towards an aiming point. The time to make functional moves is easiest in the early years, but this does require some direction – accepted by all concerned – to achieve. The trainee stage is usually directed and there is much to be said for that continuing for a few years even if the general culture is non-directive. So we should encourage perhaps the young personnel graduate to spend 12–18 months in sales before it is too difficult to get accepted – he or she can only gain from such experience. Perhaps some personnel managers are nervous about this because they fear the person will not come back to personnel – is this to the gain or loss of the organization?

What about changing direction later in life? It is always relatively easy to revert – from general management to functional; from functional management to specialization. Many ex-executives in the latter phase of their careers choose to provide consultancy in an area that has always been of interest. However, to make onwards and upwards changes does become increasingly difficult as the years go by – firstly, because the number of management positions is always limited and there are competitors who are likely to be younger; and secondly because as one becomes more senior in grade, etc, a change of career direction becomes more difficult for the organization to accommodate.

HIGH FLYER SCHEMES

Whereas most organizations seek to identify the people who have high level potential (colloquially known in some as HIPOTS), some place them in a more formal group which is given special treatment. There are those as we mentioned earlier that start such a group from graduate recruitment time, but a few years' experience leads to a better selection.

A formal scheme may have all or some of the following elements:

- Some kind of assessment event designed to confirm high level potential (ie against some general management criteria), and using high level assessors. Only a small number of places a year may be made available.
- Successful candidates become group level resources and their career is managed by either a designated HR manager or, more commonly, a committee of some kind. Placements are recommended and both parties – employee and receiving manager – need very good reasons to reject the suggestion.
- Some kind of parenting (by home division) or mentoring (by one of the assessors for example).
- Preferential selection for training events; some organizations may sponsor their high flyers for an MBA at a prestigious school.

It can be an uncomfortable label to be given for an individual, especially with the high expectations that go with it. Participants may find they are thrust unwillingly on departments, that other colleagues resent their special treatment, or that they are expected to succeed in unreasonably short periods of time. The assumption that accelerated movement to the top is good for the organization is questionable – the implication is that experience is of less value than youthful dynamism. The people with the highest potential must be of great interest to the organization; however, their career progress can be within a framework designed for the career management of all employees – and in that case a special label is not necessary. (See the section on potential in Chapter 5.)

JOB MOVEMENT PROCESSES

Filling vacancies

Making things happen in career management means having effective ways of moving people from one job to another. Here the cultural issues mentioned in Chapter 2 will influence how things are done. There are two dimensions:

- Will jobs be openly advertised, and anyone have the opportunity to apply?
- Will jobs be filled according to succession plans, career plans etc?

or a combination of both . . .

The careers manager is unlikely to be able to worry about everyone's career plan, and is probably selective, based on the populations that are of particular interest. So unless we have an army of helpers matching every job opportunity with all possible candidates, some form of open advertisement is the best way of bringing people and jobs together. It has potential problems – unsuitable applicants have to be dealt with, taking time and resource; applicants may find the job has been fixed for a preferred candidate and was not really open at all; people may not get to see the ad in time; and so on. But the advantages are stronger. An organization-wide publication helps to bridge the parochial problem and brings knowledge of other areas and jobs; the system appears fair and open; individual interest and self-help are encouraged in career development.

Are there limits on what jobs are openly published? This depends on the specific organization, but one could expect that senior jobs above a particular level might be exempt and filled by other means of selection. Another case might be when a job will clearly be filled by one candidate due to rationalization, reorganization or returning from abroad.

How do succession and career plans fit into this free-for-all? There need be no conflict. Career plans (see Chapter 5) focus on a particular type of experience rather than a specific job – the career manager or mentor taking an interest in an individual would, therefore, draw the ad to the person's attention and encourage application. The exception is where we really do want to manage the career of a person with high potential and achieve a specific career bridge – then some intervention may be needed and the job not advertised.

Selection for a position should be based on:

- the match of knowledge, skills, attitudes and experience

between the individual personal growth profile and the essential job specification requirements,
and

- what such a position does in fulfilling the individual's career plan.

It is usually said that 'the best person for the job is the one to be appointed'. One cannot argue with that except to say that sometimes the choice between candidates is marginal and the development opportunities for personal growth of a candidate should then be part of the consideration. If the position is defined as a development position then the choice should be heavily weighted towards the development gain for the individual.

We tend to think of job movements as arising from vacancies, that is reactively. There is a good case for being more proactive in job change through planned career movements and this is looked at in Chapter 6.

INTERNATIONAL ASSIGNMENTS

As a means of development, international assignments offer tremendous learning possibilities (see Chapter 7). There are a number of rationales for sending someone on an assignment, not all to do primarily with personal growth. Table 4.8 lists these reasons. Analysis of assignments by such an approach is a useful way of seeing where the considerable costs are being spent, and a check on the balance of using assignments for expedient or planned development reasons. Opportunities should be exploited for career growth reasons, however, where possible.

They are expensive. The rule of thumb normally used is 300% of the cost of employing a local, depending on the method of calculation used. However, this is part of the cost of being an international organization. If local managers are so targeted on their own profit and loss results that they wish to avoid expatriates wherever possible, and yet for people development reasons opportunities are needed, then some kind of strategic funding pot is needed. Such a pot should pay the difference between total assignment costs and the cost of a local person in the job in cases where the reason is personal development for the individual.

Most western organizations now pursue a policy of local management wherever possible, and in many mature international operations expatriates may only be needed in the developing countries. This takes away some of the best opportunities available for growth of experience. But the reality is that in developed countries the organization is best served by local nationals who understand the culture of the country and have the contacts necessary. It is not quite so important where language is not an issue – Australians in the United States for example, or Austrians in Germany. One suggestion here is to use Table 4.8 and draw up a list of those positions that can be filled by a non-national.

Re-entry presents a significant problem to many organizations. Unless they are very centrally directive, or it is understood that progress in the organization depends on international service, such as Shell or BP, then the system usually used is that of 'home and host'. Ownership for the purposes of career development, basic administration and re-entry remain with the home unit. This causes problems when the home unit gets reorganized or may even cease to exist while the individual is away. So some corporate interest is needed. If the assignment is part of a committed career plan re-entry should be easier to manage.

Re-entry is always difficult where individuals have gone from a smaller country to the homebase country. A small country organization has little scope for letting go one of its best people and finding a better position for them two or three years later, unless either they were young enough in the first place to be easily reabsorbed, or the country organization is at a stage of considerable growth. It may be a more or less permanent departure from the home country in this case, as the individual takes his or her further career growth in the larger organization.

Some organizations are finding new ways to provide early international exposure by building trainee schemes that involve secondments to other countries. This has much to recommend it, in that the practical and cost problems are much less for younger and usually single people.

Table 4.8 Reasons for an international assignment

Type of assignment	**Organization justification**
A. TRANSFER OF SKILL OR KNOWLEDGE	
A1. Use of a worldwide skillpool	Sharing and full use of highly specialized talent globally
A2. Development of local knowledge/ skill by secondment to a more developed centre	Local assimilation of skills on a permanent basis
A3. Meeting a local lack of skill by seconding a person out from a developed centre	Local need resourced quickly
A4. Meeting a local management need because existing capability inadequate	Local need resourced quickly
A5. Bringing international understanding into the homebase	Ensuring international needs are built into organization's products/services/plans
A6. Staffing an extension of an existing homebase function in another country	To take a function closer to a market, or to deliberately build a more international mix.
A7. Representation of parent company in a local subsidiary	Safeguard of the organization's interest
B INDIVIDUAL PERSONAL GROWTH	
B1. Training young entrants for local country in homebase	Efficiency of learning curve through using homebase facilities; creating early international attitudes
B2. Personal development of local nationals	Development of specific K, S, A, Es and wider organization understanding as part of career plan
B3. Development of high flyers	Ditto

SUMMARY

This chapter has been about how careers are structured. Each person finds through experience fairly quickly in life the 'anchor' that is best suited to them and in organizational terms this translates to a career direction. We have suggested four main such directions – manual, clerical and administrative; technical/specialist; functional management and general management. Within these an organization will have career structures (or ladders) for specific functions and it is helpful to formalize these so that people know how to make progress. Movements between the main directions are significant events in an individual's career path.

The method of entry into the organization determines the starting point for a career, and the management of trainees deserves considerable attention. This is a time of rapid learning, of formation of attitudes, of observing other more senior members of the organization as role models. Lessons learned in these early days last for ever – so the 'kindergarten' of the organization deserves careful management.

The greatest challenge for many is to manage the crossing of functional lines in order to provide some breadth in development, through career bridges. It is in this area that the self-development philosophy has considerable difficulty because of the need for some organizational determination to make these moves happen. However, if we describe career development as the planned growth of personal knowledge, skills, attitudes and experience towards an aiming point, then the achievement of the building blocks of experience often need cross-functional moves. The processes of career management must facilitate these.

A framework such as has been described should not be interpreted as bureaucracy. The systematic presentation and use of information is not that; although some administrators are capable of turning the simplest process into bureaucracy. Nor does such a framework imply inflexibility and a lack of ability to cope with change: these needs can be built in. In the next chapter the application to the individual will be examined.

PLANNING FOR ACTION

Problems of reality

1. Career structures or ladders are fine and well appreciated when introduced. However, they tend to give people the feeling of a path of automatic promotion; individuals watch each other's progress and weak managers compromise the standards to keep people happy or solve a remuneration problem.

All processes that require control in people management are subject to abuse by weak managers, and an auditing police force in this area is not desirable. The personnel function needs to be well aware if the lack of control is caused by a weakness elsewhere, for instance salary scales being behind the market. Investment in management education to explain how the structure fits in the total framework is recommended – not just at the time of introduction as then subsequent managers miss out. The involvement of others in promotion decisions – such as the manager's boss and a personnel person – should be sufficient to hold the integrity of the structure.

2. When it comes to new entrants, managers vary enormously in the attention they give to their development, however much care is put into the design of training programmes.

It is a reality of life that managers have different styles and levels of caring about the development of their people. Effective training of managers, well designed induction and trainee schemes, integrative manager-friendly processes, a supportive culture and clearly stated standards of performance can all encourage managers significantly to go beyond their natural style. It is in the interests of the organization, however, to give the greater responsibility for new entrants to those that are strongest in this area, and when others complain it should be explained clearly why.

3. Defining development positions is fine in theory, but in practice changing organizations mean constant reassessment and update. It is also very difficult to persuade managers that selection for such positions should be governed by an individual's development plan.

Such difficulties will reduce if and when the concepts and principles of career management are well embedded into the organization. No change is successful without a driver, who is actively supported by top management. That person has to work hard to give practical help, to influence and persuade that 'what is written in the booklet' really is in the interests of each part of the organization. A measure of success is when the top management insist that an update of development positions accompanies any organization change.

4. Determining an aiming point for several years ahead is almost impossible to do; life is too uncertain. Isn't it better to focus more on the short term and go a step at a time?

If we try and focus on specific jobs this is clearly making our plan a hostage to fortune. It is better to think of an aiming point as a level in a chosen stream in a given career direction, and having that as an objective is absolutely essential to enable the intelligent and systematic planning of development. As experience in advising people grows it becomes easier to set the aiming points, although they may need revision each year as the organization and environment change.

Indicators of success – these are set out in Table 4.9

Action for those responsible for career management

1. This chapter is about 'nuts and bolts' of a framework. Few organizations start from nothing. Draw up a list of each of the concepts in this chapter and consider whether (a) they exist, (b) how effective they are in practice, (c) if they do not exist whether they would enhance the value of career management and how you would introduce them, (d) if they do, what needs to be done to make them more effective.
2. If you do not already have them, draw up tables of development positions, bridging maps and each of the other diagrams and tables in this chapter for **your** organization.
3. Draw up a list of each of the technical/specialist/professional career streams in the organization. Does each employee have a clear idea of their career possibilities? Are career structures consistent with the standards suggested on page 117.

Table 4.9 Indicators of success checklist

Career directions	1. They are identified, labelled and understood in the organization. 2. Movement is possible between them and processes exist to facilitate that movement.
Career structures	3. Each stream within a career direction has a structure for progression within it (assuming the number of people warrant it) and this conforms to the standards laid out at the end of this chapter. 4. Operation of the structures has integrity, and they are reviewed annually for update if necessary.
New entrants	5. Each category of new entrant has an appropriate formal training or induction scheme, including mature entrants. 6. Early leavers are interviewed thoroughly to determine the cause of leaving and action is taken as needed.
Bridges, maps and development positions	7. These have been identified in the organization, and are known and understood by management. 8. A person is responsible for keeping them up-to-date in each part of the organization.
International assignments	9. These are built into the career management framework; reasons for them are clearly identified and the number of people on them for personal growth reasons is monitored. 10. The responsibility for managing the return of expatriates is clearly defined and the 'failure to place' rate is zero.
Job movement processes	11. The policy is clear and understood. 12. The policy includes flexibility to take account of career management considerations, and this aspect is supported by top management in selection choices.

4. If you have an international responsibility, draw up your own version of Table 4.8 and assess how many assignments are in each category. How does this reflect the current and future needs of the organization? Are you satisfied with the management of expatriates and their re-entry? If not, how might it be improved?
5. Evaluate the effectiveness of new entrant schemes by drawing up your own version of Table 4.4 for each type of entrant. What actions should be taken to make the schemes more effective?
6. What does Figure 4.3 look like in your organization? If it is not formalized in this way, would it be of benefit to do so?

REFERENCES

1 Schein, E., *Career Dynamics – Matching Organizational and Individual Need*, Addison Wesley, 1978.

2 Schein, E., and Delong T. J., *Career Orientations Questionnaire*, MIT, 1981

3 Pearson, R., Andreutti F., and Holly S., *The European Labour Market Review: The Key Indicators*, Institute of Manpower Studies Report 193, 1991

4 Bevan S. M., *The Management of Labour Turnover*, Institute of Manpower Studies Report 137, 1987

5 Hale A., and Tijmstra, S., *European Management Education*, ILO, 1990

6 Connor H, Strebler M and Hirsh W., *You and Your Graduates – The First Few Years*, Institute of Manpower Studies, Report 191, 1990.

7 Cole, P and Hovall, M., *Take a New Career Path Ms Jones*, Personnel Management, May 1991

5. THE INDIVIDUAL – ASSESSMENT, COUNSELLING AND PLANNING

UNDERSTANDING POTENTIAL

We define potential as 'the ability to do a bigger or broader job at some time in the future', and this may be stated in terms of 'ultimate potential' – the biggest or broadest job we can foresee, or a level we foresee within a stated period of time.

We begin with three important principles:

1. Maximizing the potential of all individuals

This should be the objective of every organization. By potential in this sense we mean potential to contribute to the organization, and sometimes that conflicts between maximizing potential as a parent, in the community, or in some other way. Many a workaholic in his 40s, having given little time to the years of his family's childhood and discovering those years are suddenly gone, swears he would not let that happen a second time. The task of the organization, however, is to provide, as far as it is able, opportunities for personal growth within the context of work.

If we want career management for all the individuals it is clear immediately that we are not just talking about those with upwards potential. One of the myths that pervade some organizations is the idea that they cannot afford to have everyone with high potential in their company . . . 'there isn't enough space . . .' This leads them to recruit second best. It never works out that recruiting the best people leads to a surplus of people pushing for the top layers of the pyramid. The best endeavours in recruitment still lead to a distribution of levelling out. The problem most organizations have is the reverse – they cannot find enough people with upwards potential. We show in Chapter 6 how to calculate the ratio of people with 'upwards' to 'sideways' potential that should be present in a healthy organization.

So we are talking about maximizing the personal growth of those who have reached their level just as much as for those who have greater heights to reach. This is an excellent message to give to both our managers and employees – that you may have reached your optimal level of responsibility but this does not mean you are a second class citizen in whom we no longer have any interest. It also puts a strong responsibility on the manager as the one primarily responsible for the employee's growth.

2. Performance does not equal potential

Many mistakes have been made believing that it is the good performer who should be promoted. From our earlier analyses of the need to match people to the characteristics of each job, it is clear that the requirements of a bigger and broader job are going to be different. This is particularly true about the first step to management, and the step to managing managers is also frequently badly underestimated in the new demands in places on people.

Whereas it is normal for people with upwards potential to be good performers in their current job, the reverse is by no means necessarily true. Potential is about the ability to do a different job with different requirements at some time in the future. It is nothing to do with being the most outstanding performer in the current job. How many organizations have lost their best salesperson/engineer and gained a frustrated, incompetent manager!

3. Potential is a perception at a point in time

It is something that is changing and dynamic. The person we see today as a future leader sometimes does not fulfil expectations as he or she moves upwards. The person for whom one manager sees no further development may blossom under another. (Hence the need for a consensus of views on the perception of potential.) But it is dangerous to label people as having a certain type of potential, and it is also unwise not to review regularly the assessment or perception that is made. Making regular assessments is important not only for channelling development actions but for checking the 'succession health' of the organization – as described in Chapter 6.

The day comes when we all run out of upwards potential. As people develop and grow and change, their potential changes too – and particularly as they move into a new position. This is why a manager should never write off a person's aspirations. He or she can be consistently honest in saying: 'As we/I see it at present, we/I don't think you have the capability to do such and such a job. It requires skills, knowledge and experience that you lack and that we/I believe would be difficult for you to acquire. However, people change and develop, and it could be seen differently in a couple of years' time.' (Career counselling is discussed later in this chapter.) For the same reason, it seems to me to be foolish to label people clearly and publicly as high flyers. Everyone has a different development plan and some include more rapid movement upwards, but the development plan of each needs annual review.

CLASSIFYING POTENTIAL

It is important to have a method of classifying the potential of people, not to label them, but to be able to understand the strength of succession in the organization. A performance rating is totally inappropriate to use for this purpose, as we have explained above.

Many appraisal forms finish with a section on career development and ask questions such as 'when would he/she be ready for the next move up?' and give a choice of three or four timescales. This approach is restrictive. The only classification that makes sense is a combination of direction and speed. Shell refers to a classification of 'current estimate of potential' which shows that it is current and changeable with time. Organizations use various shorthands, for instance:

(a) ability to rise at least two further levels, with relatively fast progression. This falls down at the top and bottom of the organization – senior management may not realistically have two levels

available and at the bottom surely nearly everybody is going to rise two levels. The designation is more one to use for the person expected to progress fast through the levels.

(b) ability to rise at least one further level, and slower than (a). This is saying we can see at least one further level of responsibility that can be achieved – or if it concerns a person lower down the organization we are talking perhaps about slower progress than in (a).

(c) reached the right level – ability to develop and broaden laterally. The system has two classifications for people who are at their right level. This category is where the greatest number of people probably lie – having reached their maximum level of responsibility, but with scope for lateral growth such as a change of function or job broadening.

(d) right level, right job. The round peg in the round hole. Typical of real specialists (for example tax consultant) and sometimes of managers who, for reasons of location and/or expertise, wish to stay in the same job. The decision to place someone in this category should be thought about carefully – it places limits on further personal growth.

(e) is at a level above his/her ability. Yes, we all have such people, who conform to the Peter Principle, ie have over-reached their maximum level of competence. As we become more professional at career management, such situations can be reduced. They are invariably the fault of a wrong management decision – promoting a person who would never gain the required competences for the job. Action should be taken, but some recognition of the contribution that the organization has made to the situation is required.

Some other methods of description of potential are:

- Variations of the above – for example Dupont Nemours, the large industrial multinational, uses High for plus three levels; Medium for plus two levels and Low for plus one level.
- The grade or responsibility level that is seen to be the

maximum achievable in the future. A problem with this is that it is always difficult for a manager to accept that a junior subordinate might reach a level higher than his or her own. So artificial ceilings may be placed on people, especially in smaller parts of the organization. The method gives no indicator of speed, and although it has the merit of simplicity it can lack sufficient distinction.

- A focus on target jobs or levels and appropriate timescales eg:- 'ready for promotion – now; 0–2 years; 2–5 years', or, better: 'ready for promotion to branch manager' – etc.

This approach is limited to one step and does not provide a particularly useful classification of a population for analytical purposes. It also encourages an insular and parochial approach to career management.

Probably the best combination is an A-E type classification. It is helpful to put it in the context of the career direction of a currently perceived aiming point and timescale, eg 'A – marketing director-plus five years'. However, this depends on the data system that is chosen – see Chapter 6.

Should someone be told the organization's view of their potential? This does depend on the openness and trust dimension of the organizational culture, but there is every reason to discuss it openly if we are concerned about planned and agreed development. (Nevertheless studies have shown that while organizations today normally conduct open appraisals, a majority are secretive about their view on potential.) We cannot have aiming points and development plans without mutual discussion. Many managers are extremely nervous about openness in this area – due perhaps to some uncertainty about the validity and reliability of their perception, but more often due to a feeling that they risk demotivation of the individual. They fear a dissonance of expectations: that to tell people they have reached their optimum level in the organization will have a devastating effect.

There is no need to fear such discussions but it is wise to assist managers with advice or training in skills in potential assessment as well as career counselling. There are two key elements to such discussions – firstly, placing in context the idea of 'current perception': that this is not something that is fixed for ever and that the door for development is continually open. Secondly we should employ the logic of 'gap analysis' ie where the person is today in his or her personal growth; the requirements of different or higher jobs and the capability of the person to close the gap. So for the financial analyst, for example, who aspires to be a country manager, we can go through the logical steps of how we might achieve the necessary characteristics of the target job, and whether it is realistic to do so. If not, we will explore more appropriate career plans.

CHOICE OF CAREER DIRECTION AND ASSESSMENT OF POTENTIAL

What we want to see for each individual in the organization is:

- A chosen career direction,
- A current perception of potential,
- A career plan, complete with aiming point,
- A development action plan for the immediate future.

It is not the easiest of tasks to ask managers to make judgements about a subordinate's performance in the current job, and to articulate it constructively. Some managers – even very senior ones – never learn to do it well. However, it is infinitely more difficult to make judgements about how a person will perform in a completely different job. Perhaps matching the individual with the boss's job can be done, where both components are reasonably well known, but beyond that. . . . And yet we routinely ask managers in doing appraisals to make such judgements and recommendations.

The problem is that we are asking whether a person has the capability to do a job in the future with a quite different set of requirements than we are able to observe today. Most managers have a limited view of the requirements of other jobs. Certainly it is almost impossible for a manager to assess capability for jobs much bigger than his or her own. So most managers' assessments are confined to the next step, or the ability 'to take my job'.

Many studies have been done on the assessment of potential and validating predictions. Most show disappointing correlations – especially on the picking out of high flyers at graduate recruitment stage. The more established and mature a person is in a career stream, the more accurate are likely to be predictions of future heights that may be attainable. Nevertheless, we want to invest in the broadening of younger people although we may not yet be sure of their real potential.

Figure 4.3 showed diagrammatically when one might make formal assessments of career direction.

Types of choice and assessment

We can identify three groups of situation which require some form of assessment and evaluation:

- Change of career stream,
- Promotion to a higher level in a career stream,
- Assessment of long term potential.

The various options are shown in Table 5.1

The forms of assessment may be classified under two headings – that which is done on a regular basis and for all employees, and that which is done at specific times and for specific groups.

Regular assessments

The appraisal discussion – or the subset of it concerned with development which may have a separate form – is the foundation of dialogue between the individual and the organization. It is normally done once a year and most appraisal forms include something to do with future development. The manager's judgement of the person's capability is an essential input because of his or her day-to-day observation of behaviour and performance. To gain the necessary ability to make those judgements the manager needs training in conducting the face-to-face dialogue of appraisal, in observing and analyzing behaviour, in understanding people growth and in the career management processes of the organization. Quite a tall order, and yet organizations permit managers to do complex and demanding appraisals with minimal or even no training. A minimum of two, preferably three, days is needed for this foundational process, which provides such an important opportunity for input by an employee regarding his or her future.

Table 5.1 Types of career direction and potential assessment

From	*To*	**Methods available**
Manual/clerical administrative	Technical/ professional stream	Mutual decision to change; some formal assessment likely; plus retraining
Technical/ professional stream	Different technical/ professional stream	Mutual decision to change; no formal assessment; retraining as needed Career interest inventory or similar tests taken Assessment based on skill requirements of new stream
Promotion within a technical/professional stream		Recommedation against required criteria Vetting/approval panel
Long term potential within a technical/professional stream		Not normally formally assessed
Technical/ professional stream	Functional management or general management	Selection on ad hoc vacancy Assessment centre Psychological tests Informal recommendation
Promotion within functional management stream		As above but rigorous methods likely to be less common
Long term potential in functional or general management streams		'High potential' panels/committees Development centres

The good news is that it is much more common these days (in the UK and America at least) to have an appraisal system for all employees based on objectives set at the beginning of the year. Better still if the system requires periodic review during the year. This is not only important for the objective review of performance, but by focusing on specific action in the year provides an experience-based platform for strengths analysis and development planning.

As part of the appraisal we should expect:

- To understand the individual's aspirations,
- To discuss them, and set a career aiming point,
- To draft a career plan,
- To arrange for discussions to take place with others that would be helpful,
- To recommend for any career guidance events/assessments that may be suitable/available,
- To structure learning events that will 'grow' the individual.

The help of a professional human resources specialist in both the compiling of the plan and associated actions, and in the implementation of the action steps should be a service of real added value. But it can only be so if the specialist has a sound and mature understanding of the organization and its career processes and opportunities.

There are those who say a blank sheet of paper is all that is needed for this process. It is true no appraisal is the same or needs the same space in every box. However, most appraisers value guidance on what should be covered and a fairly directive format is recommended which leads the manager specifically through the right areas, and is backed up by suitable guidelines. Such guidelines may include:

- Reminder notes on face to face feedback,
- Causes and remedies of performance problems (for example),
- Definitions of commonly used skill categories,
- Choices of learning opportunities,
- How to counsel and plan in respect of careers.

Part of the documentation needs to be concerned with career planning information, and a format which is consistent with the approach in this book is shown in Table 5.2.

Different people have different needs – they are in different career phases; in different stages of certainty or uncertainty about their career development. The evidence is that managers find it hard to fulfil all the objectives outlined at the beginning of this section. I have studied several years of attitude surveys in my own organization and there is consistently a perception by people that career and development issues are not handled well enough. I would be surprised if this was untypical. The careers manager seeks, therefore, to establish other processes that build on the basic appraisal.

It is recommended that there are other regular processes or reviews which provide opportunity to assess potential such as:

Pooling of opinions This approach is to be recommended as an addition to the appraisal inputs. An organizational review at a level where several managers may know an individual can provide balance, assuming all are clear about the definition of potential and do not confuse it with their knowledge that the individual is working well at the current job.

A regular review of all individuals in a working group or department, one by one, by the managerial team is highly beneficial. If this takes place before appraisals the appraising manager is not relying on his or her own view solely when he or she conducts the discussion, but has some confidence in an organizational consensus.

Specialist review A similar name by name review may be conducted by the human resource specialist on a six monthly or yearly basis, ideally with each manager in turn, or with the local personnel manager (which is only useful if such a person knows all the staff in the area well). This is an opportunity to discuss and review the appraisal and career plan and to hear the things that could not be written down – I have found such discussions to be the most valuable source of update of data.

Special events

Individuals can participate – usually by invitation but in some organizations by request – in a specially constructed event that may be for assessment of promotion to management, for promotion to a particular post, or for assessing long term potential. They may be either general or specific – the former giving an overall view of potential, the latter against a specific target. We would favour the second, as jobs vary in the knowledge, skills, attitudes and experience required.

Table 5.2 Sample career development documentation (extract from appraisal)

***Section 4* CAREER DEVELOPMENT AND PERSONAL GROWTH**
4.1 What is the employee's preferred career direction?
4.2 Should the employee attend an assessment or development centre? Which and approximately when?
4.3 What is the employee's career aiming point over the next 5–7 years?
4.4 What gaps in knowledge, skills, attitudes and experience need to be filled to meet the aiming point?
4.5 What areas of knowledge, skills, attitudes or experience could be enhanced using the current job?
4.6 What is the employee doing or planning to do by way of self-development?
4.7 What is the earliest date to consider the next job move?
4.8 Are there any constraints on the employee's mobility?
Attach a learning plan (reference Figure 7.2) and a career plan (Figure 5.3)

Testing and assessment methods can be time consuming and expensive but also the most helpful and thorough. By 'testing' we are referring to psychological tests done with paper and pencil, and by 'assessment' some more complex combination of events that may in fact also include psychological tests. Because it is not feasible to put the whole of an organization through such procedures who should be selected for them and when?

These events are particularly worthwhile when the skills required of a target job are significantly different from those of the current position, to find out whether people have the potential to change career direction and move into, for instance, a managerial role. They would also be useful during phase one of people's careers, as they can determine their optimal career direction.

More and more organizations are testing for longer term potential – identifying the skills required in top jobs and assessing people who are five or more years away from that seniority. This type of event is frequently known as a 'development centre'; some call them 'career guidance centres'. Participants are tested against the requirements of a level of job which may be up to three steps higher than currently. Assessors should be higher than the job being assessed to set the standard of expected performance, and so are usually top executives. At the end of the event the assessors have a much better view of the career direction and realistic aiming point of the participant and can give career guidance with authority and a high degree of validity afterwards. A good practice is for the assessor who gives the feedback to act subsequently as mentor if the individual does not already have one. In so doing, assessors learn more about career guidance as they watch the progress of their protégés.

The names for the centres have a positive ring and do not imply any pass or fail but a beneficial outcome for all participants. Terms of this kind are recommended rather than the more blunt 'potential assessment', because they should not be seen as giving black and white results or labels as their outcome. It is, rather, systematic guidance on development directions to all participants in the same way. One person should not emerge with a label saying 'I have potential', and another with 'I do not have potential' – but each has an appropriate form of career guidance which is positive.

Organizations using this approach to longer term potential assessment include British Rail[1] and ICL[2].

Assessment centres The centres referred to above are forms of assessment centre. This term, imported from America, is now in common use in the UK and elsewhere. One of the pioneering organizations in its use was AT&T, which has operated an 'advanced management potential assessment program' for several years covering three and a half days of tests and simulations. The purpose is to analyse personal development. A second two-day event is entitled the 'high potential career development program'; this is more exploratory for the participants using various resources such as organization information and psychologists.[3]

An assessment centre works with a researched set of assessment criteria against which performance will be measured. These are normally behavioural skills (not knowledge which can be tested in other ways) – those skills that characterize the target job or level of the assessment centre, and can be observed through simulated events. 'Integrity' is a difficult one to test in this way; certain kinds of 'leadership' are, however, very observable. These are examined in Chapter 3 in the discussion on capabilities. There are professional organizations working in this area who have built up standard packages of criteria, exercises and evaluation sheets. Many are exceptionally well packaged and they can be tempting – one example is 'Symphony' marketed by Development Dimensions International (DDI) which has been a leading firm in this area for many years. But every organization is unique; its jobs and environment are special and if professional help is used it should be in custom-building a 'centre' suitable for its needs. We have recommended throughout the creation of a common language for human resource processes in general, and this should be used in defining assessment centre criteria. Assessors have difficulty in observing more than about 10 at a time, so priorities have to be established from the many wonderful characteristics that most jobs normally demand! The choice of the criteria may be researched internally using one of the methods described on pages 88–90.

These choices are the foundation of the centre and deserve some time and attention, although one can invest in too much detailed research. The extra margin of accuracy obtained after a certain point is very low – at the end it is still a case of integrating subjective judgements.

When the choice from a number of worthy criteria proves difficult, then we should concentrate on those that distinguish the target job from others, and particularly from those at the current level of participants. Thus, for a career assessment centre using general manager criteria, participants have normally already shown management skills. Therefore, testing elementary competences like 'choosing priorities' is unnecessary unless there is a higher level of that competency that can be distinctively defined.

If it is a promotion centre (ie the successful participant may move into the target job in the near future) we can take the skills required today; but if it is a longer term potential assessment event we need to think of the criteria needed for the job a few years ahead. The thought processes outlined in Chapter 1 should help us here.

A set of exercises are used which replicate the mix of the target job in terms of working alone, in groups or in one to one situations; they also measure each of the chosen criteria on at least two occasions during the centre. Such exercises may be group discussions, group tasks, presentations to an assessor or to others, analysis of a paper, fact finding, interviewing, etc. Exercises should be 'knowledge-independent' – ie performance in them is not dependent on any specific job or company knowledge.

Some exercises require so-called 'resource people' who act as interviewees, sources of data and so on. It is always tricky to get the same standard of resourcing from different players in this regard, especially if inexperienced. Exercises chosen should be suitable for observation – which may be by watching behaviour; by listening; or by reading an output. Recording exercises has many benefits in terms of subsequent careful observation and evaluation, but it is usually impossible to take the time needed for this in a multi-exercise event.

Assessors are trained to observe, record, classify and evaluate the behaviours in the exercises. It is usual to have one assessor to every two participants, at a level in the organization at least one above the target job.The centre is organized so that every assessor observes every participant. To train assessors requires an absolute minimum of half a day and preferably two days; using a pool of experienced assessors on a continuing basis who share common standards is highly recommended.

The centre needs a systematic way of recording and rating behaviour against the criteria; summarizing in open discussion between the assessors all their observations and concluding a summary of the observed strengths and weaknesses. A professional facilitator needs to lead the discussion – and be acutely aware of the strength of the data that has led to an assessment, avoiding the mechanical averaging of marks and seeking an integrated assessment which balances the observations and looks for a common standard.

Finally, there should be a detailed write up of the conclusions and thorough feedback to the participant, which should be in a meeting with the participant's current manager and – in most organizations – personnel manager or careers manager present. Development actions should be derived, and if these affect careers, a career plan created or modified as a result.

The advantages of the assessment centre approach have been well documented and the resource and systematic thoroughness that goes into a well designed one has been shown to have the best accuracy of prediction of all available methods. It is still far from 100% reliable though, and one has observed facilitators of centres striving for a mathematical accuracy of assessment that is quite inappropriate. But the face validity with assessors as decision makers and with participants is high – everyone feels that the effort made on both sides is justified, and I have always found a readiness in participants to accept the outcome.

We look at feedback and after-care in the section below on career counselling.

Difficulties with the assessment centre approach

Only in the late 1980s have assessment centres in the UK really taken off, despite the definitive book by the Stewarts being published in 1976[4]. Some companies have been dedicated to them for many years, however, such as Mars and ICL, and experience provides caution among the enthusiasm. Here follow some cautionary notes:

- The observation and classification of behavioural data is difficult; assessors are often inexperienced and can allow their intuition to rule their objectivity; one must not be deluded by the appearance of systematic accuracy. This is particularly true where an exercise gives little data on a criterion, but it is 'scored' nevertheless *pari passu* with each other combination of exercise/criterion. The intimate knowledge of the facilitator of the exercises and their particular application is, therefore, crucial.

  Assessors who are not prepared to give up the time to be properly trained should not be allowed to participate – untrained assessors are a menace to the whole process!
- Associated with this is the difficulty of deciding what is a standard of satisfactory performance. Good assessment centre design includes writing down the expectations of good performance in each criterion at the 'satisfactory' and 'excellent' level for each exercise as an aid to assessors. This is most important for exercises like an in-tray (which should be assessed by two assessors independently) but is of value generally unless the assessor group is extremely experienced. As managerial performance is based on an inter-related group of skills being exercised, often simultaneously, the overall performance in an exercise is worth assessing just as much as the breakdown into individual criteria.
- There is also an assumption that the right things are being measured. Centres whose target job is clearly understood – like, for instance, a sales management assessment for salespersons – are the easier ones. However, those that seek to assess potential two or three career steps ahead may need regular revalidation of the base criteria.
- Exercises become known in the organization through overuse and, although for some of them prior knowledge does not influence performance, this is not always the case. I have seen a period in one organization where the enthusiasm for the centres led to what appeared to be more people taking part on a given day in assessments as facilitators, assessors,

resource people or participants than appeared to be actually working!

- Care must be exercised in what happens to the data. It is good to have a rule (and this should also apply to psychological test results) that the raw data is not made available to non-accreditated assessment centre designers/facilitators. This means that a professionally constructed assessment report for general reading is essential.

  A centre is normally targeted against a specific job or group of jobs and the results cannot be used in consideration of something different.

  It is not recommended that assessment data be held on a computer – the process of coding compounds existing inaccuracies and leads to false assumptions by the uninitiated.
- There is a great danger that the centre is seen as a decision maker in its own right. It is only an input, albeit a powerful one, and if it conflicts with other data then it must be put in context. After all, the most powerful means of assessment is being observed doing the job itself – so a good appraisal should be an equally important input. Assessment centres designed for a pass/fail decision need a facilitator who can input the other data available.
- There are potential difficulties with the assessment of women and ethnic minority participants. Assessors look for behaviour that fits their experience of successful performance and attributes. The evidence is that many women succeed in achieving results using different skill sets from men. One solution is to use senior women and people from ethnic minorities as assessors whenever possible; another is to provide awareness training to help white, male assessors overcome prejudices.

Participant selection

When it is generally known in the organization that a series of assessment events are available, it is natural for managers to recommend in appraisals that the appraisee should be put forward for a certain event. This builds up pressures if the number of events is limited. It is recommended that some clear criteria of selection are laid down as guidance for managers.

This is particularly true of the long term potential assessment events which are only for those who are perceived as having such potential, and this is likely to be quite a small number. Such events need to be restricted in number if senior managers or directors are going to be used as assessors.

A perverse aspect of nomination to corporate high flyer events may be failing to nominate a good candidate because the department concerned wants to keep that person. The solution for this lies only in all parts of the organization feeling there is a balanced give and take of good people across the divisions and departments.

Other methods of potential assessment

In Chapter 7 we discuss ways of learning through experience, and one of the most potent ways of assessing potential is to **observe live experience** in the context of a bigger job. Thus the acting role; the stand-in period for the boss while he or she is away on a project or long course; the special assignment – these are all excellent ways of observing the capability of a person in a wider, deeper context. This is providing that the objective of using the opportunity for assessment is clearly understood and the person is really stretched in a controlled way, with relevant skill criteria documented beforehand. Some macho managers despise the acting role as an inability to make a decision about an appointment. They are not usually the managers who are the best developers of people. (In some continental countries a three or six month trial period is absolutely normal, particularly with external appointees.) Managed well, this approach should be better than an assessment centre.

Psychological testing is a more traditional way of assessment in the UK; but is having legislative difficulties in the US in the area of fairness in discrimination. In a survey by Savile and Holdsworth, leading consultants in this area, in 1989 of 300 firms in the UK 47% were found to be using personality questionnaires and 37% assessment centres – the latter having mushroomed through the 1980s. A survey of management assessment methods by Shackleton and Newell in 1991[5] found that, whereas personality questionnaires were used by about 60% of firms in France and UK equally, only 19% used assessment centres in France compared to 60% in UK. However, 80% of

French firms use graphology. Research is taking place on the internationalization of test uses, and the cultural dimensions that influence the norms.[6] In Switzerland and Germany the use of external psychologists to select and identify potential is quite commonplace.

Detractors of personality testing, as opposed to occupational testing, would say they measure what a person is, rather than what a person can do. However, combined with a professional criteria-based interview probing into past experience, many would see it as a valid alternative approach. They can also be made part of an assessment centre.

Those who specialize in this area believe they can make predictions of job matching and assess potential. A typical battery of tests, such as ITT has used for many years with approved assessors across the world, might include verbal and numerical reasoning tests, logic and critical reasoning (the ubiquitous Watson-Glaser test lives on), productive thinking and a personality test such as Cattell's 16PF or the Savile and Holdsworth's Occupational Personality Questionnaire

A popular test in occupational choice is the Myers Briggs Type Indicator. It assesses thinking and decision making style in terms of four pairs of contrasting mental processes – judging, perception, introversion and extraversion. Various combinations have been linked with a large number of occupations.

Several tests exist to help people match their interests against various career options, known as 'interest inventories'. Many have been developed in America and the cultural aspect may not fit comfortably if used in another country. Two such are the Self-Directed Search, which is constructed so that the individual can score him or herself and use self-help materials to interpret the results; and the Strong Interest Inventory which is reckoned to be the world's most researched psychological test – it has to be scored by computer, and relates to over 100 occupational options. Several have been developed for UK use also.

Ed Schein followed up his work on career anchors with the design of a questionnaire entitled Career Orientations Inventory[7] which is quick and easy to use and gives an order of preference for his six main anchors; this can be combined with his Career Anchor Interview Guide which explores events, and the reasons and feelings concerning them, in the person's life. This is a helpful well-researched means of testing and/or confirming career direction.

A useful list of assessment instruments (available in the USA) is given at the end of the book by Leibowitz, Farren and Kaye on *Designing Career Development Systems*[8].

CAREER COUNSELLING

Many organizations would say that they promote a culture of self-help, and the prevalent philosophy in career development today is the same. That is the employer provides opportunities and information, but it is up to the individual to make his or her contacts, choose what they want to do and go for promotions and new jobs as they arise. There is nothing wrong with this, but to leave it at that is an abdication of responsibility on behalf of the organization for developing its most precious resource. The smart organization has a mutual involvement in creating and implementing career plans for individuals and, therefore, must be involved in career counselling.

Who might be involved in career counselling?

It could be any or several of the following:

- A person's manager,
- A human resources specialist,
- The person responsible for feedback from an assessment event,
- A mentor,
- An external consultant.

People naturally turn first to their manager in most organizations as being the representative of the organization in their eyes. 'What is the company's view of me and what should I do next?' they ask. There is a strange personalization of the organization in this question. If we were managing careers using all the processes described in this book, then there would be a shared view of the potential and development of an individual – but the manager will always play a pivotal role as an interface, as a developer and as a recommender of action. Not all managers are good at this; most have a limited view of organizational opportunities – therefore the supplementary help of a human resources specialist should be value-added. Many managers fall into the trap of providing unreal expectations to an individual, either through lack of careful analysis about the real options for the person, or through taking an easy way out rather than being honest. Honesty is not to be feared if the background value is that everybody has potential to be developed, but in different ways.

The person who is doing the counselling or helping to create the career plan does need to be familiar with the options for careers in the organization and the overall framework. There is always a problem in ensuring that all managers have the same information available, apart from the interpretation they may give from their individual experience and bias. The careers resource pack (or similar) would consist of:

- Policy statements
- Career structures
- Bridging maps
- Development positions
- Assessment and guidance events or facilities
- Essential capabilities and experience required of generic job types

Every special event should have some form of feedback to the participants. Their nature depends on the purpose of the centre, but should include, preferably in a written open report, a summary of the performance against each criterion assessed and suggestions for development. Both these require considerable professional skill to do well; development suggestions should be worked out with the person's manager, taking account of the learning style of the individual and the part the manager might play in structuring learning events. Thus feedback should be through a meeting with the manager, the participant, ideally one of the assessors and any mentor the individual has or is to have. The same applies for any external assessment made.

Steps in organizational career counselling

Counselling in its fullest sense requires considerable skill but every manager responsible for the development of people can help people go through some systematic thinking. When we discuss the career plan of a person what then are the steps we should go through?

A series of five questions are recommended.

Question one: What is the career direction that is right for this individual?

In Chapter 4 we discussed the mainstream directions in organizations: specialist/technical; functional management and general management. The start point is where the individual begins in the organization and receives most of his or her training. If a change is desired, then the person should be helped to clarify his or her interests, what he likes doing, what she is good at; and then match these against the key requirements of the stream they prefer. There are more formal ways of helping in this choice, as mentioned below.

The choice for a management career should be confirmed or otherwise by a formal assessment as discussed above. Sometimes the career counsellor needs to advise that a career in management is not the right path – this can be done objectively by comparing the typical managerial job skill requirements with the person's individual profile. A good question to ask is 'What difference do you see in the requirements of the (target) job and the strengths and weaknesses you have today? Is that a gap that can realistically be closed?'

Question two: What aiming point should we set realistically and within what timescale?

This is both important and difficult: important because without it we can only plan in a vague way; difficult because people and their managers really find it hard to think five to seven years ahead. In a specialist/technical career it is less critical because there is a natural evolution in increased knowledge, skills and experience. But for managers needing a broader experience it is a different matter. One helpful way is to consider the various end-point options after two further career moves. Here the person's degree of upwards potential has to be considered – for those in career phase one this is probably still upwards; for those in phase two it may not be and for those in phase three it is unlikely. The aiming point may be expressed in terms of depth and breadth of a particular area of responsibility if it is not to a higher level.

For people in phase three a complete career change may be attractive. Thus a senior manager who has no further aspirations in the managerial hierarchy may be happy to take some special responsibility, make some special study, or act as an internal consultant in a quite different area from his or her mainstream career.

Question three: What gap exists between the person's set of knowledge, skills, attitudes and experience today and those required of the aiming point?

The counsellor needs some knowledge of the profile of the aiming point to answer this, and that knowledge may need to be obtained specifically. On the other hand, a person experienced in the organization may have sufficient personal knowledge for the purpose of the exercise. Typically the counsellor might discuss three or four items under each element of the profile. Too many becomes impossible to handle sensibly, so the perfect answer should be sacrificed in favour of practicality.

Question four: What building blocks of experience should we look for to progress forward from where we are and get us to the aiming point, and what career bridges should we use?

In Table 4.10 we listed some types of added value experience for different positions. A table of this kind should be at the counsellor's disposal, as should a table of 'development positions' (see Table 4.7).

There may be more than one route to the aiming point. But the focus of a building block is not on a particular position in the organization but on a particular type of desired experience. Once this is specified we can look at the bridges that are available.

Question five: If the plan does not work out, what is our fallback career direction, against which we can ask a similar set of questions?

This a question for those seeking to change their direction.

Despite all our assessments a person may not succeed in a new direction – for example, the functional manager taking on a general management position – so we need to be clear what the fallback would be. It would normally be the one job in which most of the career has been established and where the employee's credibility/capability is not in question.

Other forms of career guidance

These can be grouped into three general areas:[8]

- Group activities,
- Support orientated activities – one individual assists another,
- Self-directed activities.

Career workshops have their origins in special needs, such as the need to use outplacement for a large number of people or to help specific groups like women employees. They are a form of 'group counselling' and are widely available in the United States. They are participative, small group, facilitated events typically lasting two to four days. A workshop helps individuals to take stock of themselves – to review their personal growth profile or similar, to assess their total life balance, explore options for future development and develop a personal action plan. Group discussion aids this process. Videos which explain the basic framework of careers may be used.

Courses in career planning are rare in Europe but are offered sometimes in the United States – externally, by colleges and sometimes by companies. Any course outside the organization is going to have limited value to employees, and these are, therefore, more suited to people between jobs. A course run before starting a career would seem to have limited value also, as a person has no organizational reference points and has not explored his or her personal career anchor. Internally, if other processes are working well, a special course in career planning should not be necessary.

Self-help workbooks are plentiful, as are books to help the individual make choices and plan for him or herself. One best seller (across the Atlantic) is the *Career Planning Workbook* by Dr

Barbara Moses of Toronto, Canada. John Burgoyne and Calvin Germain[9] described a workbook they developed for Esso Chemicals consisting of an 11 step process:

- Your skills and your job,
- Your life and your work,
- The world in which you live and work,
- Exploring career options,
- What you can learn that will help you in the future,
- How do you solve problems?
- What should you be planning to learn?
- How do you learn best?
- How do you keep up to date?
- Opportunities and resources for learning,
- Planning your self-development.

It is suggested that people work through this guide every five years or so.

Career resource centres are also rare in Europe. One of the leaders of the few firms of consultants specializing in career management is the Lifeskills Management Group and it offers a complete career materials library plus a counselling service. The idea is to have a central advisory point where one keeps relevant literature about the organization and careers in it – career structures, career paths, maybe even audio-visual materials. The idea supports the self-help movement, but it seems relatively unhelpful to loose employees on a mass of information without guidance. Careers are not something that can be carefully planned by an individual and carried out alone in glorious isolation. Literature should be available, but used – like training films in a training course – intelligently in a wider context.

Career advice by computer The concept here is that of an interactive program which helps the user explore interests and values, and offers suggestions for particular occupations. Again relatively unknown in Europe they are more suited to those with an open field of options – college and school leavers. My son completed a questionnaire at school which was computer analysed, and he received a report which concluded the following occupations would be worth considering:

General manager	Company secretary
Insurance broker	Hospital administrator
Underwriter	Advertising
Export executive	Economist

I think a pin would have produced a similar result!

However, such systems will become increasingly sophisticated. One available in the UK is called *Career Builder 2* and has been developed by Lifeskills Associates. This is more sophisticated than just offering possible occupations (although it scores against over 900 job possibilities) and helps the person set life goals using a workbook and several modules. The idea is that it is a 'working' program, not a once off experiment.

Leibowitz, Farren and Kaye[8] describe several models in use in the US in their book on *Designing Career Development Systems*, and a comprehensive description of the career planning and information system used by IBM's National Service Division in the US is given by Douglas T Hall and associates[10]. Entitled *Employee Development Planning System (EDPS)* it has five sections:

- Orientation and planning readiness assessment (understanding the system),
- Employee self-assessment (interest and ability profile),
- System job search (matching with generic job types),
- Employee analyses jobs of interest (reacting to job characteristics with likes and dislikes),
- Summarizing personal development needs (determining the gaps between jobs of interest and current personal capability).

An evaluation of the use of this system by both employees and managers showed it to be of great support in the career planning process. Such systems depend for success, however, on the maintenance of accurate and up to date job information, on the way the employee interest inventory is prepared, and on the positioning of such an aid in the overall framework.

Systems of this kind could be useful in organizations, and

Lifeskills offer to customize the product. It requires the coding of a lot of subjective and turbulent data in addition to the obvious career structures, job profile data, etc. Once again, it should only be a supplement to the human interface that should be present in career discussions and planning.

Mentoring is becoming more and more popular in the UK, having reached the status almost of a norm in US organizations. A survey in 1990 by the Industrial Society of 145 firms found 44% were using mentoring in some way (many only for new graduates). The term is usually used to indicate an 'uncle or aunt' figure in the organization who takes a special interest in the welfare and development of a person. The implication is that it is not the person's boss and is someone older and more experienced. In most organizations it occurs informally – often a person looks to a previous boss as an adviser. In France mentoring may be connected with Grandes Ecoles alumni networks and a mentor may be outside the person's organization; this is common also for MBA graduates from certain schools.

Formal mentoring is normally confined to particular subsets of the organization. The most common is to have a system of mentoring for new graduates. This is of great value in the early years when job changes are frequent. Those on a high flyer programme may be given them too; or those who have been through a senior development centre. (Here it is a plus to have one of the assessors as mentor.) Not everybody needs one and it is impractical to provide one for all.

Not every senior person makes a good mentor. The work requires genuine care for the development of younger people, plus spending time and thought on the task. They should be people who are familiar with the organization, its history, its politics and culture, and how things really happen. The relationship must be one of trust and confidentiality on both sides. One or two American books have explored every kind of relationship variation, trying to see, for example, whether mentor-protégé relationships of the opposite sex are more or less effective than same sex links. Like many things that are assiduously researched in the social arena, ordinary common sense can give an excellent guide in these matters!

Mentoring is recommended for certain groups. No bureaucracy is needed: the career manager needs just to make some matching, choosing those who will be mentors carefully, provide some guidance as to how to manage the relationship, and let it run for as long as it proves to be helpful. A relationship that has worked well in the past, albeit informally, should not be sacrificed in favour of a new one that 'fits the system' – we want ones that work well more than anything else.

Outplacement counselling There comes a time for some when the organization cannot develop a person's career any further. Genuine redundancy may apply, but equally frequent is the case of the individual and the organization drifting apart and becoming alienated through issues of attitudes or outdated skills. One of the least happy situations is when a person has been promoted beyond his or her capability, and becomes unwanted, because of inability to cope with the bigger job. Arguably, good career management should minimize such problems but no organization can be perfect all the time.

The characteristic of a responsible employer is to recognize the inevitability of these situations arising in a turbulent and fast changing world, and to have a policy to meet them. Short term pressures for quarterly profits sometimes lead to precipitous layoffs, but we do need to replace those who, for whatever reason, are only capable of providing 70% of the job's requirements with those capable of 110%. It is hard when those seventy percenters are also loyal and hard-working. Such recognition might lead the organization to have a 'positive external redeployment policy'. Such a policy might have the following features:

- Career counselling is not confined to internal options only and, where we genuinely believe the person's career is going to be limited **because** he or she is not going to fit well in the future or persists in unrealistic expectations, then encouragement to think about external options should be given.
- More general counselling is provided in dealing with psychological, family and financial issues.
- Job search assistance – use of organizational infrastructure.
- Making available contacts, directories and various information sources.

- Training in self-presentation and interviewing.
- Some funding assistance may be given – this may be in the form of retraining for a new chosen career; paying for external career guidance or outplacement services.

Some organizations (IBM, Rank Xerox are examples) have created schemes which encourage older staff to become consultants and which cushion them for a period of time. IBM, for example, in its search for creative ways to reduce its staff numbers without actually firing them devised in 1990 an organization called Skillbase in which it retains a 40% interest. Older employees may opt for early retirement or for joining this new venture, and they receive a guaranteed level of work as well as the opportunity to work as a consultant for other organizations.

There are many excellent well established firms offering outplacement help. They provide counselling services and resources to help the individual in the establishment of their own personal growth profiles (in effect), in self-help training, in personal presentation and interviewing and in job search methods. They provide resource centres, and workshops in a variety of related topics. Fees vary but are typically in the UK 15% of salary for an individual service. Several books are available also; one practical one is that by Charles Dudeney.[11]

Managing external redeployment effectively should lead to less spent on 'rationalization' – if the organization is funding a transfer period from one job to another this can offset the normal severance payment. Such a process should be an essential part of the career management portfolio.

Demotion Taking a step down in the organization may need to be faced in some cases, particularly those in phase three of their career. Feldman[12] quotes the Co-op Denmark as having a deliberate policy to demote at certain ages to make way for younger people, but this is unusual. It may be necessary to downgrade salary and status, but there should always be positive ways to use experience or provide new ways. Feldman recommends the advantages of managing such situations so that the individual is placed in a new area with new colleagues, and to freeze conditions and remuneration rather than reduce them.

CAREER PLANNING

A documented mutually agreed career plan should be the output from a counselling meeting. The format should be more than a few lines in a box on the appraisal form.

We cannot be specific about times and jobs. But we can be clear about building blocks, which provide the advances in knowledge, skills, attitudes and experience that are needed to get to the aiming point, and by specifying and agreeing them we have a chance of taking considered decisions about career moves and not jumping opportunistically. It may be helpful for a manager to have something like a career resource pack (referred to above under the heading of Counselling) as an aid, particularly if the individual's career needs broadening.

A preliminary to writing the career plan is to have an up-to-date statement of the various components of the person's personal growth profile. We can then use the format shown in Table 5.3. This is based on the five questions referred to above in systematic career counselling. The example has been completed for a person who has eight years experience, mostly in product development and more recently in the product specification area which is more closely linked to marketing. Having been through a career guidance assessment centre event, the conclusions would be documented as shown. If more than one aiming point is an acceptable possibility, then the lower part of the form might be written in two or three different ways, representing alternative career paths.

The career plan is a working document that should be updated certainly at each appraisal time, and after each career move. Like every plan it is a statement of intent, a form of agreement made between the individual and the organization. It should provide some continuity when managers change. The careers manager will want to have copies of those within his or her populations of interest.

Considerations in career planning for women

As we have observed, in male dominated organizations, considering the requirements for personal and career growth of women needs deliberate thought, so that it forms part of the overall framework. For women who do not have a family, the question is one of culture, stereotyping and subliminal discrimination. These may be real enough, but they will not be solved by the career management framework itself. We need to watch that the essential requirements for jobs are not discriminatory; also the selection processes. But it is for women who need a break that we have to plan differently. It is a sad thing that so many senior professional and managerial women do not have the balance of a work and family life that their male counterparts enjoy. But we cannot escape from the fact that children demand care and time from at least one of the partners in a marriage.

We observed earlier that it is in the interest of the organization not to lose good, well trained employees. So effort is required to find and manage creative solutions to this problem. I suggest that the long term thinking implied by the recommended processes in this book helps career planning for women as it focusses on a period five to seven years ahead. But if we also say that experience is key to development, then it is inevitable that it is going to take longer for a woman taking a break to arrive at a certain point in the hierarchy. It is fine and creditable for personal study to be undertaken during this time, but no manager is going to give it the credit that live experience brings.

Below are some of the options for organizations in this area:

- Some may have operations that lend themselves to having a department of home workers. Some information technology companies have established units, enabling continuing technical work and development from home terminals, and employees are treated for all other purposes like their office based colleagues. The opportunities for this approach will undoubtedly increase in the 1990s.
- The career break – a time of being at home, but more or less guaranteed a return to work within a two or three year period (at most five years). It is important to retain links (a mentor helps here), keep the person in touch with change and progress at the organization (and, if appropriate, her speciality) and invite her to organizational functions or seminars etc.
- Part time working – teachers have always found it relatively easy to continue their careers due to having (approximately)

Table 5.3 Building a career plan

NAME: John Smith **CURRENT JOB:** Marketing liaison manager, Development Division

AGE: 30 **GRADE:** 11

CAREER DIRECTION: Functional management in marketing

FALLBACK DIRECTION: Functional management in product development

AIMING POINT: Senior position (two levels higher than now) in industry marketing in European Sales Division, or responsible for worldwide marketing of a family of products. Three moves from now, approximately 6–7 years, age 37.

CAREER DEVELOPMENT NEEDS TO ACHIEVE AIMING POINT:

Knowledge/skills/attitudes	**Experience**
– Fluency in another language	– Working close to customers
– Understanding of customer priorities/problems	– Management of managers
– Direct negotiating	– Working in or closely with other countries
– Managing trade-offs	– Commercial collaborations
– Market segmentation	– Marketing promotions

RELEVANT EXPERIENCE FROM WHICH TO BUILD BRIDGES: Project management of development teams; expert knowledge of office automation and database management; studying German;

CAREER PLAN

Dates	**Job type**	**Knowledge, skills, values gained**	**Experience gained**
(+1 year)	Dealers liaison manager, Germany	Negotiating / language fluency Understanding customer priority	Working with customers / in another country Commercial collaboration
(+3 yrs)	Marketing manager, N Europe	Market segmentation Managing trade-offs	Management of managers Marketing promotions
(+6 yrs)	Industry marketing manager (Europe HQ)		

the same hours at school as their children. The possibilities for part time working – while incompatible with the heavy demands placed on high flyers and many others in organizations today – are open to many creative solutions.

- Job sharing – associated with the above is the possibility for one job to be shared between two people. This has some difficulties in the boundaries of personal accountability, but gives the possibility of continuing experiential learning and, in some cases, overcomes the barriers to promotion.
- Financial help – incentives to reduce maternity leave, pay for crèches and child minding and so on. In the UK organizations are reluctant to commit themselves to these costs, which may be a sad reflection on the value placed on their female talent.
- Training and self-development – women can be helped financially and with materials or equipment to continue personal learning and growth from a homebase. A person who understands and cares about learning back in the organization can make this a more useful experience by combining their studies with some work related project work.
- Workplace nurseries – these are not often found in the UK due to the costs to the employer of setting them up, staffing them and maintaining them. A report in 1985[13] stated there were only 80 workplace nurseries in Britain, mostly associated with factories or local government. Much publicity was given to ambitious schemes set up by the major banks, but development has been cautious. Care for the under fives is much more extensive in most continental countries. In 1989 a new magazine appeared in UK entitled *Company Creche,* asserting that 'workplace nurseries and childcare will become one of the most important employee benefits of the 1990s.'

European countries are very different in their approaches. The most advanced are in Sweden and Finland where dual careers are the norm and we may learn a lot from studying their approaches to this issue.

Women who take longer breaks may be faced with finding a new organization or even starting a new career. As the shortage of skilled people begins to bite in the 1990s it will be less difficult for women to re-enter new careers and be fully retrained. An excellent guide to this is Margaret Korving's book *Making a*

Comeback[14]. But from the organization's point of view we want to keep the talent of our female employees with us. So in career planning we can look carefully at the knowledge, skills, attitudes and experience growth that is needed for development and be creative in building the plan.

SUMMARY

The importance of distinguishing potential from performance has been more clearly recognized in recent years, but an organization needs to recognize in all its systems that **everyone** has potential to grow. The available potential in organizations is usually grossly underused. It should be assessed regularly, and at certain times in a person's career development in a formal special way.

Alan Mumford[15] points out the unreliability of many potential assessments and the degree of changeability in perceptions with time and with the values of those making the perceptions. Today's star may be out of favour tomorrow. Thus it is unwise to label employees too specifically, although we should be totally open in discussing career planning.

Each individual should have a career direction, an aiming point within that direction, and a career plan put together to enable the achievement of that aiming point. A person's manager plays a key role in representing the organization through appraisal and career counselling. Aided by others such as HR specialists and mentors, managers help employees put together career plans using some systematic steps in counselling. Other forms of career guidance may be made available but the mutual planning exercise should be the centrepoint.

Outplacement elsewhere may be the best solution for some and this should be approached caringly and positively with employees who have served many years. Likewise the continuing of the personal growth of women away from the organization is important and merits creative solutions.

ACTION PLANNING

Problems of reality

1. The textbook ideas of career plans and succession plans are based on a theory of how formal systems should operate. In reality appointments are made on the basis of whether people are known by the recruiter or recommended. Cultivating relationships is, therefore, the key to success.

This may be the reality as you see it in your organization. Undoubtedly it will be true in some national cultures where systematization is much less prevalent than the importance of relationships. We have to understand the culture in which we operate and ask if it is working in the interests of the organization's objectives. I have no doubt that the systematized approach works in the long run for the benefit of both organization and employees. If this is not natural to your organization then a staged change programme may be necessary, convincing management of the value step by step.

2. Career counselling by managers is heavily biased by their own experience and prejudices. Younger managers are too inexperienced to give a balanced view of the organizational opportunities, and yet they are likely to be managing a large proportion of the younger employees who need the help most.

This is why some special events should be scheduled at certain points of choice in an individual's career in addition to the appraisal process. Systematic guidance for the younger people is a worthwhile investment. We referred earlier to a career guidance pack and this can help to alleviate the issues raised, along with managerial training.

3. Career plans are fine in stable organizations, but those with constant reorganization and changes of management find continuity impossible and agreed actions rarely get implemented.

An individual must own his or her own career plan, and it should have the status of a 'contract' with the organization. A new manager coming in should discuss with his or her inherited people their plans and what part he or she needs to play in achieving them. This is a concept to be embedded in the culture and framework of career management.

This is one reason why plans should not specify times and actual posts, but should indicate the approximate timing and the type of post which will give the required personal growth. Precision in such plans will bring disappointment and frustration.

Indicators of success – These are set out in Table 5.4.

Table 5.4 Indicators of Success Checklist

Potential	1. Its distinction from performance, its nature as a perception at a point in time, and a system of classification are fully understood in the organization.
Appraisal discussions	2. Appraisal systems put adequate emphasis on development and career discussions.
	3. All appraising managers have been thoroughly trained.
Assessment of potential	4. Systematic methods exist to assess potential where and when needed; there is a balance of input on the potential perception, and it is regularly assessed.
Career counselling	5. Managers and specialists have clear roles and have been trained; career resource packs are available to them.
	6. Other means of career guidance have been considered and evaluated.
Career plans	7. Plans are built systematically around the achievement of personal growth towards an aiming point; and are regularly reviewed.
Considerations for women	8. A set of processes have been designed to continue creatively the personal growth of women on career breaks, and designated individuals take responsibility for their implementation.

Actions for those responsible for career management

1. What system of classification of potential are you using? Does it meet your needs?

2. Draw up a list of ways in which potential is assessed in the organization. Are there any gaps or shortcomings? Particularly look at the assessment of high potential. Prepare a plan for changes which will better meet the needs.
3. What has happened to those designated as high potential five years ago? How have their careers developed and by what means? If they had plans, how have they matched reality? What lessons can be learned from such a study?
4. Discuss with some senior executives or leaders in the organization what factors have shaped their careers and their perception of what is important. List some of the influences on their progression and evaluate whether this historical perspective has validity for the future. Did they have a plan and/or aiming point, and if so what part did they and the organization play in making it happen?
5. Find out from a cross-section of employees their views on the career counselling and planning they have received (or examine results from opinion surveys). List the areas which might realistically be improved and your proposed solution.
6. How does the organization deal with outplacement or premature termination? Is there benefit in having a different policy and if so what would it contain?
7. Examine the statistics regarding the fall-away of the proportion of women in the higher grades of the organization. Is the organization wasting precious talent? List ways in which this could be reduced through a proactive policy of promoting the personal growth of women.

REFERENCES

1 Colloff, S. P. and Goodge P., *The Open Track to Elite Status*, Personnel Management, November 1990

2 Mayo A. J., *Linking Manpower Planning with Management Development*, Industrial and Commercial Training, March 1990

3 Cairo P and Lyness, K., *Stimulating High Potential Career Development through an Assessment Centre Process*, Career Growth and Human Resource Strategies ed. London and Mone Chapter 13, 1988

4 Stewart A and Stewart V, *Tomorrows Men Today*, Institute of Personnel Management, 1974

5 Shackleton and Newell, *Management Assessment Methods in UK and France*, Journal of Occupational Psychology, 1991

6 Savile and Holdsworth Ltd, *Management Assessment sans Frontieres*, papers from Seminar, March 1991

7 Schein, E and Delong T., *Career Orientations Inventory*, MIT, 1981

8 Leibowitz, Z., Farren C., and Kaye, B., *Designing Career Development Systems*, Jossey Bass, 1986

9 Burgoyne, J. G. and Germain, C., *Self development and Career Planning: an exercise in Mutual Benefit*, Personnel Management, April 1984

10 Hall, D. T. and associates, *Career Development in Organisations*, Jossey-Bass, 1986

11 Dudeney, C., *A Guide to Executive Redeployment*, McDonald and Evans, 1980

12 Feldman, D., *Managing Careers in Organisations*, Scott Foreman, 1988

13 Truman, C., *Overcoming the Career Break – a Positive Approach*, Manpower Services Commission, 1986

14 Korving M., *Making a Comeback*, Business Books Ltd, 1991

15 Mumford A., *Management Development – Strategies for Action*, Institute of Personnel Management, 1990

6. MANAGING THE DATA

Any systematic approach requires data. In this chapter we will examine sources of data, how data is kept and controlled and how it is used to meet the agreed objectives for career management. Today, an increasing amount may be dealt with electronically; however, it should not always be taken for granted that this is the most effective way when it comes to qualitative information concerning individuals. Those responsible for personal data of this kind need to be familiar with the requirements of data protection legislation.

SOURCES OF RELEVANT DATA

Table 6.1 summarizes the sources of data for career management.

Table 6.1 Sources of data

The organization	*The individual*
Strategic plan	Personal information records
Operating plan	Training records
Organization structure	Appraisal and development
Organization demographics	Reviews
Job grades/categories	CVs
Person specifications	Personal growth profiles
Career structures	Career development plans
Career bridges	Test and assessment results
Development positions	Language capability
Career history dynamics	

Data from the organization

The strategic plan, as discussed in Chapter 1, should provide much relevant data for analysis. Thus we would expect to find manpower and broad skill requirements and, whether explicitly stated or not, should be able to draw conclusions about:

- Changes in requirements for management, geographically or in 'new business' areas,
- New subsets of the organization that may be required as the plan progresses, and those that will no longer be required,
- Changes in the numbers of particular types of job,
- The knowledge, skills, attitudes and experience that will be required of particular types of job,
- Requirements for joint venture and collaborative management,
- Changes needed in career structures.

From such a study we may find it appropriate to use some modelling, looking at the effects of various decision options, but a summary should be made of the implications for career management.

The operating plan for the organization or its parts contains the budgets for the period of the plan. The career manager will be interested in the budgeted expenditure for development activities, and in the headcount by function and the scope for new recruits and trainees. 'Control by headcount' is the great enemy of those concerned with people development and may lead to some short term and wrong decisions – it is better for organizations to control by compensation cost budgets.

The organization structure is fundamental for the scope of career management opportunities. However, it is rarely permanent, and yet people have a tendency to allow the current organization to dominate their vision of their future development. Look back over one, two or five years and see how the organization has changed – there is no reason to believe it will not continue to change at the same pace. So our conclusions from the strategic plan are important as they indicate areas of change, of strengthening or weakening in different areas.

The structure of today should not constrain our freedom of movement and flexibility. The perfect structure rarely exists, although it is constantly sought after. Some hold the view that organizations must uncompromisingly reflect the needs of the business and people have to be fitted in afterwards. This may mean there are good people who cannot be accommodated and may be lost, and it limits the opportunities for developing people proactively. The alternative is that organizations should be built around the people available. The optimum is a pragmatic approach between the two, with the needs of the organization predominating. But compromises should be made to provide a good development opportunity for someone ready for a particular type of experience although influencing the decisions of senior executives, to change or add to the organization for such a reason, can be extremely hard.

The design features of a structure were looked at in Chapter 1 and affect our capability to grow people. The careers manager should not only ensure he or she has the facts of the organization structure readily available but also has some influence on organization design to provide the necessary balance of development opportunities. Holding the organization structure on automated text libraries (if networked through the organization) or on a common module of a personnel information system is recommended for the ease of update on-line and of access.

By organization demographics we mean the way people are distributed in the organization and the flows through it. We need to have a feel for the scope available for development of people and do some modelling (see next section). In most organizations this kind of data is now readily available through personnel information systems. The careers manager needs to be a competent user of information technology.

So the career manager should know:

- Distribution and combinations of age, length of service, grade, department, job function, sex, time in job, geographic location, language, mobility.
- Attrition statistics for different groups of employees.
- Job histories – ideally in full, but at least over the last five years.

• Distribution of jobs by function and grade.

Job grades can be a great enemy of career development, particularly if linked to visible signs of status. Thus if we have people refusing to take the job or opportunity that is right for their career development because it does not give an uplift in grade immediately, or worse if we have managers using upgrading as an expedient to tempt someone to fill a job, then we are going to find good career management difficult. Some organizations are abandoning job grades – at least at managerial levels – and basing their reward system on personal value. Those with a genuine concern for career management will see considerable logic in this approach. Job grades seem to dominate in a lot of US and UK corporations but are not seen as so important in continental Europe. In France, qualifications and the job title count most; in Italy it is being a member of the *dirigente*.

Nevertheless, a common grading nomenclature is helpful if we want to understand the organization as a whole. It does serve as a useful shorthand for level in the hierarchy and an indication of job size. However, such may not exist in a multinational organization or one that has grown recently by several acquisitions. Tables that correlate the value of different jobs with the different grading systems are then needed.

A good system of job and function categorization is essential for manpower planning purposes, and for understanding the way job movements happen. If parts of the organization operate on different coding systems life becomes unnecessarily complicated. But obtaining agreement to a common system in a large organization can often be difficult.

Person specifications are not the same as job descriptions (but are linked with them). As discussed in Chapter 3 they are a summary of the requirements of a job in terms of knowledge, skills, attitudes and experience – and enable us to make matches with individuals. They are not necessarily needed for every job in the organization, but we need them for the key ones and for the main generic job groups.

A sample standard format was shown in Table 3.8. These can be coded and computerized (see section on Using information technology) – my own experience is of a number of attempts to categorize and code skills and experience which have not existed for a long period – they were used because of the need for special nuances or conditions at the time of analysis. An automated library of text is probably preferable, at least as a backup to a coded system. However, advances in information technology are providing more and more flexibility to the user.

Career structures should all be in a consistent format and compatible one with another. Whether this is so depends on the level of centralized control, but there will be problems in career management if they are not broadly consistent. The career manager needs a library of these, and normally they can be produced in hard copy to ensure availability to all relevant employees.

A library of career bridges and development positions is perhaps the most important data to generate and keep. It needs constant update as the organization evolves but the 'maps' (see Figure 4.5) of bridges and matrices of development positions (see Figure 4.7) are key tools of the trade.

Most people keep these in hard copy format as they need to be portable, albeit they may be prepared using IT tools such as spreadsheets, databases and desktop publishing.

The last item is career history dynamics. This is the pattern of things in the past. What have been typical career paths that people have trod? What have been the typical times required in a job to demonstrate some achievement? What is the speed with which really able people progress through the organization, and also those who are less able? What do the 'plateau graphs' look like? The section on Modelling the organization looks in some detail at this aspect.

This information may not be easy to acquire or evaluate: it depends on the sophistication of the information system available. However, some sampling can give the general trends.

The past is not necessarily a guide to future needs – we might want to change some components deliberately – but understanding 'the way things have been' is a sensible base for deciding on and managing changes.

Data on individuals

Personnel information system A flexible, comprehensive, automated system of holding personal information is essential for any kind of modelling and understanding of the organization's resources. We cannot cover here all that is involved in acquiring and running such a system, but we need to note its importance.

Appraisal and development reviews The appraisal discussion is a fundamental platform of career management. Quite rightly today the emphasis is on performance review, ie on the review of preset measurable objectives, and the approach of rating personal attributes has almost died. But to assess only the results themselves is not sufficient – we need to analyse why objectives were achieved or not achieved, and this leads us into the person's strengths and weaknesses. We assess those aspects of knowledge, skill, attitude or experience that require development to fulfil the needs of the current job, which leads us to choose appropriate learning experiences for the future.

The careers manager will be more interested in the future development section of the appraisal. Some organizations recommend having a separate development review from the performance review – this has merit but in practice most managers prefer to have one big meeting rather than two. What matters is the information that is collected and/or shared. Formats vary considerably, and an example was shown as Table 5.2.

The *output* should include the following:

- The person's aspirations,
- The current career direction and aiming point,
- The career plan,
- Development actions related to career plan,
- Recommendations for any specific assessment event,
- The person's mobility (local, national, international),
- The earliest date for consideration for a move,
- The current perception of potential.

Should there be an open discussion with the individual regarding all the conclusions or should they be kept for managerial eyes only? The case for secrecy is:

- Immense trouble is caused by raising expectations of career moves, etc and then not fulfilling them. It is better to say the minimum.
- Openness causes 'fudging', in order to be nice to the person; honesty becomes blurred.
- The commitment made by the manager may not be one that is finally backed by the decision maker.
- The 'label' of a potential classification may imply more to the individual than is intended, being only a perception at a particular time.

The case for openness is:

- People know that the form is being completed. It is of the greatest interest to them and they will do their utmost to find out what is on it.
- Some managers will be less 'secret' than others.
- Provided that it is made clear that it is a plan, not a commitment, what is there to lose?
- False expectations can build up just as much by the secret approach, because things that should be said are not.
- It is inconsistent with a policy of career guidance, etc, to say this part of the system is secret, ie an event can tell you things but your manager cannot.

The balance? The expected problems of the open approach rarely materialize. It is crucial, however, to train managers to be constructively straightforward, to avoid blandness and to discuss the issues clearly without an irrational fear of upsetting people. So I recommend openness, with one caveat – that is to avoid absolutes which can be logged by people as expectations. For example, dates of moves or of promotion, and maybe the classification of potential. Rather than provide a label for people it is better to discuss the perception of potential with them.

The careers manager would be expected to have a copy of this part of the appraisal – and there is, therefore, merit in making it a separate piece of paper. He or she should also visit each unit once or twice a year and discuss each individual to check whether what is written is still seen as valid, to update the current perception of potential as seen by the manager, to discuss any development actions that can be facilitated and to listen to supplementary information that does not get written down. This is a most important part of the career manager's job – it is a great mistake to operate by paper and computer alone!

A CV should be kept up to date for each individual, and a training record. More important perhaps is the personal growth profile (see Table 3.5). This is the person's portfolio of knowledge, skills, attitudes and experience that should be updated at each appraisal and provide the foundation for our building blocks of career growth. The careers manager needs to maintain copies of these for some, but not all employees.

Data from tests and assessments The main other source of data on individuals is from different kinds of tests and assessments.

An integrated language of describing capability and experiences throughout the human resource processes in the organization is of great importance as discussed in Chapter 3. So if personal growth profiles, person specifications for jobs, appraisal strengths and weaknesses, development plans, career plans, assessment reports and so on are all built around the same language of capabilities, all the right linkages can be created. Outputs from tests and assessments, therefore, should be consistent with our chosen framework and language.

The following types of tests and assessments can be useful for our purpose:

Personality tests such as 16PF and the OPQ from Savile and Holdsworth. These are frequently used to support recruitment or promotion decisions, but essentially describe how a person 'is' rather than what they 'do' or 'can do' in work. For career development purposes they are not ideal – although they can test certain skills and attitudes reasonably well.

Career interest tests – for example the Myers Briggs test and others outlined in Chapter 5. These tests may be made available to employees through a career resources library if the organization has one. They enable employees to focus on particular occupations they are likely to succeed in through testing mainly personal interests.

Results from assessment centres. These may be promotional centres or general development centres, as described in Chapter 5. Professional practitioners are aware of the caution needed in interpreting and sharing results from assessment centres, and a set of standards or guidelines is needed to control their use. The report given to the participants is more important than the detail, and the careers manager would have access to this. The output may be a combination of skills assessment and career direction advice.

MODELLING THE ORGANIZATION

Career demographics

It is surprising how often those concerned with the development of people see quantitative studies of manpower flows as the job of some other professional, and their concern as essentially with individuals. But we can only progress individuals within the limits of the organization, and its dynamics. We may want to change those dynamics but we need to know what to change and why.

Career managers, therefore, need a sound understanding of not only the structure of the organization and the jobs in it, but the way people move through it. It may be confusing and unhelpful to look at the organization as a whole if it does not contain any common career structures, but in this case one can take sensible subsets. For a particular chosen subset we can draw a line around it and treat it as a system, with flows in/out and within it. Wendy Hirsh[1] in a pioneering study based in three large different organizations, drew heavily on the work of Bennison and Casson's *Manpower Planning Handbook*[2] in developing this concept of a system, and showed by mapping the reality of movement in those organizations how to draw conclusions from the resulting models.

The data of interest includes:

The grade structure and how it relates to hierarchical levels of responsibility. We are interested in those promotions which are to significantly different levels of responsibility, and not those which are mainly to recognize added personal value and give a higher salary scale. Few organizations have more than ten hierarchical levels, and yet may have twice or in extreme cases three times the number of salary grades. Theoretical hierarchical levels can be calculated simply by making assumptions about spans of control. For example, if the bottom level has groups of 20 reporting to the first level boss, and thereafter the span of control is six, even an organization of 100,000 people does not need more than seven levels. This compares to four levels for an organization of 1000.

Bennison and Casson in their modelling suggest six main levels in a typical organization – trainees, first job employees, first level of responsibility, supervisory responsibility, managerial responsibility and general management. This may be too simple for many organizations, but it illustrates the principle of grouping salary grades into layers of responsibility.

In 1989 General Electric in the USA moved to a structure quite similar to this, even in terms of visible grades. It put all its professional and managerial staff (some 100,000) into five bands only – officers (about 100), senior executives (about 350), executives (about 4000), senior professionals (about 30,000) and professionals (about 50,000). Here we may have more than one hierarchical level within a grade band.

It may not be so easy even to define a distinct hierarchical level in complex and technical organizations, so some intelligent judgement is required in grouping functions and levels.

The numbers in each hierarchical level, by age, length of service, sex, and length of time at that level. This enables us to get a picture of how quickly people have progressed through the organization, whether there are dissimilarities for men and women, and the level of plateauing at a particular level.

If it is possible to go back in history to understand the length of time in the last two or three levels for all or for a sample of the population this can also be very helpful.

The flows in and out of each hierarchical level over, say, the last three years. Here we want to know the level of external recruits and promotions each year; the losses from each level through promotion/transfer to another manpower system in the organization/retirements/redundancies or other involuntary departure/ natural wastage.

The career pattern of individuals in a particular group intake – eg the graduate intake of year X. Ideally we would like to track what has happened to all members of a group joining the organization say five to ten years before, to understand rates of retention, speeds of progression and the career bridges that have been made.

The limits of possible change to the manpower system in relation to the business plans. By limits we need to know the upper and lower limits of change through expansion or contraction to the numbers in each level in the system. In modelling, the basic characteristics of a manpower system are not very sensitive to changes to the quantitative numbers in each level – but much more so to assumptions of attrition, speed of promotion, external resourcing policies etc.

This information enables us to create a number of models and pictures. The simplest is to depict the flows as shown in Figure 6.1

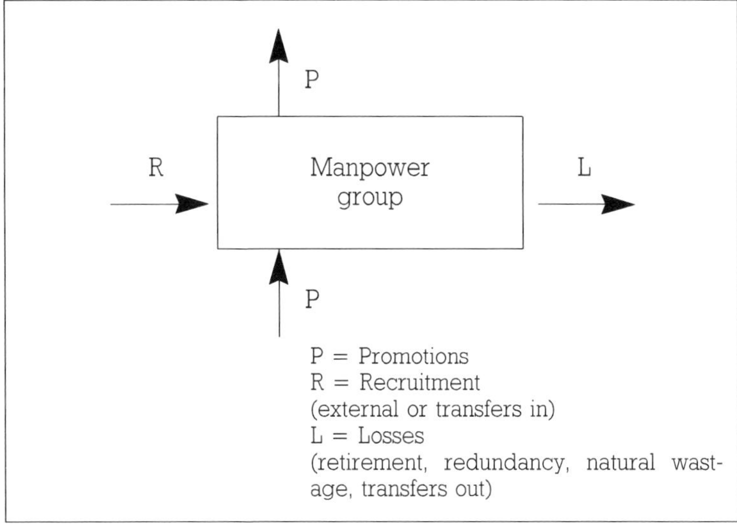

Figure 6.1 Module of a manpower system

The size of boxes and thicknesses of flow lines can be drawn to a scale reflecting the actual numbers involved, to give a useful visual expression of manpower in the organization. It shows where potential bottlenecks in promotion may occur, but this is dependent on the aspirations and capability of the group concerned. Although there may be relatively few supervisory positions on the shopfloor they are not necessarily desperately sought after, and many an organization has had a headache in filling them. So the classification of potential becomes important in completing the picture, as we show below.

What then can we do with this data and what questions can we try to answer?

The distribution of age in itself has limited value unless linked with level or other factors. However, it may show peaks of recruitment due to business growth, and is of most value in showing imbalances such as a particularly high proportion in the 50s age group. Young companies show imbalances in the other direction and, unless high growth continues, they suffer crowding for senior opportunities when they arise.

The distribution of age and grade (or level) This is extremely useful and shows us the speed with which people progress in the organization – the earliest and normal ages for entry into a level; and the number who appear to plateau at each level. Bennison and Casson express this in the form of a 'career progression diagram', drawing curves for each level in the organization of the percentage in or below that level by age. Figure 6.2 shows an example.

Such curves show relative, not absolute, numbers because of the use of percentages, and need to be treated with care if the absolute numbers are low. The curves fluctuate wildly with small numbers and grouping of say five year age bands can help to smooth them. They have value in that they show the historical time between promotions, at least for those who have always been with the organization, and they reveal potential difficulties with the organization's policies.

The data can be shown in different ways and a look at the absolute numbers can also be interesting, although it is but a snapshot at a point in time.

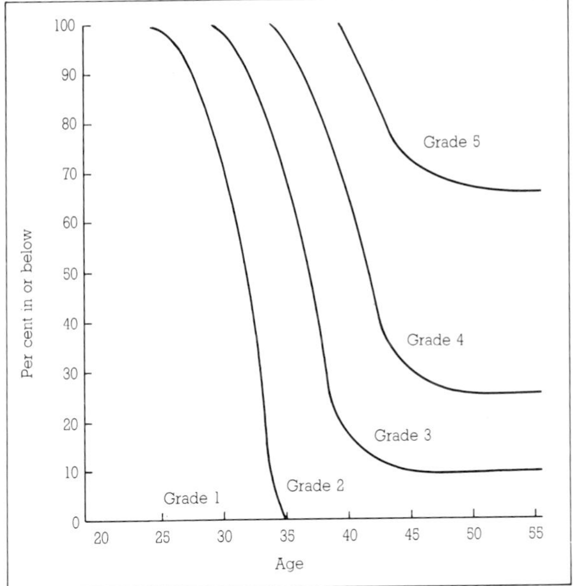

Figure 6.2 Example of a career progression diagram

One would expect a statistically normal distribution of ability in an organization.

The distribution of length of time in a grade (or level) This will give an understanding of speeds of promotion that, together with the age distribution, provide a good picture of the career dynamics. Better still is to have the distribution of length of time in the **two previous grades/levels** and then we have an excellent picture of average and high flyer speeds of progression.

It is instructive to look at different functions – are there faster ways to the top? I chose to set my sights on a top personnel position partly because I observed that this was a fast way to reach a position of functional leadership with limited competition – albeit not a good route to a chief executive role. Organizations show historical preferences for their top leaders to have certain backgrounds – but when it comes to functional leadership how different is the speed of progress?

The distribution of external recruits by grade (or level) Any vacant position can either be filled by an external recruit or by an internal promotion. An organization should know what its policy is in this area, and monitor it. Thus, if its policy is that 90% of posts above a certain level should be filled internally this has significant implications for the pools of available people to promote. Certain levels – or functions – may require more external top-up than others and may want to make some resourcing and career management changes as a result.

The distribution of grade (or level) with sex This shows us how the percentage of women in each grade changes, and may cause us to ask some questions about the result. The percentage of women managers that is often decried as too low is partly a function of the numbers of women who have been available to come through the organization – and to stay coming through. Analysis may lead to questions that, in themselves, might cause change in our career management policies.

Drawing the manpower system for women and men separately, showing the relative flows in, out and upward, give a useful indication of any differences that may need explaining. Likewise separate career progression diagrams for each sex are particularly useful, being based on percentages. Specific career streams should be taken for comparison and not the whole organization, as certain functions in manufacturing and administration with a predominance of female employees can distort the total picture.

The loss rates at each level and their distribution by age, sex, potential and length of service. Labour turnover rates are important in planning, but we need to understand more than cold numbers. We want to track for each chosen population to be studied:

- First the reasons for the losses, particularly 'voluntary', retirements and early retirements, and the various forms of involuntary termination.
- The 'survival' patterns; meaning the variation of voluntary loss rates with length of service. Particularly interesting is the loss rates of new entrants, plus the main causes.

- The reasons for losing women at various stages – particularly those having upwards potential.
- The reasons and age/length of service for losing all people with potential. We particularly need to understand whether there are frustrations or blockages in the career management system that we can put right. An example would be finding that an undue number were leaving because they wanted an international appointment and the organization is poor at enabling these, or leaving after five or so years of service because of a perception that the wait for further promotion is too long.

All this analysis does is to give us an understanding of what has happened in the past: but this understanding reveals weaknesses in the systems and processes of the organization and provides a guide to what changes should be made to meet the needs of the future.

Types of models

The Institute of Manpower Studies[3] has published a summary of career planning models. The authors examined the practice of career modelling in five commercial organizations and four government departments. They naturally found great variation in the use of models, which they group in three categories:

Aggregate deterministic box-flow simulations – dealing with total flows in and out of a manpower system, and useful for predicting the numbers of vacancies to be expected and possible promotion opportunities for groups of staff. This is based on the box-flow approach depicted in Figure 6.2. Each run of the model produces one answer.

Individual box-flow simulations – this is similar to the above but tries to make predictions for an individual based on a large number of characteristics. It is a stochastic model (based on probabilities) and, therefore, there are a number of possible outcomes.

Both these models rely on historical data to predict the future and this is a limitation. In the first, the boundaries of the system may be difficult to draw in complex organizations and, whereas it is simpler to use larger units as the modelled manpower system, the usefulness of the results to smaller parts is reduced. The second is more suited to smaller staff groups, is flexible and comprehensive as it seeks to get closer to reality. It requires a lot of effort to run and its complexity can be an enemy to continued application.

Promotion models use the career progression diagram approach as in Figure 6.2. to look at the ages and chances of promotion at different levels. Such a model sold by the Institute of Manpower Studies in the UK is known as CAMPLAN. The information to apply the model is usually easily obtainable, but it needs large numbers of staff to be valid. It has severe limitations in that it assumes promotions are equivalent to a grade move, and it does not take account of all the growth opportunities available. It also assumes one profile of recruitment and attrition which may be an average of quite different local situations. However, the model is useful for giving broad pictures and an understanding of what is happening in the organization.

For further technical details of these models readers are referred to the IMS paper.

Most models are limited by the assumption that staff have the same potential to be promoted and this is clearly not the case. The model described below was developed in the course of my work in two large organizations and seeks to take account of the distribution of potential in a population.

Linking manpower planning with individual career development

What practical link can we find between manpower planning (organization flow and movements) and individual development planning? The majority of the models that are described for career analysis seem to be based on the premise of 'for ever upwards, if there is enough space'. But the higher we go in the organization the fewer we find with the capability to progress further, never mind the ambition. The model described below attempts to answer some of the following questions:

- What is the effect of **internal promotion policies** on manpower planning?
- How many **people with potential** can an organization cope with effectively? Or, looked at another way, how many should we have to meet our needs?
- How can we plan for adequate **succession in the longer term?**
- How fast should we plan careers for **high flyers**?
- How can we tell if our organization is healthy in terms of building the **quality** of its future manpower needs?
- Is there a rational way of determining the **intake of young people** each year?

These questions go beyond the traditional short term approach to succession planning. The model described below has the following outputs:

- It shows the required ratios of people with upwards potential to those who have reached their level – at each level – needed to ensure future resourcing needs,
- The annual input of young entrants,
- Expected annual resourcing plans at each level,
- A basis of comparison with today's reality leading to actions in resourcing and development to come closer to the desired position.

Manpower planning is traditionally concerned with relatively short term flows in, out and within an organization. Its timescales are significantly shorter than those necessary in career planning. Figure 6.3 illustrates an organization shown as a broad pyramid, and divided into levels of accountability. Not all organizations are this shape – some are like a box with a funnel on top (the higher levels being a mixture of management and specialist jobs), or like an uneven hour glass with a middle bulge – as in most computer companies that have a high percentage of specialist staff who are well paid. However, for the management structure – which is the major resourcing problem – the pyramid basically holds good.

The first question to ask is 'what ratio of internal versus external resourcing meets the needs of our business?'. This may not be the same at all levels in the pyramid. For example, many

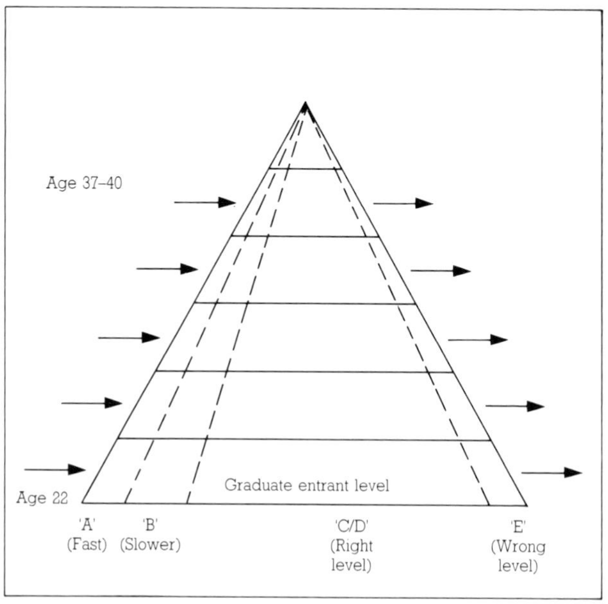

Figure 6.3 Distribution of potential in an organization

organizations would say that, whereas they wish to hire and train all their own young people, they do not want to buy in externally at the top. They would, however, like perhaps a 10 to 20% replacement rate at mid-levels from outside. Others are 'cradle-to-grave' companies, which try to avoid any external recruits above the bottom two levels and promote entirely from within. This is good for the careers of individuals but such organizations often have excessively low attrition rates, which means that opportunities are dependent on organizational expansion or retirement rates and that there is an excess of people drifting to the higher levels. A 100% internal promotion policy with a high attrition rate gives an opposite problem – a requirement for a larger number of promotable people than the organization contains.

The combination of internal promotion policy and loss rates is thus significant both in terms of the opportunities made available and the number of people required with promotional capability. Not all organizations have articulated a policy – some have unofficially accepted norms – but most are pragmatic: if there is someone promotable internally, fine; if not, call the headhunter or agency. Such an approach is mismanagement of the organization's resources. It is extremely expensive to hire externally, apart from the neglect of the growth potential of one's own employees. There needs to be a *deliberate* policy. This may for good reasons be a policy of majoring on external recruitment – to bring fresh thinking into a stale organization; or to supplement the stock of people with talent at a particular level or in a particular function. Some companies have done just that – convincing themselves that their internal people were inadequate for today's competitive world and recruiting significantly outside. However, the life of the new recruits may be limited because of difficulties of cultural absorption and lack of further prospects, so eventually the turn of the company faithful come round again. Most mature business organizations today would find a policy of internal promotion at the level of 70–90% in the senior levels acceptable, with a mix at the lower levels of hiring trained recruits *plus* training their own. For start up or fast growing organizations more pragmatism is needed.

Whatever the policy, it has a significant influence on the career dynamics. Every loss from the organization requires replacement from without or within. An internal replacement will come – eventually if not immediately – from a promotion up the ladder of accountability. The more who come from within, the more we need people capable of upwards movement. Modelling requires, therefore, some division of the population at each level into bands of 'potential'.

This is shown in Figure 6.3: on the left hand side is a fast stream – the 'A' stream – which includes people perceived at the time of assessment to be able to go at least two levels further forward, and to move relatively fast. The second, 'B' stream, is that which includes others with upwards potential – but perhaps not more than one level, and generally moving slower. Whereas everyone at any time has potential to grow, not all will grow upwards, so the next two classifications are those who have reached their right level (as currently perceived). The majority have lateral potential, ie will be able to move sideways or take greater responsibility. There is also a group of those who are truly round pegs in round holes and want to stay that way. Lastly, few organizations escape from having a few people who have, according to Professor Peter, reached their level of incompetence.

Before we start modelling, some further questions. We need to find out the numbers at each level and the best estimates of attrition from the manpower system we are looking at – this should include all losses at each level other than promotion to the next level. Then we should ask: **what is the speed of progression we would expect the two streams with upwards potential to have?** Our analysis of the career dynamics should tell us this. It will vary considerably between organizations and slowly with time within an organization – in young, turbulent, highly competitive ones getting to the top happens to younger people than in established slow-moving organizations. But today's young company is tomorrow's mature one, so in looking at history projections need to take account of this.

Table 6.2 A model for manpower planning

SETTING UP – See Figures 6.4 and 6.5	
STEP 1.	Choose a discrete population of statistically significant size (>100). This could be a unit, a function, or a whole organization.
STEP 2.	Define the levels of accountability, ie real promotional rungs, and determine the number of jobs at that level. (It is of interest to do the model both with the existing number and that projected by the traditional manpower plan for a time in the future.)
STEP 3	Set the 'speed of progress' parameters for the A and B streams. Figures should reflect the reality of the organization, or how it would **like it to be;** the A stream might enter the most senior level at 40; the B stream top out at the next level down at 45 (on average).
STEP 4	Determine the voluntary attrition rates for each level, the anticipated level based on the best information available. (This is an attrition rate requiring **replacements**, so should not include forced separations through redundancy).

NOTE if this is a **subset** of the organization it must include transfers out of this subset.

STEP 5. Estimate at each level what proportion of the annual losses might typically come from each stream. (Note, due to career plateauing, mid-career comfort, etc, above middle levels it is mainly people of potential who leave voluntarily. It is useful to track this in the analysis of attrition.)

STEP 6 Determine the percentage of internal promotion that is desired at each level. (Note that if we have taken a subset of the organization 'transfer in' counts as external resourcing).

STEP 7. Estimate the average annual promotion rate out of Level 2 to the top level. (Express as decimal if necessary).

CALCULATIONS – See Figures 6.6 and 6.7

STEP 8. For Level 2, add all promotion and loss figures to give the 'annual resource requirement' for that level.

STEP 9. Based on the assumption in STEP 6, split the annual resource requirement between internal and external.

STEP 10. Cascade downwards by distributing the 'internal requirement' to the 'promotion pa' boxes of the A and B streams respectively at the next level.

STEP 11. Repeat steps 8–10 until the bottom right hand box is filled. This will be the 'annual young entrant intake'.

STEP 12. For each level determine the number required at that level in the A and B streams as follows:-

N = (Promotion pa + Losses pa) × average time between levels.

STEP 13. Calculate the ratio of A: B: (C + D) for each level.

Population:

Date:

ORGANIZATION RESOURCING

Level / Grade	No at This Level	'A' Stream				'B' Stream				C/D Streams All Losses	Annual Resource Reqd				Target Ratio A:B C+D	Attrition Rate
		Entry Age	Promotion P A	Other Losses P A	Number Required	Entry Age	Promotion P A	Other Losses P A	Number Required		Total	% INT	INT	EXT		
2	40	38				45										5%
3	150	34				40										7%
4	600	30				35										10%
5	1800	27				30										10%
6	3000	24				25										12%
7	5000	21				21										15%
8																

A: Substantial potential; 2 levels min
B: Some potential; ½ levels further
C: Sideways potential
D: Right job, right level

Figure 6.4 Steps 1–4

Population:

ORGANIZATION RESOURCING

Date:

Level / Grade	No at This Level	'A' Stream				'B' Stream				C/D Streams All Losses	Annual Resource Reqd				Target Ratio A:B C+D	Attrition Rate
		Entry Age	Promotion P A	Other Losses P A	Number Required	Entry Age	Promotion P A	Other Losses P A	Number Required		Total	% INT	INT	EXT		
2	40	38	1 (to Level 1)	1		45	–	–		1		100				5%
3	150	34		3		40		3		4		80				7%
4	600	30		20		35		20		20		80				10%
5	1800	27		60		30		60		60		70				10%
6	3000	24		120		25		120		120		80				12%
7	5000	21		250		21		250		250		–				15%
8																

A: Substantial potential; 2 levels min
B: Some potential; ½ levels further
C: Sideways potential
D: Right job, right level

Figure 6.5 Steps 1–7

ORGANIZATION RESOURCING

Population:

Date:

Level / Grade	No at This Level	'A' Stream				'B' Stream				C/D Streams All Losses	Annual Resource Reqd				Target Ratio A:B C+D	Attrition Rate
		Entry Age	Promotion P A	Other Losses P A	Number Required	Entry Age	Promotion P A	Other Losses P A	Number Required		Total	% INT	INT	EXT		
2	40	38	1 (to Level 1)	1		45		—		1	3	100	3			5%
3	150	34	2	3		40	1	3		4	13	80	10	3		7%
4	600	30	6	20		35	4	20		20	70	80	56	14		10%
5	1800	27	35	60		30	21	60		60	236	70	165	71		10%
6	3000	24	90	120		25	75	120		120	525	80	420	105		12%
7	5000	21	240	250		21	180	250		250	1170	—	—	1170		15%
8																

A: Substantial potential; 2 levels min
B: Some potential; ½ levels further
C: Sideways potential
D: Right job, right level

Figure 6.6 Steps 1–11

Population:

ORGANIZATION RESOURCING-

Date:

Level / Grade	No at This Level	'A' Stream				'B' Stream				C/D Streams All Losses	Annual Resource Reqd				Target Ratio A:B: C+D	ACTUAL RATIO	
		Entry Age	Promotion P A	Other Losses P A	Number Required	Entry Age	Promotion P A	Other Losses P A	Number Required		Total	% INT	INT	EXT		Div^N 1	Div^N 2
2	40	38	1 (to Level 1)	1	8	45	—	—	—	1	3	100	3		20:0:80		
3	150	34	2	3	20	40	1	3	20	4	13	80	10	3	13:13:74		
4	600	30	6	20	104	35	4	20	120	20	70	80	56	14	17:20:63		
5	1800	27	35	60	285	30	21	60	405	60	236	70	165	71	16:23:61		
6	3000	24	90	120	630	25	75	120	975	120	525	80	420	105	21:23:56		
7	5000	21	240	250	1470	21	180	250	1720	250	1170	—	—	1170	29:34:37		
8																	

A: Substantial potential; 2 levels min
B: Some potential; ½ levels further
C: Sideways potential
D: Right job, right level

Figure 6.7 Steps 1–13

In the example shown, the span of control (looking at the second level) may seem far too low and there is a clear case to take out a level of management. However, this is not untypical of technical organizations where a number of specialists are employed in small teams.

We could conclude from the example that this population of 10,600 people with the desired internal/external resourcing percentages as shown:

1) Needs a resourcing intake of some 1,170 pa at the bottom level.
2) Requires some 40% or so at each level to be people with some potential.
3) Requires a recruitment plan as shown in the column headed EXT.

(1) and (2) would be reduced by lower loss rates, slower progression up the ladder, and a lower internal resourcing rate.

The model tells us where we should be and we can then compare that with where we are. We can do this by undertaking an 'organizational audit', ie assessing the potential of each individual at each level and then compare the actual ratio of people with upwards potential to the remainder at that level. When this model was applied to one particular large organization in the UK it was used in three ways – for the overall UK organization; for each separate division; and for the personnel function as a whole.

As a result, firstly the number of young entrants was increased substantially – previously it had been at the whim of the budget makers each year and the under-recruitment was showing in an excessive external recruitment at higher levels. In the personnel function a graduate recruitment scheme was restarted after many years' lapse. Several weaknesses were discovered in various parts of the company in respect of future long term resourcing, and action was taken to strengthen those parts over a period. This was partly to pursue external recruitment of talent and partly to engineer transfers of people from other parts of the organization. In understanding the 'speed of progress' dynamics it was realized that high potential people were not being accelerated fast enough and frustrated ones were leaving for greener pastures. The age of entry to senior management grades for exceptional people was reassessed and steadily reduced. A strategy of internal promotion versus external hiring at senior levels was quantified and articulated. Looking five years later at the same organization, all these actions have had their desired effects in creating a more balanced, healthy company.

The model lends itself to a simple spreadsheet format and this is to be strongly recommended. It is dynamic and needs review every six to 12 months to ensure the validity of the assumptions. Using different assumptions the organization's sensitivity in different areas can be measured: for example, taking out a whole level of accountability will have a significant effect.

Why is this approach helpful?

- It focuses attention on future resourcing, beyond the normal horizons of manpower planning. It looks at long term succession capability.
- It models an ideal organizational dynamic and comparison with the actual situation provides a basis for intelligent resourcing strategies.
- It works against a stop/go policy of resourcing, particularly with young entrants.
- It disciplines an organization to concentrate on potential, and assess it regularly.
- It can show relative strengths and weaknesses across parts of an organization and lead to actions for a better balance.

USING THE DATA FOR DECISION MAKING

How much data to hold?

Whereas all the processes described so far should operate to the benefit of all employees, the careers manager has priorities within subsets of the population. The majority of the employees in a given year follow natural career movements, stay in their jobs or take up lateral opportunities. Special attention is needed for those who:

- Are particularly key to the success of the organization,
- Are in need of a move that requires some 'management' to achieve (eg cross-functional moves, cross-divisional moves, returning expatriates),
- Are believed to be at risk (of leaving).

There are populations of special interest where all the members of that sub-group are of interest to the career manager continually. Examples of such populations might be:

The senior management group. Management development specialists sometimes spend a disproportionate amount of their time on this group, monitoring and planning their moves. They are important but they have the least need for career planning and career management as their options are both limited and well understood. Typically such a group would embrace the two levels below the chief executive.

People on high flyer schemes. Such schemes are normally monitored centrally and moves of the participants carefully planned.

People perceived as having high potential. Arguably the career manager should take interest in all those who have been identified as having significant potential, at least to two levels below the top slice referred to above. They, after all, represent the future of the organization, and we need to be sure that they all have a clear career direction, aiming point and career plan. In a large organization there may be too many for individual attention – but then the task is to ensure that the career manager's 'agents' are doing so down through the structure.

We can redraw Figure 6.3 as below to show these groups of interest.

Expatriates seconded for personal development. Employers vary considerably in their capability to manage international moves from a career point of view. Out of sight, out of mind often applies, and it is of benefit for someone to take a special interest in this group.

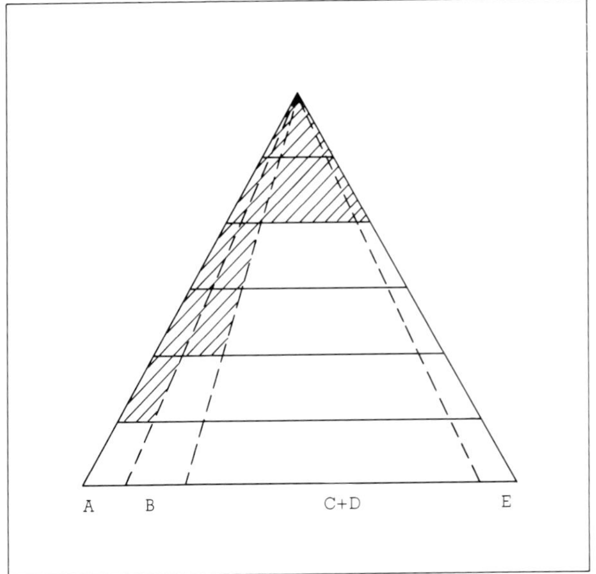

Figure 6.8 Population of special interest

MBA recruits or other special intake whose success we want to track. We may wish to monitor over a period of time specific intakes who will help us to understand their value as a resourcing input, and to see how successful we are in managing their career development.

People on special secondments either internally or externally. Particularly cross-divisional and cross-company, and anything external. One reason for doing this may be that the originator of the secondment may not be in post at the end of the period, and the continuity is lost with the secondee.

Subgroups such as all the professional HR people. The careers manager may take an interest in complete sub-pyramids, either to manage development on behalf of a senior executive, or to understand the career dynamics involved (for example the complete finance function).

From all the data that is available for the chosen populations of interest what should be distilled from it?

- A database with at least the following fields:

Name	Location
Date of birth	Growth potential code
Job title	Earliest date for move
Date commenced current job	Mobility
Date of entry to the organization	Languages

  It is not necessary to have many more fields than this, as full details should be available on the main personnel information system. Each entry should have reference to a CV and personal growth profile, together with a career plan which gives details about career direction and aiming points etc.

- The people (within our populations of interest) who have an 'earliest date for move' within the next six months. This can be derived from the database(s), and is an action reminder that it is time to be thinking about the next step for specific individuals.

- Other subsets of the populations that may be of current interest for special reasons, eg people who are willing to move internationally; people who have a defined level of capability in a language.

SUCCESSION PLANNING

Succession planning is normally taken to mean the identification of particular individuals as possible successors to key or senior posts. Most organizations have some kind of activity here – concerned at the very least with the immediate succession to specific current posts.

Lynda Gratton in her study on succession strategies[4] looks at the differing needs of different organizational structures. She distinguishes between those which specifically seek to perpetuate a cadre of like minded and like experienced executives (such as IBM) and those which see themselves as young and fast moving and for whom the pragmatic decision is best. She distin-

Job title:					
Incumbent:					Grade:
Age	DCJ	EDM	MOB	CPP	LPR
Successors:					Ready:
1.					
2.					
3.					

DCJ = Date commenced current job
EDM = Earliest date for a move
CPP = Current perception of potential
MOB = Mobility level
LPR = Last performance rating

Figure 6.9 Succession planning for a specific post

guishes further between those groups of companies which see a layer of management as of common interest (like BAT) and those whose corporate HQ is no more than a financial holding company (like Hanson). These types of companies naturally have different sets of career management objectives (see Chapter 1) and their approach to succession planning varies accordingly. Thus all or none of the options described here may be taken up depending on need.

The textbook approach concentrates on taking each senior post in today's organization and identifying possible successors to the current incumbent. An adaptation of the organization chart may be used as shown in Figure 6.9.

Some scepticism is attached to this activity, however – here are some of the questions that can be associated with it:

- Is it relevant in a fast changing world to treat a dynamic organization as if it were static? The traditional approach focuses on today's organization and its current positions. The answer is that it is useful to do it as one part of a system of career management processes. If it is the only activity it has very limited value.
- Do the plans provide really credible candidates when the time comes to make changes? Are not the plans frequently ignored when it comes to making a decision?

  All the relevant parties must be committed. Credibility is impaired if:
  - names are filled in for the sake of box-filling and completeness,
  - names are the subjective input of a small number of people and not derived from an integrated set of career management processes,
  - the plans are not kept up to date as fast as the speed of changes in the organization,
  - a lack of trust exists between line and staff (or central HQ and subsidiary organizations): game playing and separate agendas can result – 'you fill in your plans, but I know what I am going to do if I have to'.
- Is it not as effective to look around at the time when we have the vacancy and see who is available? In practice, this is what we do anyway, but we will start with the names on the succession plan. Is there any advantage in having the names specified? It gives us a head start to deal with a vacancy, but a major argument for doing this exercise is to see where there is no successor available. These succession gaps prompt us to take corrective action.
- Does this approach sit comfortably with a policy of open job advertisement? There is no need for conflict here, in the sense that both processes can operate simultaneously.
- Should we not be more concerned anyway with long term development of pools of people ready for particular types of jobs? Yes, this is an important measure of the organization's

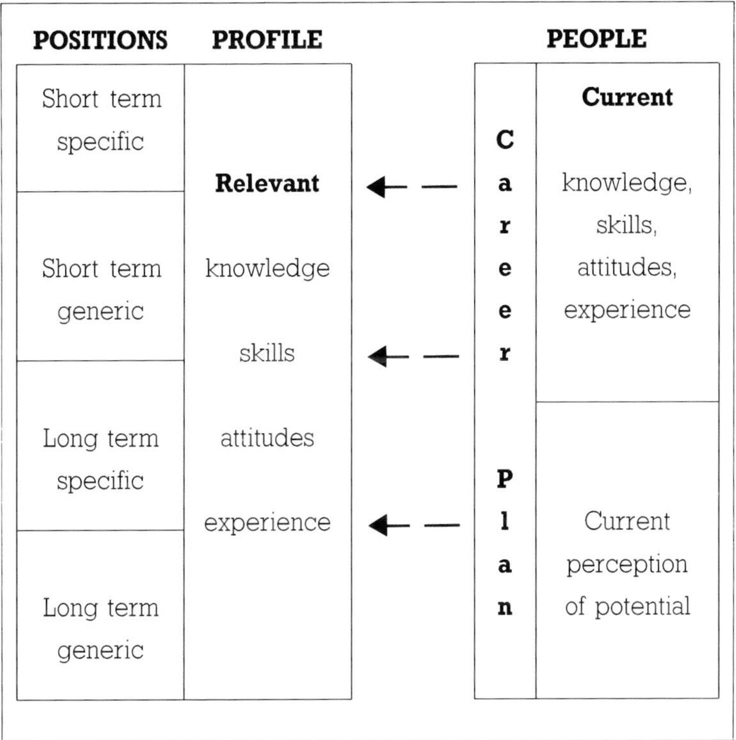

Figure 6.10 Matching people and posts

health and readiness for the future. It is certainly as important as planning the 'next step' inherent in traditional succession planning, although both have their place. Our concern in this book has been to emphasize longer term career planning for people.

The full set of options for matching people and posts was shown in Chapter 3 and is reproduced again here in Figure 6.10.

Succession plans often lie unloved and unused. The careers manager will nevertheless want to make succession planning useful and successful. If we follow the general thesis of describing the personal growth profiles of people and person specifications for jobs in the same terms – ie in knowledge, skills, attitudes and experience requirements – and we are regularly assessing potential and building career plans then we should be in a position to do the following:

- Against each type of job, name those individuals who are ready and able to take such a position should it become vacant now,
- Name those individuals who are being prepared through development planning to take up such a position.

Figure 6.11 shows an example of a way in which this might be described.

Note that we have said 'type of job' (the generic approach). In some cases there may be only one of a type, and we can replace with just 'job'. But many jobs are members of a group having similar profiles. This approach removes the objection that the organization structure is not static, and moves us into the area of resourcing for the future. It also helps us to look laterally and not feel comfortable just because a box is filled – even though it is with the most obvious candidate.

Many organizations have succession plans and they are not built on a managed or systematic basis at all. They are prepared from subjective discussion, often coloured by political agendas. One would question the value of plans which are not the result of an interlinked set of processes. But even in the most sophisticated career management environments the 'successor in the box' is often not chosen. A typical series of questions in the event of a key vacancy is:

- Who is on the succession plan?
- Do we agree they are candidates for consideration?
- Let us look at all the relevant population which would be a source of candidates and see if there is anyone else to be considered.

This process ends up sometimes in choosing a name not on the list. This can be frustrating to the careers manager – but those on the plan may not be suitable because they have just changed jobs, or are unwilling to move to the job location, or were put there for political or parochial reasons. The *effective* careers

Type of post: **Grade:**

Specific jobs	Division	Location	Date to job of incumbent

Available candidates (next 3 years)

Name	Current job	Div	Grade	Locn	DCJ	EDM	AGE	CPP	MOB

Locn = **Location**
DCJ = **Date commenced current job**
EDM = **Earliest date for a move**
CPP = **Current perception of potential**
MOB = **Mobility level**

Figure 6.11 Generic succession strength

manager needs to be up to date and have the data on all the angles of matching individuals and posts, and may find that even after the three questions above have been asked, the final answer is the answer to the first.

Proactive planning

Succession planning tends to be related to 'what we would do if we had to' scenarios. But the careers manager wants to be proactive. Can we create opportunities driven by our objectives of people growth? Events and organizational change often pre-empt the time one would like people to spend *doing* a job. The length of time in a job should be the sum of the learning time, the time to consolidate and do the job effectively, *and* time to achieve results and leave the job in a better state than when it was inherited. For a management job these periods are, typically, three months, nine months and nine to 12 months respectively – depending on the complexity of the environment. So two years would be a guide. In Japan they place much more emphasis on the third stage and a typical time is five years. In more stable organizations (and more directive) it is easier to achieve these 'job-lives' and to plan ahead.

The question to be asked is: can all the information available be used actively to plan some moves? It is a complex task in a large organization and, as we discuss below, people have tried to provide computerized solutions.

The starting point is the field on the data described as 'earliest date for a move'. This is a trigger to set up a sequence of moves which are consistent with the career plans of individuals. This can be done using a table as in Figure 6.12 where each sequence or chain of moves is scheduled for a particular period such as a quarter. A table such as this can be made more sophisticated by specifying actions on particular people and so on, but they are really useful for regular monitoring of planned moves.

USING INFORMATION TECHNOLOGY

It is unusual today for even small organizations not to have some form of computerized personnel information records, and to be able to do basic analysis of the employee population for

Move sequence	M	M+1	M+2	M+3
Chain 01 (period)	Person A from Job J to Job K	Person B from Job L to Job J	Person C from Job M to Job L	Person D from Job N to Job M
Chain 02 (period)	Person E from Job P to Job Q	Person F from Job R to Job P	Person G from Job S to Job R	Person H from Job T to Job S
Chain 03 (period)				
Chain 04 (period)				
Chain 05 (period)				
Chain 06 (period)				

Figure 6.12 Sequencing moves table

the purposes of manpower modelling. However, what about the computerization of career management processes? In complex organizations the process of classifying, searching, comparing, integrating, summarizing and updating facts about job requirements, structures and individuals are candidates for automation. Systems which give all the information needed using consistent coding are gaining greater interest as those available become more flexible.

The use and effectiveness of automated data handling in this area depends on the orientation of the careers manager. Some are much more at home with paper lists and models and plans, and use these most effectively. Browsing, retrieving and quick visual searching can be much quicker for a person really familiar with the files. However, the number in this category decreases annually as personal workstations and familiarity with them rapidly increases. The norm will be to use computers, albeit in various forms. Computerization has a significant advantage in visibility – it is more difficult for departments to hide their good people from so called predators.

For whom? The careers manager needs to concentrate on those populations of interest that have been defined. It is not necessary and is an unproductive and labour intensive task to secure the same level of data on everybody – although an output of the appraisal and development review exists for everyone.

Wendy Hirsh[5] in Chapter 8 of her IMS *Report on Succession Planning* covers the subject admirably. As in all process management, there are **inputs, outputs** and **processes** between them. Table 6.3 shows a summary of the input data that is required.

Inputs

A few notes are called for on the coding of some of these:

Post identifiers – both in the coding of career history and in the categorization of positions in the organization a consistent system of coding is needed. It can be numeric, but if preferenced by some alpha-codes indicating major functions this is probably more helpful.

The identification of **development positions** is important also – these are the ones that must not be blocked and should feature regularly in career moves.

Time related items – should always be coded as dates and not elapsed time – computers are perfectly capable of calculating the elapsed time and actual dates do not change.

Mobility – need not be complicated. It needs to cover the four eventualities of – no significant location move; commuting Monday to Friday; national move and international move. Some try to code all the places people would or would not move to – the lesson is always to keep it simple and never forget that the more complex it is the less likely it is to be kept up to date.

Knowledge, skills, attitudes and experience – perhaps the most difficult area to code is the data from personal growth profiles and the person specifications of jobs, which need to be consistent with each other. Taking the language of this book, areas of knowledge need to be coded for the depth of that knowledge. As used on the sample personal growth profile in Table 3.5, three levels were suggested:

01 Working knowledge
02 Competent enough to do a specialist job in this area
03 Known expert

Skills and attitudes can be coded as 'strengths' using an alpha abbreviation. They could be qualified in a simple way, depending on the nature of the organization. Experience should be qualified with the number of months or years in the particular field.

Table 6.3 Inputs to career management processes

Type of input	Type of source
Individual data:	
Personal details: name, date of birth, sex, date of joining, qualifications	Personnel information database (preferably an automatic link)
Career history post, grades, time in each	as above or written CV if special coding needed
Training history	ditto
Earliest date for move Last performance rating Current potential code Mobility	These come from appraisal information or supplementary discussions/assessments
Knowledge, skills, attitudes and experience; languages	Personal growth profile
Career plan including plans for significant training	From development review with individual
Other information (textual)	Careers manager's input
Organizational Data	
Characteristics of posts Division, department Post identifier Title (s) Development post identifier Manpower category Location (s) Earliest date available Grade/level Current post holder and date appointed	Organization charts
Essential knowledge, skill, attitude and experience requirements	Person specifications for jobs
Other textual data	Careers manager's input

Coding experience can be done simply by using the code for the functional area, or by adding further elements to show subdivisions of that experience and elapsed years of involvement in the area as defined.

What has to be remembered in these areas is that describing the attributes of people in a coded form will never be adequate, and there is a great danger in using such a system mechanistically as if it were scientifically accurate. There is a sense in which the less sophisticated the system is the better it will serve you, because it will not delude you into thinking the computer can do everything for you.

The career plan may not be easy. One is primarily interested in the next post for the purposes of the processes the computer will undertake – the type of job sought in terms of experience needed, timing and so on. So it is useful to reference the full career plan (who has it, what was its last date of update) but only to code the key information regarding the next type of post(s) that are being sought.

Languages – an international company needs to know who speaks what language, but again these must be coded for proficiency. The person who says he or she speaks French because they know how to ask for another beer in Calais is not quite what the marketing division seeks in a posting to France . . .

The last date of update – should always be shown on any set of individual or organizational data.

Processes and outputs

The system must be able to manipulate the data as shown in Table 6.4.

In specifying the system requirements it is necessary to input some rules for these processes. For example, the links between individual career plan data for the next job and succession requirements – how will we distinguish the *essential* matching requirements from the *desirable*? A system that interrogates the user on the particular details of an enquiry is ideal – together with the facility to override the general rules of the system if

Table 6.4 Processes and outputs

PROCESS	OUTPUT
1. Job/people matching	Options of candidates for posts available
2. Move sequencing	Chains of planned career moves
3. Succession strength assessment	Availability of potential in specified areas
4. Succession plans	Successors for particular posts or types of posts – with 'ready dates'
5. Order, list, search	Lists of people according to specified search or ordering instructions
	Manpower planning data, such as percentage of people with potential, ratio of women ++

needed. It is better to risk getting some inappropriate names or jobs in the answer to an enquiry, than to eliminate possibilities by having the rules too tight. The careers manager can add value by using the superior human brain to evaluate the computer's answer.

Specifying and choosing a system

The ideal system will:

- Be linked to the main personnel information system,
- Have the capability of processing in a defined way, reporting in a predetermined way, and doing both these functions under a query system,
- Be accessed globally within the organization, but absolutely secure,
- Be easy to update,
- Be easy to link/integrate with standard spreadsheet, database and word processing software.

There are a number of packages available that claim to track careers and/or computerize succession planning. Savile and Holdsworth market their *Work Profiling System* which claims to link appraisals, assessment reports, career development needs and person specifications and obtain job matches thereby. Another popular system is *Executive Track*, a software program 'that matches the right person to the right position at the right time'. Developed in Iowa, US, it claims to be the world's leading system of its kind with over 1000 users, giving the following facilities:

- Organizing and storing individual information (CVs, career plans, etc),
- Organizing and storing position-related data,
- Matching candidates with positions,
- Producing succession plans (immediate and five years),
- Producing 'ready for change' lists,
- Identifies positions blocked,
- Enables tracking of special populations,
- Monitors equal employment parameters,
- Picks up data not recently updated,
- Organization and succession charting,
- Links with (some) main personal information systems.

Peter Deen of Dow Corning, Europe, in a paper presented in 1991[6] based on his experience in computerizing succession planning in a global business provided a number of lessons. I quote some of them as good advice, with some added comments:

1. **Don't do it yourself . . . look for a PROVEN package** – others have been down this route before and learned some things; better to capitalize on that than go through all those lessons yourself. Besides, internal systems people in an organization love to computerize the most complex system you can dream of – an outsider can ask the sensible systems analysis questions.

It always seems to be the case that no package quite fits **our** situation. This may be true, but see if you can go to the limits of flexibility first.

2. **Students are very clever and they love special defined projects** – Dow Corning used students to do a lot of the set-up work with great success, and many have had the same experience.

3. **It always takes longer and is more difficult than you had**

imagined – so be careful of what you commit to whom by when . . .

4. **The needs of managers and personnel are not the same** – Managers want summaries and key data, and personnel are interested in the detail. So in report design remember the two sets of user needs.

5. **Run a pilot with the full data for a small group** – get it working and credible in one area before investing massive effort in data entry and then finding problems.

6. **Computers are incredibly stupid** – if you want a system that will be subject to a multitude of data entry staff with different native tongues do not forget that the computer cannot sort out errors of entry; so it has to be foolproofed by simple, systematic coding and one must recognize what **cannot** be sensibly coded and use text.

REVIEW COMMITTEES

The careers manager cannot work alone. He or she is but an adviser, a coordinator, a facilitator, a process manager of the systems in place. It is necessary for the significant outputs of his or her the work to be 'owned' by the management of the organization, and to have a means of decision making on key posts or movements that involves all the right people. Furthermore, the senior executive group needs both to share and own the people who are key to the future of the organization. Those who are coming through as high potential need to be visible and known at a level beyond their own part of the organization to avoid their careers being narrowly restricted; likewise each sub-division must not guard and hide its best people lest they be poached. This is a natural risk of territorial decentralized structures – however, the top team ought to rise above this for the corporate good.

It is a common practice for organizations today to have a committee chaired by the chief executive and consisting of a representative group of senior line and functional managers. The personnel director or, more normally, the person responsible for career management acts as secretary. The composition of such a group must include all the major sub-divisions within the scope of the organization, so that members can discuss each other's areas. Typical names given are the executive review committee; the succession planning committee; or executive development committee. These may be replicated on a cascade basis down the organization, and each autonomous operational unit will probably justify one.

The typical standing agenda of such a committee might be:

- To review and update succession data – for specific and senior generic posts,
- To resource key vacancies, or new ventures/expansion,
- To decide next moves for those ready for their next step in the coming period,
- To review the organization's 'pools of potential' and take action if they are inadequate,
- To review the list of high potentials and their development,
- To decide on changes to career management processes as needed by the organization to meet its short and long term objectives.

Such a committee is a powerful instrument of the career manager, and he or she will serve it and the organization well by careful preparation and staff work, and by making the decisions happen.

In a turbulent organization there is merit in this committee meeting monthly. Some only meet annually or six monthly – a frequency of quarterly is the maximum interval I would recommend. After all, nearly all senior managers admit they spend insufficient time on the development of their most precious resource . . .

Some organizations have formal 'sign-off' of succession plans. The question is what the sign-off is meant to mean – is it that the senior executive doing the signing agrees with the contents; or is it ratifying the collective view of the management; or is it approving a definitive plan of action? No amount of signing will ensure that the document is used when needed. Organizations are dynamic entities and no plan stays up to date for long. The ongoing interest and commitment of the senior management group, therefore, counts for much more than a piece of paper.

Is it possible to keep career management and people growth issues permanently on the agenda throughout the business? Some have found ways to do this. For example, one large international company operates a process it calls the **Organization and management review**. The fundamental strengths of this process are:

1) Each time there is a formal review of the business situation – quarterly in this case – a time is specifically allocated for the discussion of organization and development issues, on an agenda similar to that described above;

2) The **business manager** presents the status and issues to his or her boss, with the equivalent level of human resources managers present, and no other attendees other than the specialist responsible for career management, if such exists;

3) The process is cascaded from the chief executive downwards, so that everyone is embraced within the process;

4) There is the opportunity to specify a common agenda item for the quarterly series which is important to the business objectives.

A typical agenda is shown in Figure 6.13. Multitudes of forms are not required and it achieves its objectives through flexibility

- Organization review
  - Current issues
  - Changes needed
- Resourcing issues in general
  - Skill shortages
  - Attrition by category
  - Reprofiling
  - Rationalisation
  - Succession strength
- Review of key staff
  - Performance
  - Career plans
  - Stability/risk
- Review of lists of
  - People with potential
  - Key skills
  - People for international movement
  - 'Development positions'
- Strategic training priorities
- '*Local* development processes'
  - Projects
  - Secondments
  - Task forces
  - Junior management boards
  - Mentorship
  - Appraisal schemes etc.

Figure 6.13 Organization and management review – an agenda

and in the involvement and commitment of the key line managers in accounting for and planning for the development of their organizations and key resources.

The message for review processes is to keep them continuous and flexible, rather than, for instance, annual formalized rituals. This way they can keep in tune with the constant change of the environment and the people in it.

SUMMARY

A wealth of data is potentially available, both about the organization and about individuals. Controlling the various inputs and providing intelligent and efficient processing to give the outputs that management finds useful is a significant task. Using information technology to do this clearly enables a greater range of data to be handled, and enables modelling of the organization to check whether what is actually happening is in line with the needs of the organization. One has to beware, however, of immersing resources in the creation of a wonderful system instead of doing any effective career management, and remember that *talking* with people should take up more time than manipulating data.

Ideally, the systems in use embrace all individuals in the organization, but each careers manager needs to be selective in working with certain parts of the overall population that deserve special attention.

Providing succession plans and (probably more important) defining the succession *gaps*, short and long term, is one major output for the organization. However, careers managers should strive to be proactive in job movements rather than only reactive to vacancies and reorganizations. The specialist in this area is not a decision taker and, therefore, some form of review body should exist which includes key line executives. This reviews the succession plans, initiates career movements, and recommends changes to the career management framework.

ACTION PLANNING

Problems of reality

1. One person's system is not always easily used by another; nor is one person's mix of electronic data handling and paper handling. Likewise, different careers managers have different priorities and interests in modelling, or in the parts of the population they regard important. Continuity is such a problem that it is best to keep systems as simple as possible.

This chapter set out to be fairly comprehensive; even so a whole book could be written in dealing with the subject. It is always better to have some simple processes that work and add value than a multitude of complex ones understood by only a few, or worst of all one person. However, we must always come back to the question of what the organization needs to achieve its objectives and ensure we can give the answers speedily and correctly, and also that we know which questions to ask. Anyone responsible for creating data management systems must think about other users, either elsewhere in the organization or his or her successors. One benefit of a review body is that it can ensure consistency in the overall framework of career management.

Elementary information technology tools, such as readily available spreadsheets and databases, can be very useful, and referencing text files may be more effective than sophisticated coding systems.

2. A lot of time can be spent in collecting and analyzing data, and feeding it through sophisticated models, and the final conclusions are those that were self-evident anyway. Time would be better spent on more practical career management activities.

This is always felt when research or analysis yields the obvious. It does not always do so, however, and much can be learned that can influence career management practice. But a balance has to be kept; the more sophisticated and complex the model used the more assumptions and uncertainties are included and the less valuable the outcomes. Naturally when a problem is obvious to all it is better to start solving it than to go on proving it exists in different ways.

3. In a fast moving, fast growing, turbulent organization it is unrealistic to keep track of all the data which quickly becomes out of date. It is better to react to situations than to spend time on files and lists and plans.

Organizations have different needs to be met in different ways. What is important is to know what **could** be done and make a selection given the needs.

Indicators of success – these are set out in Table 6.5.

Table 6.5 Success in data management

Organizational and individual data	1. Sources of data are identified, and data is available in formats that are consistent with one another and lead to ease of analysis and coding. 2. There is a system of 'change control' which enables data to be kept up-to-date or reviewed at prescribed intervals. 3. Populations of special interest are defined and agreed with the senior executives.
Career demographics and modelling	4. The factors listed under 'Career denographics' (page 209) are regularly monitored. The flows of people through the organization are well understood and modelled where added value can be obtained.
Succession planning	5. Succession planning exists both for short and long term, considering not only specific posts but generic job types. 6. The number of matches between what was planned and the eventual selection of posts is sufficiently high to validate the planning exercise. 7. Proactive movement takes place as well as reactive.
Review bodies	8. A body of senior decision-takers meets regularly to manage both the overall career management framework and to take specific decisions regarding career movements.

Actions for those responsible for career management

1. List, from discussion with senior managers, what outputs the organization should have to help it meet its objectives. (Compare with any exercises done from Chapter 1.) What implications does this have for the inputs and processing needed?
2. List the information sources available in the organization based on Table **6.1**, and against each their current usefulness in career management and their frequency of update. Make a list of the changes required to make the data consistent in format and language.
3. If not already available, conduct some analyses of how people move through the organization and the flows in and out. Refer to some of the models in the literature, or discuss with some organizations which use modelling in practice, to choose an approach that will yield helpful outputs.
4. List the terms of reference for an **ideal** review body to realize the career management and people growth objectives for the organization. If such bodies exist, how well do they meet such a list? What changes might be proposed?
5. How, honestly, is succession planning regarded in the organization? What measures of effectiveness would you propose in this area and how well are they being met? What improvements might be made?

REFERENCES

1 Hirsh, W., *Career Management in the Organisation*, Institute of Manpower Studies, Report no 96, 1984

2 Bennison, B. and Casson, J., *The Manpower Planning Handbook*, McGraw Hill, 1984

3 Morgan, I, Seccombe, I. and Such J., *Career Models for the 1990's*, Institute of Manpower Studies Paper no 161, 1991

4 Gratton, L. and Syrett, M., *Heirs Apparent: Succession Strategies for the future*, Personnel Management January 1990

5 Dean, P. of Dow Corning Europe, *The Benefits and Pitfalls of Computer-*

ised Succession Planning, Institute of Industrial Research Seminar in London, March 1990

6 Hirsh, W., *Succession planning: Current Practice and Future Issues*, Institute of Manpower Studies report 184, 1990

7. MANAGING PERSONAL GROWTH

The careers manager will not just be interested in personal growth through job change, but also in how a person's personal growth profile can be *continually* enhanced. The elements of growth – knowledge, skills, attitudes and experience – are developed most significantly by a job change, but this chapter looks at how they can be grown within the context of an existing job through experiential learning.

Several excellent books have been written on this subject. A good proportion work on the assumption that self-development is the key. While not denying the validity of this, *assisted* self-development as part of a mutually agreed plan together with other learning experiences, is surely the best mix.

HOW PEOPLE LEARN

Not only are there a great many ways of providing learning, but people learn in different ways. 'Learning' is the activity undertaken by the user, the employee, and therefore where the emphasis should be, rather than on the more passive terms of 'training' and 'education'. The careers manager needs a sound understanding of how people learn if he or she is going to advise on personal growth.

The American Professor Kolb, one of the foremost figures in this field, gave this definition[1]:

> *'Learning is the process whereby knowledge is created through the transformation of experience.'*

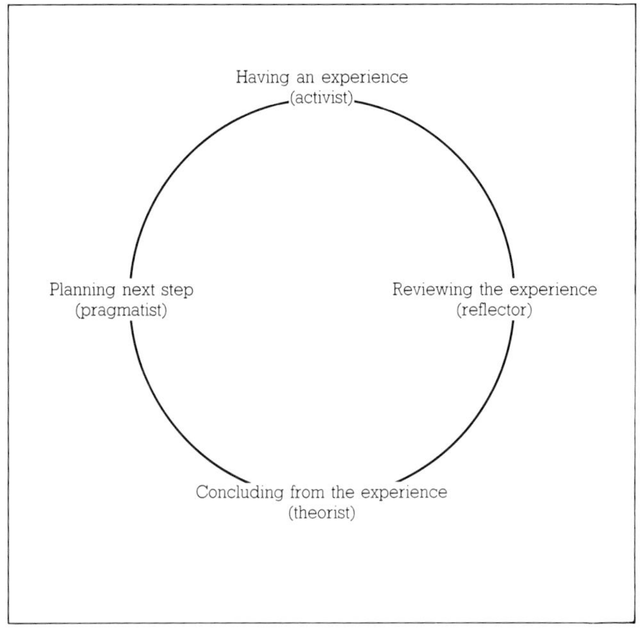

Figure 7.1 Honey and Mumford's Learning Cycle

Professor Alan Mumford in several writings has probably argued the case in the UK for a 'learner orientated' approach more than anyone. His very practical definition is[2]:

> *'A manager has learnt something when either he knows something he did not know earlier, and can show it; or he is able to do something he was not able to do before; or both . . .'*

This kind of thinking leads to a logical assessment of the effectiveness of various methods, rather than, for example, feeling good about a charismatic set of lectures which did not change the way the listener actually did anything. However, people do learn in different ways (and can improve their learning capability by **learning to learn**). The choice of particular learning routes should take this into consideration.

Figure 7.1 reproduces Honey and Mumford's Learning Cycle.[3] All learning includes each element, but different experiences provide a different opportunity for the respective elements. Individuals have preferences and abilities also for parts of the cycle – their preferred 'learning style'.

Table 7.1 The skills of learning

Effective learning behaviour

1. Set standards of performance,
2. Review achievement,
3. Identify learning needs,
4. Identify learning opportunities,
5. Analyse personal learning preferences and stoppages,
6. Develop learning plan.

Crucial learning skills

Listening	Taking risks
Sharing	Accepting help
Monitoring achievement	

(from Mumford [2])

Table 7.1 summarizes learning behaviour and skills. The first summary looks like a traditional performance appraisal sequence but the addition of the fifth step is rarely considered before arriving at the sixth, except perhaps intuitively and subconsciously by some managers.

Honey and Mumford have developed a learning styles questionnaire[4] (and others have created similar instruments) based on these four main styles. The characteristics of the styles are reproduced in Table 7.2.

In Mumford's studies only 20% of managers studied came out with at least three strong preferences – ie were good allround learners. In contrast, 35% had one strong preference. So standard prescriptions for learning are not as effective as custom-made structured experiences, taking account of both the need and the style of the learner.

Table 7.2 Characteristics of different learning styles

Activists:
• Try anything once, • Tend to revel in short term crises and firefighting, • Tend to thrive on the challenge of new experiences, • Are relatively bored with implementation and longer term consolidation, • Constantly involve themselves with other people.
Reflectors:
• Like to stand back and review experiences from different perspectives, • Collect data and analyse it before coming to conclusions, • Like to consider all possible angles and implications before making a move, • Tend to be cautious, • Actually enjoy observing other people in action, • Often take a back seat at meetings.
Theorists:
• Are keen on basic assumptions, theories, models and systems thinking, • Prize rationality and logic, • Tend to be detached and analytical, • Are unhappy with subjective or ambiguous experiences, • Like to make things tidy and fit them into rational schemes.
Pragmatists:
• Positively search out new ideas or techniques which might apply in their situation, • Take the first opportunity to experiment with applications, • Respond to problems and opportunities as a challenge, • Are keen to use ideas from management courses, • Like to get on with things with clear purpose.

Research by Mumford[5] and Margerison[6] into the influences that chief executives see as prime in their own development highlighted early responsibility, early leadership experience and a breadth of functional experience together with being stretched by their bosses as the most important. They listed also several personal characteristics – such as a need for achievement and an ability to negotiate – but off-the-job managerial training was bottom of the list.

A book entitled *The Lessons of Experience* by three American authors, McCall, Lombardo and Morrison[7], reports the study of 600 learning experiences from questions given to some 200 successful executives (although from six major corporations only). These experiences are described as 'assignments, bosses or hardships/setbacks' and they use a master table of 'lessons learned' in studying them. This master table is of interest and is reproduced in Table 7.3.

It is helpful to recall a variety of learning events over the years and ask which were the most effective in enhancing one's profile (with organizational progress as the goal) and which were the least effective. I can recall some as follows:

More effective:

- My vacation student project in my first real industrial experience,
- My first course in presentation skills,
- My first boss who nurtured me systematically as a new manager, taking me through decision making processes step by step,
- My first job as a training manager which exposed me to a whole new set of external points of view,
- A week's course in discussion leading, including immense amounts of practice and feedback, built around leading a supervisory course,
- My first sales presentation and the feedback from an experienced salesman afterwards,
- Numerous 'deep end' experiences in actual work projects and challenges.

Less effective:

- A week's T Group in Tunbridge Wells,
- A course in marketing strategy,
- Being given additional responsibilities but of exactly the same type as those that I already had (more work for no learning).

The object of learning is to cause some change – an increase in knowledge, in learning a new skill or enhancing effectiveness

Table 7.3 Lessons of experience

Setting and implementing agendas

Technical/professional skills
All about the business one is in
Strategic thinking
Shouldering full responsibility
Building and using structure and control systems
Innovative problem-solving methods

Handling relationships

Handling difficult political situations
Getting people to implement solutions
What executives are like
How to work with executives
Strategies of negotiation
Dealing with people over whom you have no authority
Understanding other people's perspectives
Dealing with conflict
Directing and motivating subordinates
Developing other people
Confronting subordinate performance problems
Managing former bosses and peers

Basic values

You can't manage everything all alone
Sensitivity to the human side of management
Basic management values

Executive temperament

Being tough when necessary
Self-confidence
Coping with situations beyond your control
Persevering through adversity
Coping with ambiguous situations
Use (and abuse) of power

Personal awareness

The balance between work and personal life
Knowing what really excites you about work
Personal limits and blind spots
Taking charge of your career
Recognizing and seizing opportunities

from McCall, Lombardo and Morrison, *The Lessons of Experience*, Lexington Books, 1989 Figure 1–2 in others, in changing values and attitudes, and in having real experiences that are going to be drawn on in the future. In career development we try to define the levels of these elements that are required by a particular target post. An individual therefore has a set of **learning objectives** relevant to that target – or if the target is an expansion of the current job, relevant to that expansion or enhancement. It may sound fascinating to go on a course on 'Management styles of the 1990s' as a 'part of your general education' but how does it fit with the current learning objectives?

A classic error is to define a requirement for better understanding of the organization's financial management processes and to send the individual on an external 'Finance for non-financial managers' course. He or she comes back knowing all about balance sheets in theoretical organizations and nothing about the management accounts of the real organization. A learning experience is not complete until it has had real and immediate application to the practical job situation and is seen to be effective. I observe many keen individuals burning midnight oil on part-time MBAs, and then being very perplexed on graduation that the organization does not seem to recognize their achievement. The organization has only observed what they do day-to-day and there is rarely any obvious and visual change in their behaviour from their studies. It is the same for many classroom experiences, especially in management development – less so for specialist and technical learning. Management trainers have become more creative and innovative in their methods of learning over the years, including simulations and exercises – but only if a clear association with reality can be made are they likely to be effective. This is why Reg Revans left the Manchester Business School to set up a quite different type of management learning – which he called Action Learning – built around structured job-related experiences based on real work rather than simulation and case studies; his ideas, however, are still not universally accepted. Among many writings his book *Action Learning*[8] gives case studies from around the world of practical learning application.

DEFINING A LEARNING NEED

The nature of the need should arise from a person's appraisal (if it is to consolidate the learning potential of the current job) or the career plan (if it is in relation to some future job). The induction period in a new job is frequently handled appallingly badly – the lost productivity and delayed learning involved in the casual approach to new incumbents is quite unnecessary. The first few weeks in a new job (whether in a new organization or not) are critical in terms of personal growth – we look at how this can be done more effectively later in this chapter.

Some planning should be done in a disciplined way in defining what is to be learned in a specific period. People cannot learn everything at once, nor make giant steps in a short time. Therefore, for each quarter the needs should be specified, how the need will be met, who is responsible for initiating what has to happen and how it is to be monitored. A simple format such as in Figure 7.2 can be used.

NAME:	**JOB TITLE:**		
Learning need	**Learning action**	**Action on**	**Review date**
This quarter:			
1.			
2.			
3.			
Next quarter:			
1.			
2.			
3.			
Date of this plan:			

Figure 7.2 Format for a learning plan

A need should always be specified in behavioural terms, ie what the person will be able to do at the end of the learning. Here are some examples:

1. (**Knowledge**) To understand how to recruit graduates in another country in order to be able to do so effectively and at minimum cost in the coming year.

   The context of this might be in the expansion of the job of the graduate recruitment manager.
2. (**Skills**) To be able to handle a TV interview effectively and in the interest of the organization.

   The context here might be that this is a skill that will be required of the next job, and can be acquired in advance.
3. (**Attitudes**) To create an attitude that believes customer problems deserve greater priority than internal organizational problems.

   This is a need for anyone aspiring to a senior job, especially general management.
4. (**Experience**) To have personal experience of setting up and managing an exhibition stand in another country.

   This might be for a marketing communications person expanding to or aspiring to a more international role.

WHO HAS A ROLE TO PLAY?

The individual has the prime responsibility for personal growth; after all he or she will only grow and develop if the motivation to do so is there. But whereas there are many excellent ways of self-development, the organization is not helping itself by leaving all the effort to the individual. Mutual interest demands mutual help.

The boss must always have a responsibility for the development of his or her staff, and needs to define the requirements clearly. However, research shows that there is only a minority of managers who make this a priority on their time – in coaching and managing the growth of their staff. Frequently their responsibility is discharged by merely providing the required appraisal interview once a year and sending the person on one or two training courses. It is the easy option to look down the catalogue and pick a course. However, other efforts in this area are time consuming, difficult sometimes to construct and monitor, and require an attitude of mind that places time spent in staff development as a priority over other demands.

Many a person remembers a boss from whom they learned an immense amount. In Alan Mumford's study of the making of directors[5] he found this to be a common thread. What is it that the boss can do?

The appraisal of performance – not just the formal annual affair, but constant feedback on things done well and things done not so well that can be improved.

Dialogue along the lines of 'how else could you have approached that problem?' and 'what are you going to try and do differently next time?' are extremely powerful and helpful.

The formal appraisal, taking stock of the strengths and weaknesses of the individual, is little use if it is bland and superficial. But if the manager and the employee analyse each area of performance using examples thoroughly, lead on to agreeing some precise learning objectives, and choose intelligently (perhaps with the help of a human resources development specialist) the right mode of meeting the need – then this will be a significant event for the individual. The involvement of the appraisee in the thinking processes – which is appropriate for all other than the very young – is crucial in achieving mutual ownership of the needs: the 'tell/sell' style may be quicker but misses a significant opportunity.

The review of career development and potential – the boss–subordinate discussion is critically important. It may not be the only input individuals have regarding their career direction and plan – at least at some points in their career there should be some additional inputs. But it remains the foundation discussion – of the individual's aspirations, the manager's view of their reality, and the planning of the future. A manager does his or her people a disservice if he or she takes the soft option of setting the sights of the individual higher than their capability.

The involving of others in development of his/her staff – the good boss cares enough to involve others – specialists, his or her own boss, colleagues – in development planning and actions. If the boss does not have a natural interest in staff development then this is the second best route – to ensure it happens anyway.

Delegating specifically to grow subordinates – not just giving away the bits that are no longer of personal interest but looking for possibilities to delegate some parts of the job that would provide a needed experience for a subordinate. For example, putting together a monthly report, representing the department at a meeting internally or externally, defining the scope, terms and reference for a project, or choosing the resources to be used.

Looking for opportunities – for new experiences which are consistent with the development plan, and making them happen. For example, a trip abroad, an external seminar, a special project, membership of a working party, taking part as a trainer, giving presentations . . . and many others.

Showing by example – how things are done, how to handle problems and so on. The developer–boss asks all the time whether something he or she is doing today could be a learning opportunity for a staff member. It is often not practical to make it so – people have their work to do and cannot be specifically learning all the time. But it is an attitude of mind that is key. So, after chairing a meeting perhaps, the boss may discuss with the subordinate who was present, how things were handled, what the subordinate would have done 'if', etc.

Acting as a model – His/her own behaviour in situations, ie what is done rather than what is said, is a model to be observed – if it is a positive model it provides a powerful means of learning for subordinates. Often it is a cause of criticism as perceived from below! However, people do learn from perceiving what not to do – the basis of the famous set of John Cleese VideoArts training films was first to illustrate the wrong way to do things.

Discussing objectives of off-the-job courses and monitoring application afterwards – a course has little use if it cannot be applied and often that application needs a supportive environment. The boss should want to see some things being done differently as a result of the course, and should discuss the content immediately afterwards, set some application objectives and monitor them a while later. Few bosses take the time to do this well.

Allowing risk-taking – people learn more by mistakes than by doing it right, because it forces analysis of the best way to do things and some determination to improve next time. This is not to recommend encouraging everyone to make mistakes all the time – but the question for bosses is: 'Am I prepared to allow this person to go into this new area, to take this risk, to do something it would be safer for me to do personally?'

One option is to let a subordinate stand in for the boss when away on holiday or for some other extended period. The subordinate gets a real appreciation of the scope of the boss's job – and even if all the normal demands do not arise in the period many new problems will need to be handled. A manager whom I visited on an induction course said 'If you want to know what my job is about, go through the mail I have received in the last couple of days'. It was extremely revealing about the real nature of his job. Standing-in for the boss achieves the same feeling.

Another area of risk is to step back from making all the presentations and reports oneself, and get a subordinate to take the stage, field the questions and show his or her capability. The willingness of managers to do this seems directly related to their own feeling of personal security.

Sharing their own job – in the sense of communicating to subordinates some of the tasks and difficulties that have been faced and what was done, or seeking input for those that are about to be faced. I recall learning an immense amount from a boss who shared every Monday morning in the staff meeting some of the discussions of the board meetings, negotiations on mergers and acquisitions and so on. His approach was that the risk of indiscretion on our part (zero in fact) was less than the importance of our understanding the issues that were key to the division's business.

Budgeting for costs of development – when the inevitable squeeze comes, is the staff development budget the first to suffer? (Despite this, the best development need not be expensive if we focus on learning from real situations.)

This is a tough portfolio for a boss to worry about, especially if he or she has a large number of subordinates. Even with the best will some selectivity is inevitable. It is unrealistic for human resource people to pursue the theoretical line that managers are responsible for the development of their people, that the HR job, therefore, is to design and communicate sophisticated systems to 'help' managers in this task and to train them to do them effectively – and then to abdicate their assistance. The only reason an organization has specialist help in areas like human resources is that it reaches a stage of growth where the directors cannot do or know everything themselves. So there needs to be a sensible balance between the expectations of good people management and a quality specialist service to managers.

So next we should consider the role of the **human resource development specialist**. This may be a grand term in some organizations – the role being done perhaps, if time permits, by a hard pressed generalist personnel practitioner. Larger organizations or subsets may have specialized training and development advisers. In general it is an under-resourced area, but we have to recognize that this may be as much to do with the perceived added value of such people. There are very few who are so in tune with the organization's objectives and the consequent people development needs that their help is sought as being critical for success. So what is the nature of the added value that could be given? Leaving aside the design of policies and processes, and taking a central overview of the population, consider what the adviser on the ground can do working with managers on the growth of all their staff. (The two roles may be done in fact by one person, but they are distinct.)

Here are some of the activities that can be done:

- Ensuring managers understand the framework of career management and people development processes in the organization.
- Working with managers pre-appraisal in how to handle potentially difficult situations.
- Working with managers post-appraisal in refining learning needs and structuring learning experiences.

- Providing support to both manager and subordinate in implementing the agreed learning experiences; choosing and organizing resources as necessary.
- Assisting the manager with assessing potential and defining career plans.
- Jointly with the manager, undertaking career counselling and recommending/facilitating special events related to career direction or potential assessment.
- Resourcing any local committees or review panels looking at the potential and growth of the population as a whole.
- Liaising through the network of specialists in the organization to facilitate movements or special learning experiences.
- Helping specify the elements of job profiles and helping individuals describe their personal growth profiles.

Some of these tasks are not intellectually easy and they demand considerable time. Establishing personal credibility is crucial in getting that time. That credibility is a function of:

- The genuine interest taken in the manager's operation,
- The understanding of what people really do in their jobs,
- The professional added value that is given,
- The perceived ability to make things actually happen.

It helps considerably if the adviser has experience outside personnel or training and development, and there is nothing worse than someone whose main interest is in the latest theories.

Colleagues do not have the burden of responsibility that the boss has, but nevertheless may be helpful. Some of the ways in which they can do this are:

- Acting as a model to be observed.
- Sharing knowledge and experience ('I had that problem once').
- Social sharing and discussion of common challenges, analysis of others (like the boss!) and of the organization's strengths and weaknesses. (This social sharing is a major benefit from most formal training courses and happens on the job all the time.)
- Giving feedback – on behaviour, on written work, on presen-

tations and so on. The non-threatening input of a colleague can often be more freely given and received than in a boss–subordinate relationship. Such feedback needs to be constructive and illustrative rather than generalized statements such as 'You did a great job there' (which may give a warm feeling but little direction as to what exactly was done well).

Choosing a colleague to help you and establishing a helping relationship can be a constructive aid to personal growth. Many do it unconsciously, perhaps more could and should do it consciously.

Mentors were mentioned in Chapter 5 in their career counselling role. Some managers continue to act as mentors for many years for people who have worked for them, taking a continuing interest in their development and sometimes opening doors for them. However, the term is usually applied formally to a system of assigning a senior person to somebody who does not work for them, usually from another department or division, sometimes from outside the organization.

Several books have examined the practices of mentoring and the resulting relationships[9,10], and the role can extend beyond just counselling. A mentor can help by:

- Helping define the person's career direction and aiming points,
- Advising on the appropriateness of opportunities that arise,
- Creating opportunities through personal influence,
- Sponsoring for projects and programmes,
- Acting as a coach, trainer and role model.

A mentoring relationship is of particular potential value to women on career breaks, where the mentor can take responsibility for maintaining links and suggesting continuing learning ideas during the period, as well as help smooth the re-entry into full time work.

TYPES OF LEARNING EXPERIENCES

Alan Mumford[11] chooses the word 'opportunities' rather than 'methods' because many learning situations are not methodically designed. Planned learning is better than accidental learning, but opportunities arise constantly in an unplanned way also. The majority of effective learning comes through work related situations rather than formal teaching; thus we realize after a particular challenge has been handled how much we learned from it, without having set out with learning objectives.

For example, from a manager's **people management** responsibilities we could list the following as some of the experiences he or she ought to learn from:

Hiring a new subordinate
Choosing a subordinate for promotion
Firing someone for performance or misconduct
Making someone redundant
Reorganizing the department/division
Conducting appraisal and development reviews
Preparing salary reviews
Briefing the staff on a major change
Inducting a new subordinate
Coaching a subordinate for development
Counselling a subordinate in career development
Merging with another department . . . and so on

Some people are managers for several years before they experience all these things, and the first time are unlikely to do everything correctly, despite having attended training courses in the relevant subjects. The second time, however, the learning from experience will really show. The individual and the boss can capitalize on new experiences if they recognize the learning potential of the experience and treat it as such by discussing and analysing what did happen and what might have happened.

Relying on one experience as the source of expertise in an area clearly has its pitfalls and a phrase often heard in organizations is 'he thinks it should be done the way *he* did it 10 years ago!' Generalizing from the specific, one-off experience is dangerous – a common fault of mankind, especially when it comes to forming judgements of people – and many experiences become less relevant with the passing of time. Readers will have observed experienced new recruits working hard to apply their knowledge of another organization and culture and finding it frustratingly difficult. What has to be learned is how to be effective in the current environment and there are always unique elements.

We need a balance of different learning opportunities and that balance should vary based on the learning need. Skills training particularly benefits from an off-the-job, almost experimental environment. To believe that a manager knows all about appraisal interviewing just because he or she has carried out many is a false and dangerous premise. Table 7.4 gives a suggested hierarchy of desirability of learning mixes for skills learning.

Table 7.4 Hierarchy of desirable learning experiences – skills

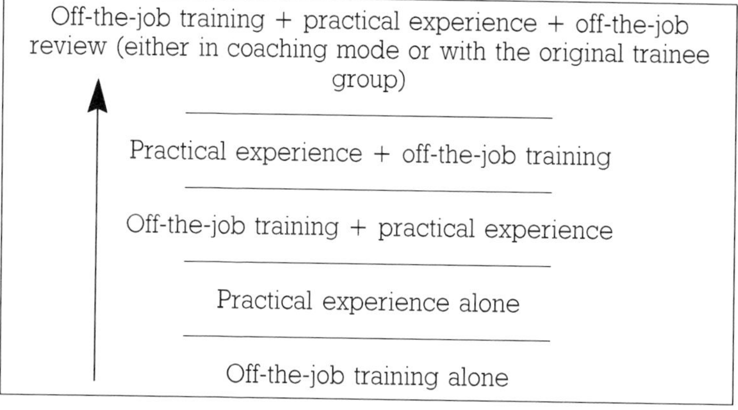

Table 7.5 gives a list of possible learning experiences and their relevance to the elements of knowledge, skills, attitudes and experience. Individuals do not make these distinctions day-to-day in their analysis of personal effectiveness: any learning experience is an integration of shifts in most if not all the elements. Live experience calls on the other three, but is the most powerful and desirable of the four elements. It is certainly what recruiting managers want to discuss first in an interview.

Table 7.5 Choosing learning opportunities

Type of opportunity	Knowledge	Skills	Attitudes	Experience
Off-the-job:				
Lectures	**		*	
Case studies	**	*		
Group discussion	*		**	*
Reading	*		**	
Demonstration/practice	*	**		
Role plays	*	*		
Simulations	*	**		**
Business games	*	*		*
Outdoor training		**	*	*
Distance learning	**		*	
Additions to current job:				
Task force membership	**	**	*	**
Special project	***	**	*	***
Delegated from boss	**	**		***
Visits to customers etc	*	*	***	***
Junior board membership	**	***	*	**
Committee membership	*	**	*	**
Standing in for the boss	**	***	**	***
Visits to other organizations	**	*	**	**
Assessment event participation		**	*	*
University or school liaison	*	**	**	*
Speaking on training events	**	**	*	**
Using the current job:				
Reading about other parts of the organization etc	*		*	
Listening to others with more/different experience	**		*	
Presenting ideas/products internally or externally		**		**
Watching/questioning those worked closely with	**		*	
Coaching/counselling from boss	**	**	**	*
Visiting other parts of orgn.	***		**	*
Social mixing	*	*	*	*
Foreign travel	**	*	**	**
Managing a new challenge	**	***	**	***
Taking on new responsibilities	***	**	**	***
Beyond the current job:				
Secondment	***	**	***	***
'Tiger offices'	***	***	***	***

Specific options in off-the-job learning

Events involving other participants The great benefit of going off-the-job is that the mind is focused on learning, rather than on activity at the end of which one might reflect on any learning that has resulted. Some skills simply cannot be enhanced by experience or watching others alone (for example, presentation skills) – they need the experimental environment of the well constructed course. Knowledge and attitudes may also be improved effectively away from the practical demands of work.

We should recognize specific informal benefits from events involving other participants – listening and observing others, sharing experiences, solving problems in a group, team building (strengthening of personal and work relationships) and time to think.

Here are some conditions for effectiveness for off-the-job learning events:

- They are as closely linked to the reality of the workplace as possible.
- They have objectives that are defined in an action-orientated way – 'at the end of this event, participants will be able to . . .'
- If in-house or custom designed for a particular organization they are in tune with the values of the organization.
- They provide opportunities for participants to apply inputs to their own work, or to think and plan how they will do so on return.
- They provide opportunities for the experience of participants to be shared.
- They are linked to follow-up activity, preferably first on-the-job and then a subsequent review in the experimental environment.
- Any assessment of how much participants have learned is not seen as a threat to free experimentation and learning – nobody should be marked down for saying or doing something stupid.
- There is a feedback loop of effective evaluation and restructuring of the event in place.

Choosing external events Some off-the-job learning events should always be conducted in-house or to an in-house design; e.g. areas that are interwoven with the culture and practices of the organization. For instance, appraisal interviewing skills relate uniquely to a particular organization – every form is different, the availability of development and career opportunities is different and so on. In learning about finance and accounting the real need of most people is to know how their own organization does things, not to play with academic balance sheets of European Widgets Ltd.

However, there are sometimes good reasons for choosing an external event – some are:

- There is a pool of knowledge to be gained that is unavailable inside the organization but is or will be needed:

(example: to learn about European legislation.)

- There is a learning need to understand how other organizations do things and how they have tackled particular problems:

(example: open international executive course.)

- There is a need to experiment/learn away from colleagues:

(example: a senior manager needing to improve a personal skill.)

Nevertheless, the time spent by people attending external events, salving the conscience of their managers that they ought 'to go on some kind of training this year', can be wasted when, for the same time and expense, alternative learning options would be far more effective. A manager should always sound out previous attendees of an event on the practical usefulness they experienced before making a choice.

Outdoors learning The UK fascination with this form of learning has spread elsewhere. Its popularity, particularly for managers, is undoubtedly due to the rich personal experiences many participants have – not only physically but in the understanding and strengthening of relationships. Team building and leadership development are the most common sales pitches. The question is whether slinging a rope bridge across a river is really an experience with relevance to the management of, say, a distribution depot. It certainly can provide real learning for young people in interactive, planning, organizing and team leadership skills; but for managers it depends very much on the objectives defined for the event. Such an event will appear on the personal list of memorable learning experiences for many but in making a choice one has to ask how this option relates to the learning need and what it can achieve for the time spent. There are other more productive learning experiences in many cases.

External committees and associations Belonging to a professional association on a personal basis or representing the organization on an association of interest is a useful opportunity to meet other people with similar interests. Learning comes from the contacts themselves and from events like seminars, dinners, lectures and so on. Younger people can be encouraged to attend some events as guests or, if appropriate, invited to join. An organization such as the European Women's Management Development Network is an example of a low cost opportunity to involve women working with people development in meeting practitioners from many countries and learning from them; we could quote numerous other examples. Organizations should not see the cost of membership only in terms of immediate benefit and pay-offs, but count in the benefits of learning for the staff involved.

Distance learning Distance learning involves a packaged course designed to be used solo by the user at his or her convenience. They are certainly useful for providing knowledge simply and flexibly, and the cost of preparation is justified by volume of use. Examples of such effective use are in company induction (part of it), or in providing product or market information (particularly to different parts of the world). This mode can give the knowledge background to many skills but cannot give the skill itself.

Some prestige institutions in the UK have invested in distance learning for training in management effectiveness – indeed there are distance learning MBAs. This is intended to be a substitute for the busy manager with no time for a traditional event. Many feel they have benefited from completing such a course, although a study in 1988 showed only one third of students were completing it. But it is hard to reconcile this approach to management skills with any criteria for effective learning.

Self-development Many an employee pursues various areas of self-development despite of or in addition to anything that happens in a specific work context. Naturally, organizations want to encourage this and some go so far as to provide resource centres with libraries, self-teach materials and so on. Self-development places responsibility for learning with the learner and people choose options that they consider relevant to their individual growth. However, there is a divorce from the experiential reality of learning, and self-development needs to be supplementary to assisted learning in the workplace.

Employees may read – in areas relevant to their current job or beyond it. This may include books on self-development such as the excellent *Manager's Guide to Self Development*[12]. This is a collection of exercises to work through in self-understanding and in basic management activities. Others are plentiful, of varying value. An excellent introduction to how self-development should be approached is in Chapter 5 of Alan Mumford's *Making Experience Pay* and is entitled 'The self directed learner'[11].

They may undertake part-time study courses. For some these will be logical steps in obtaining professional qualification. Studying languages is (good news) on the increase. Some take part – usually for amusement – in computerized competitive business games. (The most unlikely people seem to win these!) Others may study business or management – such as the part-time MBA which is so popular in the UK. In the milestone Constable/McCormick Report[13] Iain Mangham's section on management education stated the following:

'The future of all forms of management education, including MBAs, seems to lie in a pattern of modular, part-time, flexible, transferable provision both in-house and external, by distance and direct methods and subject to some form of accreditation.' The last point may be debated but the other characteristics seem to make a lot of sense; we could add 'as closely linked with real life application as possible'. However, the main thrust of the Constable report was to encourage more MBA courses, and some employees have been led to believe that this degree is some magic passport to management and promotion. This is hardly the German or Japanese model of effectiveness. At least a full time MBA gives the social benefits of mixing with others for nine to twenty months, depending on the course. Except for certain special organizations such as management consultants one should think hard before sponsoring employees on a full time MBA. They find themselves at the end of it with expectations of reward that cannot be met internally after such a short time, and in a job market that makes them uncomfortable if tied to a home organization.

If your organization believes in the benefit of extensive formal management training and a qualification, then the action learning approach of (for example) Roffey Park or the International Management Centre at Buckingham is preferable to straight academic study. Here the organization, the individual and the institution share the responsibility for the learning. These may be custom-made, jointly constructed and managed courses between the organization and a teaching institution, with strong practical involvement using the reality of the organization's issues. An example of such a collaboration was that between Trafalgar House, the civil engineering group, and Buckingham. This four year programme leading to a certificate, a diploma and finally a master's degree in business administration, incorporates projects and studies built around the business operations of the company.

All these have their place, but an individual needs advice on how they fit into their personal current learning objectives.

Women on career breaks or maternity leave Distance learning and self-development are particularly useful options for women on career breaks, or less so (time can be limited!) for those on maternity leave. However, their organizational manager or mentor should advise carefully, and wherever possible choose options that are part of planned personal growth and can be combined with some project work that is relevant to the organization.

Options in on-the-job learning

Few of the above do much for the enhancement of experience and it is this that we aim for in career management. A change of job which adds to personal growth provides the greatest inherent learning opportunities. Just moving in the same function to another similar part of the organization is not as productive in new learning as a change of function or moving to an unfamiliar environment.

The importance of good induction Having said that a new job is the best way to get increased experience, we still need to structure some of that experience to maximize the learning potential. The first contribution we can make is by getting the person off to a good start. Does your organization see induction as only for new recruits? Or does it provide a programme for all new job entrants?

A Cooks tour of new colleagues is not sufficient: induction should be a real and thorough introduction to what the job requires. Here is a format, based on what I was taught 25 years ago at Procter and Gamble, which followed this practice systematically, and has worked well for people new to my own departments.

1. Contents
2. Summary of the job and how it fits in; welcome
3. Job description (or profile)
4. Timetable (approximate) for the induction
5. Sections covering each area of the job and specifying:
   - **Learning objectives**: what the induction should enable the person to know or do,
   - **References**: people or written material,
   - **Learning assignments**: a number of specific self-directed assignments either to meet people and discuss things; to study reference material; to analyse and synthesize.
   - **Check questions**: to self-test on the depth of knowledge attained.

An example of the Contents and one section is shown in Table 7.6. for the job of a management development consultant.

If it is well constructed, this format helps the individual to understand quickly the issues surrounding the job; to know where to look for things subsequently; and to have the opportunity of thinking through some of the challenges ahead. The manager plays a major role in guiding the person through this

Table 7.6 Extracts from an induction programme

MANAGEMENT DEVELOPMENT CONSULTANT

Contents

(*Sample Section*)

5. MANAGEMENT DEVELOPMENT IN THE COMPANY

Learning objective: To bring you up-to-date with the history and current state of management development policy and practice; to enable you to assess where we are and where we should be heading, and thereby to formulate objectives to aim for.

References: People: Mr A, previous incumbent
Ms B, personnel director
Mr C, chief executive
Mr D, head of training
Ms E, external consultant, ABC Ltd
Mr F, international sales director
Ms G, training and development manager, main subsidiary

Material: R1 Management development policy 1988
R2 Performance appraisal system
R3 Succession planning database
R4 Career structures manual
R5 Standards for use of assessment centres
R6 Career counselling course material
R7 Organization review committee minutes

Learning assignments:

1. Study R1, R3 and R7. To what extent are the objectives outlined in R1 being met in practice? What seems to be missing? Does R3 give any indication of problem areas – where are they?
2. Arrange to see Mr C and discuss with him his vision of the future and the characteristics of the managers that will be needed. Discuss

Table 7.6 Continued

also your findings from the previous assignment to see which are of concern to him.

3. Discuss with Mr A his view of his successes and failures; achievements and frustrations. Study R3 and ask him about any queries you have; how it was used, and how it needs developing. What would be Mr A's objectives in the next year if he was still in the job?
4. Discuss with Mr F the needs of the international part of the business as he sees them. How do they match up with current policy and practice? Make notes on issues of concern.
5. Meet with Ms G and similar colleagues, having first made a checklist of items to ask about regarding local practice. What are their expectations of your role? What local initiatives are being undertaken? How does their practice match up to R1?
   Ask them about R2 – how comfortable are managers with it? How useful are the outputs in people development actions? Are managers well trained in this area?
6. Meet Ms E and discuss the work that is being done with the organization on development centres. Make notes on their history, their design and the challenge she sees regarding their future development. Go through R5 with her and note any problem areas.
7. Discuss with Mr D how training for management is commissioned and designed, implemented and evaluated. What role should you play in the specification of off-the-job learning events? Which courses are the most popular and why? Which are shown to have the greatest value in improved job performance?
8. Study R6, and in discussions with Ms G and others assess how valuable it is. Are the messages consistent with the needs expressed by the people you have met?
9. Arrange to spend at least half a day with Ms B. Prepare beforehand an agenda for discussion. It should include the history of the various processes and committees in operation; the political aspects of succession; the inputs received from your various contacts, and your preliminary ideas for priorities in the job.

Check questions:

This part of the section should include a few well chosen questions relating to key issues, practices or people that should be known and should have been discovered through the learning assignments. For example:

* What innovations in management development in XXX division were introduced in 1990?
* Where do we have a real problem in medium term succession?

period and reviewing progress from time to time – even though managing the assignments is self-directed. This induction needs to be a full-time occupation and not confused with getting started in the job at the same time. (This is not always possible, but should always be aimed for.)

Secondments A secondment may mean different things in different organizations but the idea is that people leave their main job or function temporarily, but the 'home link' is maintained. The Institute of Personnel Management has produced a code on secondment, published in 1988, which says 'the secondment provides a unique development opportunity for employees to learn in challenging new situations'.

A secondment may be to another division, another function, another organization, another country. If we go back to our three phases of career growth, some examples of types of secondment that are appropriate are:

Phase one:

* Trained graduates to another country to use their training and at the same time learn about another culture.
* To another function for experience as part of a career growth plan.
* To be PA or shadow to a senior executive.
* To a special project team (eg a special customer proposal; a merger integration team).

A special application appropriate to the younger high potential people is the secondment to a 'tiger office' – a group of young secondees working for three to six months closely with the chief executive on special projects at a senior level in the organization. The 'tigers' may not be universally appreciated in the organization, but as a learning experience for them it is hard to beat!

Phase two:

* To a senior position in another country.
* For a line person – to a staff role such as training or strategic planning (to provide an overview of the organization).
* For a staff person – to a line supporting role (to understand specific operations in the organization).

* To another organization, such as a customer, to appreciate a different culture and obtain an outside perception of the organization.

Phase three:
* To an external government or industry related body to use the person's knowledge and experience.
* From the private sector to the public and vice versa, to improve the perspective of one in relation to the other.
* To academia (rarely *from* academia in the UK, although more common in other countries).
* To charities or similar, as a contribution from the organization.

The potential of a secondment in enhancing personal growth is clear and it has the advantage of not 'losing' the individual. However, many fail to live up to their expectations; this is often because the learning objectives (assuming this is the main purpose) need to be owned by the receiving party – and this may require a lot of work and liaison to achieve. On return, a person may not want to pick up their old job – which if it was a long secondment will be filled by someone else – and, therefore, considerable forward planning is needed.

An **international secondment** provides rich possibilities for personal growth as well as being a key part of the career management strategy. Some of these possibilities are summarized in Table 7.7.

In addition many secondments provide special opportunities – in the level of government or customer relations, or in the need to train local staff for example.

The short assignment of some weeks or months, which is far less disruptive to families and much less expensive for organizations, can bring much learning potential – although secondees miss out on the 'stand on your own two feet' aspects.

Another specialized form of secondment is that arising from mergers and acquisitions. Events of this kind offer excellent opportunities for learning through experience, although caution is needed in putting bright young high potentials into very sensitive situations. Wise managers say that a merger integra-

Table 7.7 Learning opportunities from an international assignment

Knowledge: Moving into a 'centre of excellence', – Wider understanding of operations, people, organization, strategy, technology, help available, political constraints. Moving out from a 'centre of excellence' – Understanding local environments, constraints, requirements, capabilities, cultures.
Skills: – Enhanced planning and organizing; independence; initiative; communication skills; adapatability; interpersonal skills; stress tolerance and resilience.
Attitudes: – International thinking, flexibility; realism; multicultural understanding

tion manager should be an elder statesman/woman in the organization – totally loyal and not out to prove him or herself. Nevertheless, supporting positions offer excellent learning, not only in the secondment to an integration team but in the possibilities of a future full time position capitalizing on the experience gained.

Job rotation This term specifically refers to the transfer between jobs at the same level to give additional experience. It is a particularly useful way of learning all the jobs within a department, and of giving new challenges to those who appear stuck at their level.

Job exchange This is a variation of job rotation but refers to the planned exchange, between departments, divisions, companies or even countries, of staff for a fixed period. It is easy to administer, and has the obvious advantages of planned endpoints and mutual involvement between the two instigators. In practice it may not be as simple as it sounds. Firstly there are problems finding two willing parties where the exchange is going to meet the learning objectives of two individuals and the timing is right for both; and secondly individuals do not necessarily want to return to their old job at the end of the exchange.

Additions to the current job

When people have mastered the requirements of their current post, they should not automatically move on to another one but should have time to achieve some change and improvement in the job. However, new challenges are frequently needed – either for motivation or for personal growth – and people cannot always change jobs for this. This is particularly so in the smaller organization. We can either arrange for some additions to the current job, or look for expansion of the job itself. Some additions could include:

Working parties and task forces These are not to be found in every organization but the careers manager would want to encourage them as they provide significant learning opportunities. The purpose may be defined as seeking a solution to a problem by using the input of people representing various interests. Some may just require a cross-section of good people; others may need particular departments represented to give their point of view.

Their value is in the bringing together of people with different experience and perspectives, and in forcing the participants to understand and think through what is likely to be new ground for them. Indeed, the manager who cares about people growth may deliberately choose this route rather than a more obvious one of giving the task to one person. In my current organization we are using this to help in our goal of creating greater cross-cultural understanding in Europe – setting up a task force of several nationalities with agreed terms of reference to work together instead of just appointing an individual to undertake the project. Faced with the choice of recommending someone for such an opportunity, the obvious choice (the person with most relevant experience already) should be the subject of second thoughts. Who is the person who will gain the most personal growth from this? Here we go back to the role of the boss in risk-taking.

Committee membership Most organizations – even the most

unbureaucratic – have standing committees, review bodies, etc. Not always regarded as a reward, membership can offer a lot to those who can gain from the additional knowledge, communication/political/influencing/listening skills, and exposure to others that this opportunity can bring. This is particularly true of those committees which are outside the person's local area of operation or even organization.

Projects The assignment of special projects officer or similar is a standing joke in many organizations and indicates someone is on the sidelines, in waiting or something similarly pejorative. This is a great pity, for anyone who has had experience of being allocated to a special project will say it was a significant learning experience. But what is a project? The enterprising job-holder normally has a few projects he or she is working on as time permits in addition to the day-to-day requirements of the job. Indeed, if the organization operates a managing by performance system each person will have a set of objectives agreed at the beginning of the year, many of which will be of a project nature. But we are talking here of projects that really stretch people, that provide enhancements to their knowledge, skills, attitudes and experience. These can be obtained by:

- The opportunity to gain a deep knowledge of a particular subject.
- The opportunity to explore outside the boundaries of the current department – either internally or externally.
- The opportunity to enhance a number of personal skills – in planning, prioritizing, analysing, presenting, communicating and so on.
- The opportunity to gain specialized experience of a particular area.

One job I had was a series of projects under the title 'market planning consultant'. My task, based in New York, was to visit a large number of multinationals in the USA and discover what their information technology purchasing policies were and to recommend to the company how we should resource the accounts. This involved travelling all over the States and visiting companies in a wide range of industries – from Tampax to toys, from aerospace to oil. I do not think the organization (or more correctly, my then bosses, saw this as the superb learning opportunity that it was: rather, I fear, they were wondering what to do with me at that juncture.

The key is to understand the wealth of opportunity for learning available through this approach and to use it creatively for individuals. Projects need to be real and of clearly perceived value and not artificially manufactured – as some student trainees find happens for them.

The action learning approach uses projects widely in its mix of learning methods: individuals discuss their projects with other students and cross-fertilize ideas and potential solutions. Some organizations use this as a specific form of management development and it has much to recommend it. For example, the Phillips Group has for many years run events called 'Octagons' – where eight people with potential, reasonably senior, are given six months or so to study an issue of importance to the main business and to make recommendations to the board. They continue with their current jobs but are expected to devote up to six weeks to the project. Participants speak in glowing terms of the experience and the network of colleagues in different parts of the organization that continues afterwards.

Stand-in roles For someone who has potential to rise to the next level, an excellent opportunity is to stand in for the boss while he or she is away – either on holiday, an extended course, a special project, or some other reason. However, the event should be managed. It is not just a case of making sure that nothing of any consequence will arise during the period, or of leaving instructions that anything other than routine matters should be left for the boss's return. The boss should ask 'What could my subordinate learn from this opportunity and, therefore, how should I plan my absence to ensure the potential learning can be realized?' This may mean briefing others that they should expect the subordinate to be handling certain matters, standing in at meetings, taking signing authority, etc.

Equally important is the post-event review by the two parties – looking at work that was done well, what gave problems, drawing out the lessons, and perhaps reassessing the personal profile after the event.

Another aspect of deputising is in making presentations, preparing reports or looking after visitors – all of which might normally be done by the boss. Sometimes there is a problem because of the expectations of others, but exposure to new situations is good experience.

Visits to customers, colleague departments, suppliers, and other organizations Simple but effective, the learning visit can be used for a variety of purposes. Discussing an issue face to face with an individual gives an added dimension both in the learning effect on knowledge or attitudes, and in the establishment of contacts for further use. Thus a design engineer may change his whole outlook by actually seeing first hand the problems caused in another country by his parochial design or documentation; a salesperson will be more careful with her paperwork after a visit to the factory to see what has to be done as a result; a training manager may change his whole approach after seeing how training is managed in another company. Most people are willing to cooperate with such an arrangement when asked. One clever variant in this area was a training manager in Holland who had persuaded customers or, more interestingly, prospective customers, to train (for a fee) his salespeople in understanding their business and relevant needs – so that they would in future be able to offer something that was right first time.

Once again, the post-event review by the manager is a necessary completion to such an exercise.

Junior boards The idea here is to take a group of younger people with potential and expose them to the bigger problems of the organization by creating a junior board that meets once or twice a month and looks at some key issues with a view to analyzing them and synthesizing some conclusions. These are then presented to the main board or a subset of it. Open access to information and people who can help is given.

Few of these work well, because they do depend for success wholly on the consistent will of the senior executive or team to make it work and to take it seriously; on having the time to work on quite difficult problems; and then for the recommendations to be worthwhile and not just what has been thought of before.

It is probably a mistake to put people on such a board with less than say three to five years' experience in the organization. Less experience limits their capability to deal with the issues as well as the credibility of their final results.

The development potential of this approach is significant – if it can be made effective. Many careers managers find that it is not easy to organize – and my own experience is that without the champion being the chief executive, the benefits are minimal.

Participating in training or assessment events It is said that there is no better way to become an expert in a subject than to be asked to teach it. Participating in the design and management of a learning event is a developing experience in itself and frequently underestimated as such. My period as a training and development manager in what was a new industry for me was one of my fastest learning periods. I undertook any training request given to me as in those days I did not believe in using consultants: I thought that was what I was paid to do!

Likewise there is no better way to be an effective observer of people's strengths and weaknesses than to be a trained assessor in an assessment centre. Not only does the person make his or her own observations but they listen to others' views and perspectives and sharpen a number of skills in the process.

Using the current job

Job expansion Another option open to us is to look for ways of expanding the current job itself. So can we stretch the boundaries by, for instance:

- Delegating a part of the boss's job permanently
- Increasing authority levels
- Transferring responsibilities from someone else
- Increasing the scope as part of an overall expansion of the department
- Cross-training to increase flexibility in a department
- Mentoring a more junior person in another department
- Taking on an external liaison role, for example with a university, college or school.

We are promoting these things for the purposes of **personal growth** – not to overload already hard-pressed people, who will not learn by having insufficient time to do anything well.

Coaching and counselling These are frequently linked together to describe the on-the-job development activity of a manager, although we have seen there are many aspects to this. We are referring to learning from the current job itself, with the active structured help of the boss. It is not a critical matter to separate distinctly the two terms, as they are closely inter-related, but one can distinguish a difference as follows:

Coaching – a deliberate attempt to help an individual learn by another person (usually the manager) using discussion and guided activity, which is instigated, monitored and reviewed by that other person.

Counselling – a process whereby a person listens, advises, helps, and discusses issues and problems with an individual – but with the objective of guiding him or her to find their own solution. This may be on specific work problems, on performance and career related matters, or on personal difficulties.

Whereas the latter happens from time to time in most boss–subordinate relationships – at the instigation of either party but often by the employee – the coaching process is less common and few managers have the natural instinct for it. As Mumford[11] points out, there are few managers who concentrate on the learning needs of their staff, although they may do such activities in the interest of getting the job done well.

Edwin Singer wrote the best known work in the UK on this subject[14] first published in 1974. He defined five key skills of coaching – **observation, listening, appraising, discussing and delegating**. So the manager looks for opportunities through observation of subordinates, takes the time to listen carefully to what they say, is a good appraiser and evaluator of what he or she observes, and is open and mutual in discussing development and issues rather than having a 'telling' style. Thus the effective coach is capable of dealing with feelings as well as actions and is able to receive feedback as well as give it. He or she will also be willing to share parts of their own job through delegation as a learning experience.

As a manager comes to the point in an appraisal/development review where actions are planned, we want to discourage a list of training courses as the answer to every issue identified. A manager benefits by first asking 'Is there any way that I can help this person grow through the work that we are doing?' So, for example, a manager might identify a problem of relationships with other departments. Is the answer going to be to go on an interpersonal skills course? We can consider some of the options for coaching.

- The next time a problem occurs, to spend time with the individual talking through the alternative approaches that could have been taken; agreeing a different line to be taken next time, and to review it again after the next contact with the other department.
- To set an exercise for the individual to observe and make notes on the approach that other people take when faced with inherent conflicts of interest and to discuss these with the boss at regular intervals.
- To role play with the individual a real situation that has occurred, or is about to, and tape the proceedings for subsequent analysis and review.

The BACIE *Guide to Coaching*[14] is helpful in its discussion of the process and in its suggestions for developing coaching skills.

SUMMARY

We should be interested in personal growth for everybody in the organization – not just for management and not just for those with upwards potential. It is not practical or even desirable in most organizations constantly to change people's jobs, even though job changes offer the greatest potential for learning. So we need to be creative in looking at the options available to us.

Megginson and Boydell[15] state boldly that 'Adults learn best when they are trying to solve a problem.' The importance of understanding how people learn in general, and how individuals learn best for themselves has been deliberately emphasized. The evidence that most learning comes from live experience is overwhelming; either we can hope things happen through luck and circumstances or we can manage it. To do so we must first define a learning need as precisely as we can – whether it is for performance improvement or career development – and list in a systematic way the options open to us and their appropriateness to the individual case. The choice is then only a start, as we go on to design and monitor the experience.

We have recognized the number of roles that the good developer boss can play, and they are very demanding – in caring, in systematic management and in time. The specialist should be capable of adding value through advising and helping in as many situations as can be practically coped with.

Guides to help managers produced by and in the context of the specific organization can really help. A listing for example of the specific development options that can be used by managers under separate headings of knowledge, skills, attitudes and experience is a worthwhile investment. Examples of coaching projects, of special project or committee opportunities, of self–development activities, of courses and seminars can be given. Self-initiated development is to be encouraged as a desirable personal attitude, but if we want to aim together for an agreed objective in career planning we have to invest some effort and initiative in working together.

PLANNING FOR ACTION

Problems of reality

1.Interest in how people learn is dependent on an individual HR specialist. Few line managers will be interested unless stimulated to do so. It is much easier for them to choose some good courses for their people to go on than to go through the intellectual rigour of exploring all the options.

If we look at three roles we would like the manager to play – first to care about the development of his or her people; second to be prepared to work systematically on that responsibility, and third to give personal time and take some risks in achieving results – then typically the majority do care, most will be prepared to work systematically with some hand holding, but very few – despite best intentions – give the time needed or take enough risks to fulfil their total role in people development.

The exceptions are in those organizations where the culture is such that all managers know that it is expected that they will fulfil a certain role, or the reward system specifically relates to people development. Internal pressures of this kind are fine, but the internalizing of the need by managers is not necessarily achieved through them.

The careers manager can help by:

- Preparing a 'development options guide' as a reference for managers.
- Take a personal interest in a selection of appraisals and career plans with managers and explore options together.
- Offer to help structure learning experiences, but in such a way that a manager could learn to do it for him or herself on a subsequent occasion.
- Write, for example, a job induction programme jointly with the manager so that the next time it can be done by him or her.
- Arrange training in the practice of coaching.
- Work with the chief executive to look at ways of reinforcing values of people development in the organization.

2. The organization is structured and managed on as lean a basis as possible: task forces, committees, projects, external work, etc, are actively discouraged as being against clear management accountability for results and, anyway, taking people away from what they are paid to do. Short term results override any long term considerations in practice.

Some organizations are like this throughout, some in parts, depending on the style and values of a local leader. Some go through periods when they take actions of this kind dictated by economic circumstances or because they have become top-heavy. Typically this thinking extends to formal training also, and it is likely that a careers manager (under whatever name) would be regarded as a luxury also . . .

Influence needs to be on the grounds of economic benefit –

so if there is a careers manager or personnel director wanting to see more opportunities for individual development they need to choose their ground carefully.

It is worth estimating the amount spent on formal education and training and that being invested in experiential activities such as task groups, international assignments, special projects and so on – versus results in real learning. This is hard to do, but rough estimates may make the point.

Indicators of success – these are listed in Table 7.8

Table 7.8 Indicators of success checklist

Learning plans	1. Each individual has a learning plan updated quarterly which specifies clearly the need in terms of knowledge, skills, attitudes and experience; the chosen actions and a review date.
Managerial responsibilities	2. All managers have their roles in staff development specified in writing.
Managerial training	3. All managers have been through training in staff development, coaching and counselling.
Mentoring	4. A mentoring policy exists, is understood and is operating in practice.
Investment	5. The investment in formal off-the-job training and that in the various experiential options are balanced in favour of the latter.
Range of learning opportunities	6. A good range of the options listed in Table 7.5 are available in each part of the organization.
Induction	7. All newcomers to jobs receive a systematic induction programme based on their individual learning needs.
Women on leave	8. Special attention is given to the continuing development of women on career breaks.

Action for those responsible for career management

1. Draw up a table similar to Table 7.5 of all the options available in your organization and your judgement of their relative contribution to knowledge, skills, attitudes and experience growth.
2. Consider some of the options that you believe you would like to add and could do so practically, and make a plan for each in respect of the steps needed to make them a reality.
3. Evaluate carefully the real contribution that formal training and education is making to personal growth, and the effort and resources expended in that area compared to the experience-based options.
4. Check that appraisal systems are designed to give the right outputs in terms of learning plans.
5. Develop a guide to learning opportunities for managers to use.
6. Design and implement training material for managers for their role in staff development and in coaching, delegating and counselling skills.

REFERENCES

1 Kolb, D., *Experiential Learning*, Prentice Hall, 1984

2 Mumford, A., *Learning to Learn for Managers*, Journal of European Industrial Training Vol 10 No 2 1986

3 Mumford, A., *Management Development – Strategies for Action*, IPM, 1989

4 Honey, P., and Mumford, A., *A Manual of Learning Styles*, Honey, 1982

5 Mumford, A., *Developing Top Managers*, Gower, 1988

6 Margerison, C., *How Chief Executives Succeed*, Journal of European Industrial Training, Vol 4, No 5, 1980

7 McCall, M., Lombardo, M., and Morrison, A., *The Lessons of Experience*, Lexington Books, 1989

8 Revans, R. W., *Action Learning*, Blond and Briggs, 1980

9 Kram, K., *Mentoring at Work*, Scott Foreman and Co., 1985

10 Clutterbuck, D., *Everybody Needs a Mentor*, Institute of Personnel Management, 1985

11 Mumford, A., *Making Experience Pay*, McGraw-Hill, 1980

12 Pedler, M., Burgoyne, J., and Boydell, T., *A Manager's Guide to Self Development*, 2nd ed, McGraw Hill, 1986

13 Constable, J., and McCormick, R., *The Making of British Managers*, BIM/CBI, 1987

14 Singer, E. J., *Effective Management Coaching*, IPM, 1974

15 Megginson, D., and Boydell, T., *A Manager's Guide to Coaching, BACIE, 1979*

8. MAKING IT ALL HAPPEN

THE TOTAL FRAMEWORK

Figure 8.1. links together all the processes discussed with the responsibility areas of an organization. It looks at:

- The manager–individual interaction,
- Those appropriate for divisional management,
- Those appropriate for the top level of the organization.

In some, the last two will be combined. In others (decentralized conglomerates) only the minimum may be needed at the top level.

In addition to these processes, we may provide a number of resources to employees to assist them in self-development and career information as discussed in Chapter 5.

This framework needs to be backed by a statement of policy, which is publicly available – it might be in a booklet, a manual or an employment handbook. It should not be concerned only with management development but cover all employees. It should cover areas such as:

- Beliefs about potential, personal growth, organizational and individual roles in career development.
- Processes such as appraisal and development reviews, vacancy filling, selection, career guidance, mentoring.
- Personal development opportunities – training and education, professional qualifications, on-the-job learning.
- Managerial commitment – review bodies, expectations.

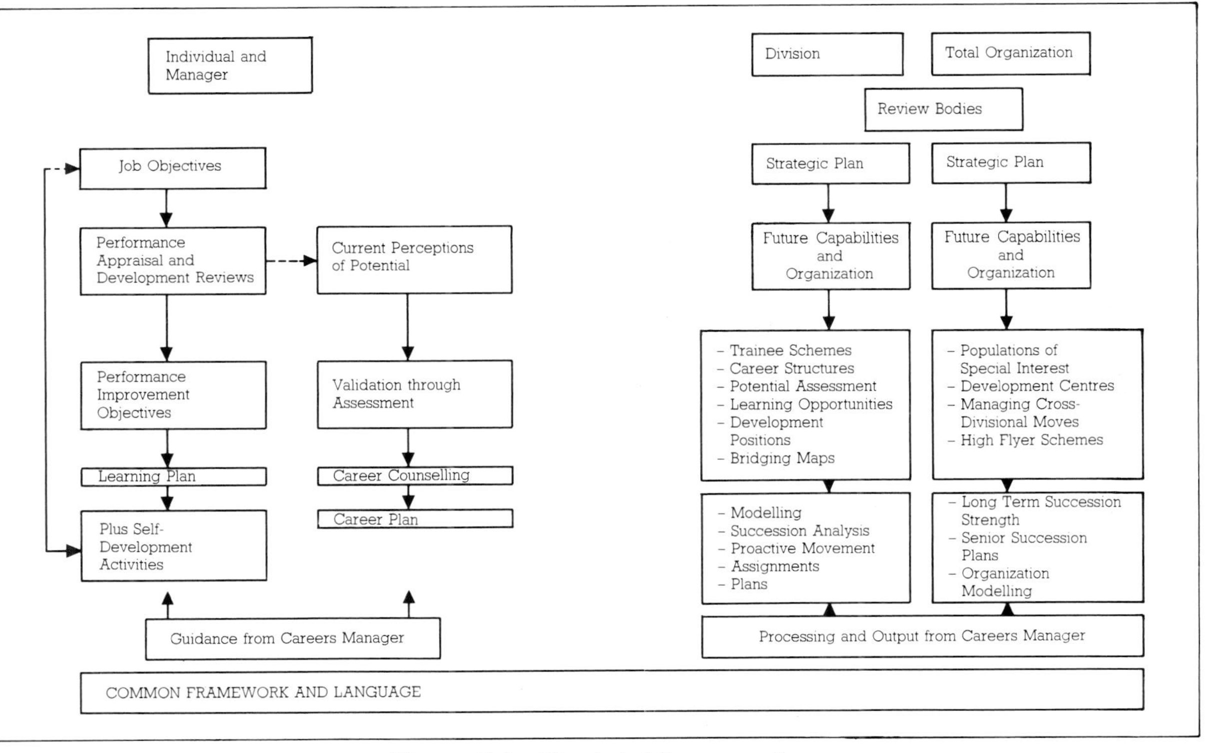

Figure 8.1 The total framework

DEFINING RESULTS AND MEASURING SUCCESS

At the end of each chapter we have suggested some indicators of success. Career management aims to develop people for the future, and must always be ahead of the trends and thinking about the needs in the years to come. Over a period of time, what are the measures that might tell an organization that it is effectively matching the personal growth needs of its people with the capabilities it needs to meet its objectives?

The following are suggested:

- Each year the organization finds itself able to meet its resourcing needs, with people who have developed the necessary capability and had the required experience (according to its policy relating to internal promotion).
- Employees indicate through appraisals and opinion surveys that they believe the organization effectively considers their personal growth and career development needs.
- Very few people leave because of frustration in personal growth and career development.
- The chief executive and his or her team make visible their commitment to personal growth and give time to reviewing progress and initiatives.
- People do not fail in jobs through lacking the capability for their appointment.
- The best specialist and technical people do not leave because they cannot achieve adequate reward and status.
- All levels in the organization operate the agreed processes with integrity.
- Development of people is valued and rewarded as an essential managerial accountability.
- The potential that exists in the organization to meet today's and tomorrow's needs is known and quantified.
- Appointments are made taking into account career plan and personal growth needs.
- A range of learning opportunities are used in the organization.
- Best practice is benchmarked externally to ensure that the organization is not operating with a competitive disadvantage.

- The mix of nationalities or breadth of functional experience in teams reflect the need of the organization.

It is strongly suggested that a set of such measures is included in any definition of the policy and framework, and there is a regular review (say, annually) of where the organization stands against them. In addition, a regular survey of the opinions of employees is a great help in checking how employees perceive the practical implementation. Questions to be asked might include:

- How helpful do you find your manager/superviser in assisting you improve your performance and skills?
- How satisfied are you with the career counselling you have received?
- How satisfied are you with promotion and job movement processes?
- How aware are you of opportunities in the organization?

Opinion surveys have the most value when they measure trends, ie comparisons with the responses to the same questions the last time the survey was carried out.

MANAGING CHANGE

One thing is certain, that systems and processes need to evolve and change with the changing needs. We have argued for defining the overall frameworks and objectives and ensuring the various processes fit into them in an integrated way. However, a programme of change will almost certainly not start from a blank sheet of paper and aim for the ideal realization of all the measures of success in one programme. It will be a move from a mixed and variable position existing today to what we believe to be the needs of the organization's objectives in some years time, by a series of steps. Thus we plan where we want to be at certain points in time – quarterly or half yearly. We have referred earlier to Wendy Hirsh's 1984 study *Career Management in the Organisation* (Institute of Manpower Studies Report No 96), which is probably the most thorough study made in the UK of our subject. Sections 6 and 7 of this report are particularly helpful, and an appendix is included entitled 'Summary of Questions for Aspects of Career Policy Review' and gives some 100 or so questions for an organization to ask itself. Using an instrument such as this and/or some of the checklists in Chapter 1 should enable a change programme to be defined.

It is not within our scope to cover the complexity of managing change, and there are many excellent books and consultants available. Leibowitz, Farren and Kaye in *Designing Career Development Systems* (Jossey-Bass, 1986) devote the whole of Part Three of their book to implementing change, and in particular gaining the support of top management; not all of it crosses the Atlantic easily but it has some helpful messages. We should recognize that managers will not automatically be enthusiastic about career management processes that might encourage their staff to become restless, or to have expectations beyond the manager's capability to deliver, or to require more work from them. Staff who attend self-help workshops particularly become proactive and demanding, so that it is essential to secure the general support of management groups before initiating change in this area.

The following steps are, therefore, essential:

- Understanding clearly the benefits the change will bring to the achievement of the organization's objectives (the 'nice idea' must always be subjected to this test).
- Making sure the priority is high enough among the many calls on time and money investment, the problems needing to be solved, and the benefits to be gained.
- Checking that the expectations that may be raised can be met realistically.
- Evaluating alternative solutions which will meet the needs and not jumping to conclusions as to one particular route.
- Consulting with the people who will have to implement the change.
- Ensuring the organizational culture will not stifle change; understanding the positive and negative forces that will affect its implementation. (Some culture change may be necessary first.)

- Piloting the change in one area.
- Investing in materials, publicity, training and education for those affected.
- Monitoring and reviewing progress and adjusting accordingly.
- Obtaining the active commitment of the top management: the most important step.

Some points to remember in this process are:

- Care with language: obscure human relations jargon is not helpful in gaining credibility.
- Identifying and using senior executives who are convinced of the need for the change and are opinion leaders among their peer group to act as champions for the cause.
- Being able to articulate benefits in terms of business objectives, saved costs, more revenue, etc.
- The knowledge of competitive practice and any real competitive disadvantages that the organization has through its current practices.
- The importance of visible commitment to the change through talking with employees, tapes and videos, written materials backed by the chief executive, and – perhaps most important – attendance at some or all of the relevant courses and seminars.
- Regularly monitoring success and providing feedback on it.

PUBLICITY, TRAINING AND EDUCATION

Selling ideas and internal processes to users is little different from selling products and services to customers. Identifying benefits, packaging, introduction planning and promotion all play their part. No organization should be internally focused at the expense of customers, but some time, effort and money needs to be spent in implementing change.

We referred in Chapter 5 to a career resources pack to be at the disposal of managers. Employees need a booklet (or similar) which is more explanatory, describes what they should expect, and the part they should play personally. Many examples of employee material are available from the library of the Institute of Personnel Management in the UK.

Managers like easily referenced factual material: they leave comprehensive summaries of the theory involved in the bookcase; a manual clearly indicating the procedures to be followed, factual material, contacts, resources and so on will be well thumbed. It will be needed, because the demand from employees for factual information will increase as a result of greater awareness of the career management framework.

The ideal way of introduction of new processes is through live management briefings, where the manager is visibly seen to own his or her part in the process. Receipt through the mail, internal or external, is cold and impersonal, whatever the words may say in the literature that is sent.

Training

Both managers and the specialists who may be available to help them need training, and thoroughly. A two hour introduction to a new process – and some organizations give no more on appraisals for example – is a recipe for problems and failure. The training should be sufficient to ensure participants have learned fully the level of skill or change in attitude that is involved; they own the process intellectually, are committed to make it effective and are capable of doing so.

There are many external courses available in areas such as appraisal interviewing and staff development. In the UK only a few exist on career management: examples include the Institute of Manpower Studies, Lifeskills Associates and Sundridge Park Management Centre. It is strongly recommended that such culturally sensitive issues should be dealt with in-house, perhaps collaborating initially with external advisers.

As a general rule training should only be given to those who have an opportunity to use it in practice quickly. Specialists will find themselves applying their knowledge and skills much more frequently and we should naturally expect them to develop a deeper level of expertise. It is important to recognize – despite our desire that managers should have continual concern for the development of their people – that most managers will use the skills involved infrequently, and as we know, it is practice that makes perfect. Just because a manager went through a training event at some time does not guarantee at all that he or she is an effective practitioner of the skills involved. The specialist, if available, therefore needs to guide and counsel managers in sharpening their skills. A role model boss is the ideal coach for subordinates who are inexperienced in developing their staff.

Areas of relevant training are summarized in Table 8.1.

Table 8.1 Modules of training relevant to career management

TRAINING MODULE	Knowledge, skills or attitudes	Line or specialist? (Typical duration in days)
Appraisal processes	K	L,S (½)
Appraisal interviewing	S	L,S (1½)
Giving feedback	S	L,S (2)
Mentoring	S	L,S (2)
Career counselling	S,A	L (2); S (3)
Career planning	S	L,S (1½)
Life balancing	K,S,A	S (2)
Career development framework	K,A	L (1), S (4)
Designing career structures	K,S	S (2)
Succession planning	K,S	S (2)
Computerization of career development systems	K	S (3)
Creating career help resources	K	S (2)
Assessment and testing	K,S	S (5–10)
Potential assessment	S	L,S (2)
Selection methods	K,S	L (3); S (5)
Manpower planning	K,S	L (1)
Manpower planning and modelling	K,S	S (3)
How people learn	K,A	L,S (1½)
Planning and monitoring Learning; using learning opportunities	K,S,A	L (2); S (4)
Managing change	K,S,A	L,S (3)
Formulating strategy	K,S	L,S (3–5)
Influencing skills	S	S (3)

THE ROLE OF THE CAREERS MANAGER

The responsibilities and requirements of the effective careers manager are significant, however simple or complex the framework may be. To be able to assist the organization to meet all the measures of success listed earlier is demanding and it is unlikely in larger organizations to be achieved by one individual. We have used the term throughout to indicate people responsible for aspects of career management.

On the unlikely assumption that it is one person, Tables 8.2 and 8.3 show a job description and a person specification that embrace the full role. This is a job for people with considerable experience of how organizations work, the ability to influence senior managers and demonstrate they can match the business or service needs of the organization practically with ideas and processes for people growth. Because history and culture are so important, anyone coming from outside must be particularly culturally and politically sensitive. Bringing in new ideas is a plus; transplanting them into practice is a skilled process.

Working in this arena provides development in itself. The personal growth possibilities inherent in the breadth of this type of job, in the enhancement of skills needed to do it effectively and in the observation of people learning and developing, these are all invaluable experiences. Such a job can be considered as a 'development position' for people with the right mix of basic skills.

The roles described are often merged with others, such as responsibilities for training or general personnel. Whereas at the lower levels in an organization this would be normal, at the highest level focus and dedication on career management would be recommended. It is a demanding and important job.

PITFALLS AND DIFFICULTIES

Problems of reality have been discussed at the end of each chapter but it is worthwhile covering by way of a summary some of the difficulties one might experience in introducing and managing a systematic careers management framework.

Table 8.2 Careers manager job description

Job purpose: To design, communicate and facilitate the implementation of processes which aid career management and personal growth within a framework that meets the needs of the organization both for today and tomorrow.

To provide a service, through advice, help and management of information, to managers and to the senior management team.

Accountabilities:

1. To prepare from the strategic plan information concerning the capabilities of people, organization and culture that the organization will need in order to fulfil its strategies.
2. To recommend a framework of career management consistent with the goals and culture needs of the organization for the future.
3. To design, gain approval for, publicize and implement specific processes as parts of the overall framework.
4. To recommend how much integration of these processes is needed across different parts of the organization.
5. To define through agreement a common language for describing personal capability that will link people and jobs consistently.
6. To train managers and other employees in skills needed to create effective and continuous personal growth.
7. To suggest innovative learning opportunities for achieving personal growth.
8. To design and agree formats for 'personal growth profiles', job specifications, and career plans.
9. To define the career directions that are relevant to the organization, the career structures that should support them, and the processes of movement between them.
10. To define a policy of when and how career direction should be assessed.
11. To prepare and maintain libraries of 'development positions', 'career bridges', and secondment opportunities.
12. To define a classification of potential, and methods for assessing and updating perceptions of potential.
13. To define 'populations of special interest' in which a personal interest will be taken.

Table 8.2 Continued

14. To define appropriate formats for succession planning and proactive job movement that will be used effectively by senior management.
15. To recommend candidates for positions who are ready and suitable, and for whom the move represents a positive step in personal growth in line with their career plan.
16. To maintain regular dialogues with managers concerning the development of key individuals.
17. To ensure that the different parts of the organization have trainee schemes and manage them in a way that is consistent with the overall career management framework.
18. To organize and control up-to-date information regarding structure, jobs and individuals using information technology as appropriate.
19. To understand and model the flows of people through the organization, monitoring the pools of potential management where necessary.
20. To service one or more appropriate senior management review bodies.
21. To maintain up-to-date knowledge of external practices and developments in the field of career management and personal growth.

Resourcing

The quality, credibility, maturity and consistency of the people driving and supporting careers management influence, as always, its continuing success. Responsibilities for the various aspects should not be split between conflicting specialists and, as seen in the person specification in Table 8.3, considerable maturity is needed. Credibility with management will result from producing results and real help – new careers managers should therefore look for ways to help managers solve short term problems, but also concentrate on an aspect of change that can be achieved relatively quickly and effectively. The traps of being swamped by the detail or the development of an information system must be avoided. A real interest in and knowledge of the operations and objectives of the organization is an important step in credibility.

Table 8.3 Person specification for a careers manager

Job name: Careers manager		**Grade/level:** 12
Expertise key: 1=Working knowledge; 2=Fully competent 3=Known expert		**E=Essential; D=Desirable**
Knowledge:	**E:**	Organization history and culture (3) Organization structure (3) Company strategies (2) Career management framework and activities (3) Appraisal systems (2) Testing and assessment methods (2) Learning opportunities and styles (2)
	D:	Manpower planning and modelling (2) Personnel information systems (2)
Skills	**E:**	Career counselling Preparing career plans Selection interviewing Assessment of capabilities Political and organizational awareness Communications skills; presentation, clear writing Planning and control of complex data Influencing others in authority Priorities and personal organization
	D:	Future orientated Personal use of information technology Designing on-the-job learning
Attitudes	**E:**	Care for people growth Commitment to company goals and strategies Perseverance to achieve objectives Creative but practical rather than theoretical Concerned for needs of women's careers Belief in discussion rather than paper communication
	D:	Resilient against setbacks Proactive and creative Concerned about young people development Cultural sensitivity
Experience	**E:**	of both line and staff roles of training and development management (5 years) of consistent achievement from influence rather than authority of the industry sector or similar (5 years)
	D:	of at least three parts of the organization or two other organizations of people management of cultural change programmes of strategic plan formulation of designing and managing trainee schemes
LAST UPDATED:		**BY:**

Pursuit of a personal agenda

Perhaps the greatest pitfall of all is for the specialist to be carried away with his or her own enlightenment or perceptions, and forget that, whereas it is their job to concentrate on this area all the time, others have a wider range of responsibilities. The specialist must therefore take much time and trouble to consult, listen, modify ideas, choose a language people can work with, influence and finally convince others of proposed change. The success of a career management process will not be in the brilliance of its conception, but in its practical implementation by others.

Chief executives frequently have personal agendas also, through their personal values or through listening to opposite numbers in other organizations. Examples might be insisting on a high flyer scheme, on particular structures of organization, or on a belief in particular forms of tests. Sir Michael Edwardes for example is well known for his belief in continual testing of senior management groups. The specialists responsible for career management need to be those with whom the chief executive can discuss his or her ideas and who can place them in the overall framework.

Management of conflicts and contradictions

'We have all kinds of excellent policies and procedures on career management around here, but unfortunately they don't seem to all work well in every part of the organization.'

Why is this such a common complaint? It is because there are mismatches and disconnections that arise for all kinds of reasons – between what we would like to do and the resources available to do it, between what the personnel people say and what management is prepared actually to commit itself to doing, and sometimes the particularly British desire to do something differently from the way prescribed by someone else, and so on.

It is not so difficult to convince managers of the value to the organization and individuals of a solid framework and supporting processes. However, continuing maintenance of that commitment in the face of all the pressures of today's managerial environment is a significant demand. Career management is an investment and needs to be looked at in the same way as other longer term investments. This is why it is the legitimate concern of senior management. However, line managers have a series of conflicts that they face in this area, for example:

- The wish, even need, to retain their best people rather than lose them to career progression elsewhere.
- The stronger pull of the expedient short term decision against the longer term payoff of more strategic choices.
- The choice of an already experienced candidate for a job against a person who needs it for his or her personal development.
- The pressure of each day versus the need to spend time in coaching or updating people on career breaks.
- The easy choice of training courses for personal growth rather than the disciplines of defining a learning need and choosing the best option.
- The desire to decentralize accountability and the need to coordinate the development of capability for the good of an organization as a whole.

Each manager has different degrees of freedom – these tend to increase with higher levels of responsibility but not necessarily so, because the most senior managers have to be more circumspect in some situations about what they do because of their visibility. Within the scope for freedom of choice conflicts will be resolved by a combination of three pressures, as illustrated in Figure 8.2. Some managers make their choice based on their personal interest and set of values; others because they are rewarded and motivated to do so by the way rewards are constructed, by pressure down the line or by sanctions. The third influence is the strength of the cultural norms and expectations, and the acceptance of a common philosophy on people development which overrides the multitude of individual approaches. The relative strengths of these factors will determine the final resolution of the conflict.

Importance of the appraisal dialogue

The appraisal dialogue between manager and employee remains a fundamental platform in our whole framework, and it is for the individual usually the most important event in the year.

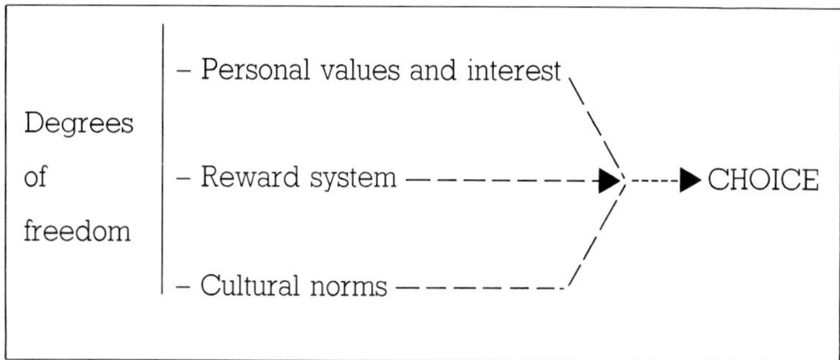

Figure 8.2 Managerial choices

Organizations are continually frustrated with their appraisal systems – studies show that a high proportion of respondents feel a need to improve them. Others experiment with abandoning it, introducing peer and subordinate feedback, and so on. It is helpful to distinguish between the two aspects of **performance reviews** and **development reviews**. There are different options for both: in the former case, a collection of feedback mechanisms may be used and in the latter we can use assessment centres and so on. However, it seems to me incontrovertible that a person's manager has the greatest opportunity to assist with both performance improvement and personal development through learning opportunities.

Some of the problems experienced are:

- Excuses to miss a year (lack of time working together, unavoidable pressures).
- The style and capability of many managers in giving feedback and developing mutually agreed plans.
- The lack of depth and analysis that many appraisees receive.
- The desire of some managers to shelve learning on to third parties such as training courses.
- Superficial or non-existent training of managers.
- Discomfort experienced by managers in being straightforward and honest, leading to blandness and woolly improvement objectives.

- Vagueness or lack of honesty in career counselling giving rise to unrealistic expectations.
- Unreliability of potential assessments made (they are often made on the grounds of performance in the job).

Readers could add more I am sure. One large organization felt it so essential that they lifted the appraisal completion level close to 100%. As part of a cultural change programme the chairman decreed every manager's bonus would be subject to a threshold of appraisal completion of his or her subordinates. Personnel protested that this would affect quality; but he insisted and it achieved its objective most effectively. After two years the sanction became unnecessary.

It is crucial to recognize the pivotal nature of this dialogue and invest in every help for managers to ensure a high level of skill and commitment.

Managing expectations

The more an organization and an individual are involved in discussion about futures the more we create expectations. Commitments to training and learning opportunities from appraisals, feedback from assessment centres and tests, career guidance in various forms, agreeing a career plan – all these create pressures in the organization and frustration with individuals when they see hopes unrealized. These are exacerbated in times of cutback and reduction in available positions. Some would use this as an argument for leaving career management to the individual to seize opportunities as they arise.

The key here is to ensure that the message is always in terms of 'this is our perception of the future. Given what we know today about you, the organization and the future, then this seems the route we should aim for. But we are going to review it regularly to take account of changes in any of the elements that make up our perception . . .'

Inherent prejudices

Whenever a person is in a minority group he or she is laid open to prejudices. However apparently equitable all the systems and processes are, an organization needs to be particularly aware that people naturally like to work with people like themselves – recruiting in their own image, recreating their own success through arranging similar experiences for their staff, enforcing their own values in their departments, and so on. Special care needs to be taken to look after groups such as women on career breaks, older employees, different nationalities or ethnic minorities, ex-employees of acquired organizations . . . and so on. It is important to ensure that there are inputs in addition to that of the person's manager in these cases.

The need to control complexity

The whole field of understanding organizations and individual capability lends itself to complexity. One organization came up with 85 key capabilities needed to be effective as a senior manager in the future . . . It is a great temptation to be too clever, to look for the fine distinctions, to try and describe every aspect systematically, to design the most comprehensive information system. This can be a real enemy of acceptance and practical implementation. Not only are managers very busy but there is an element of intuitive judgement in these matters that is helped by systematic processes and analysis but does not necessarily need fine diagnosis. In our suggested person specification for a careers manager we included the desirability of experience in an operational role so that the manager can have a balanced perspective of how some staff activities may be viewed.

OVERVIEW

Organizations in the 1990s are said to be moving towards greater flexibility, more down-the-line empowerment, decentralization, networked and integrated structures with minimum reliance on central hubs and headquarters. Classic structures and systems give way to project teams, multinational centres of excellence and stronger local cultures. There are certainly organizations (for instance, BP and ABB Asea Brown Boveri) which are actively moving in this way.

Competition increases as deregulation and privatization are adopted by governments, and markets are less protected. Home markets are losing protection and customer expectations of price and quality force globalization of manufacturing and development and at the same time local customization of products and services. Acquisitions, mergers and strategic alliances multiply. Managers are faced with increasing and potentially confusing change, with trade-offs of contradictions and a constant drive for productivity and efficiency. Controls by central 'overheads' are pushed down into autonomous business units.

Grading and job evaluation are giving way to personal and market values; and boundaries are falling away in Europe in terms of resourcing and recognition of qualifications. The strengths of local cultures are being emphasized even within a context of worldwide strategies. Managers seem to be less willing to relocate their family, but more prepared to commute long distances for the working week. Increasing numbers of dual career couples place constraints on the mobility of people in their critical first career phase; on the other hand young single people, inspired by experience in another country during their education, increasingly seek working experience outside their homebase. Loyalty to organizations is decreasing, especially in the early years when more and more feel that gaining experience in more than one environment is essential for them.

Does all this mean that the approach of a systematic framework of people development processes is inappropriate for the future, and the principle of empowerment should be extended to every individual to determine his or her own growth path?

I believe nothing in this book is invalidated by these trends. However much large organizations change in their strategic approaches to meet the needs of global competition, there are multitudes of others for whom the changes are slower. Even for those that are experimenting as described above, it mainly affects structures at the higher levels, and underneath are millions who will continue to pursue careers under more or less hierarchical structures. The principle of understanding strategic direction and its implication for career management processes becomes even more important; the need to comprehend the capabilities needed of managerial and specialist staff to meet future challenges even more imperative; and the necessity to plan personal growth to provide those capabilities essential for organizational success. Flexibility, involvement of the individual in planning development, and consideration for the total life balance must be key elements. But an integrated committed career management framework, appropriate for the needs of today and the future, is as valuable as ever.

INDEX